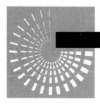

The Video Performer

Gary Dreibelbis
Solano College

Boston • New York • San Francisco
Mexico City • Montreal • Toronto • London • Madrid • Munich • Paris
Hong Kong • Singapore • Tokyo • Cape Town • Sydney

Series Editor: Molly Taylor
Editorial Assistant: Michael Kish
Marketing Manager: Mandee Eckersley
Editorial-Production Administrator: Deborah Brown
Editorial-Production Service: Susan McNally
Text Design/Electronic Composition: Denise Hoffman
Composition Buyer: Linda Cox
Manufacturing Buyer: JoAnne Sweeney
Cover Administrator: Kristina Mose-Libon

For related titles and support materials, visit our online catalog at www.ablongman.com.

Between the time Website information is gathered and then published, it is not unusual for some sites to have closed. Also, the transcription of URLs can result in unintended typographical errors. The publisher would appreciate notification where these errors occur so that they may be corrected in subsequent editions.

Library of Congress Cataloging-in-Publication Data

Dreibelbis, Gary.
    The video performer / Gary Dreibelbis.
        p. cm,
    ISBN 0–205–35865–9
        1. Television acting.   2. Interviewing on television.   I. Title.

    PN1992.8.A3 D74 2003
    791.45'028—dc21

                                                    2002018551

Printed in the United States of America

10 9 8 7 6 5 4 3 2 1   RRD-IN   08 07 06 04 03 02

Contents

CHAPTER 3

Credibility and Appearance   39

CHAPTER 4

Vocal Aspects of Performance   55

CHAPTER 5

Nonverbal Communication and the Video Performer   77

CHAPTER 6

Working as a Team with Production Personnel   95

CHAPTER 7

What Performers Need to Know about Equipment   117

CHAPTER 8

Interview Programs   141

CHAPTER 9

Being Interviewed on Television   173

CHAPTER 10

"And Now the News, Weather, and Sports . . ." 201

CHAPTER 11

Commercials and Public Service Announcements   245

CHAPTER 12

Finding Work as a Video Performer   269

Preface

Over 50 years ago, the first video performers discovered, by trial and error, what worked onscreen and what didn't. Many of these people made the transition from stage, screen, and radio to perform in front of large, boxlike cameras and hot lights.

Most of us have watched many hours of television over the years; however, beginning video performers still face some of the same questions as performers did half a century ago, such as where to look, how to move, and how loud to speak. Many effective public speakers or performers are frustrated by not knowing how to communicate via television.

Some things haven't changed over the years, but others are changing rapidly. Because of new technologies and the use of video, there are now more opportunities for people to be seen on television than ever before. Several years ago video performers trained for specific jobs in the industry—news anchor, reporter, commercial spokesperson, and the like. Today, teleconferencing, distance learning, teleconference employment interviews, video training sessions, and other such contexts require a wide variety of professionals to appear on a screen of some kind.

This book is written both for those who want to become professional video performers and those who use video performance in other professions. For years, video performance training merely has been included in television production books or in books featuring both radio and television announcing. Video performance deserves its own book due to the amount of information the effective performer needs to know.

Chapters 1 through 5 deal with the unique aspects of the medium and provide general information concerning vocal aspects and nonverbal communication. The emphasis is on demonstrating how the performer must adapt to the medium.

Chapters 6 and 7 feature user-friendly approaches to equipment and working with technical personnel. For years there was a clear separation between those in front of the camera and those behind it; however, station downsizing has blurred that line. Some news reporters are now reporting, shooting, and editing their stories, even starting the camcorder and running in front of it to do a stand-up. The thinking at some news operations is that one person can do the work of two. Also, the more you know about what can be done in a facility, the better prepared you will be as a performer.

Later chapters deal with specific performance situations. Interviews in Chapters 8 and 9 concern news and weather, Chapter 10 deals with sports, and Chapter 11 with commercials.

Chapter 12 offers specific advice on getting your first job, including information concerning cover letters, resumes, and resume tapes.

Ratings pointers featuring advice or stories appear throughout the book. Many of these come from industry insiders.

Other insiders, such as performers and production personnel, have been interviewed for this book, and these interviews have been included at the end of each chapter.

Acknowledgments

This book is the result of the contributions of many talented people. First, thanks to all who allowed their interviews to be included:

Fran Andrews, Client Coordinator, Golden Gate Productions

Kate Botello, Host, Tech TV's *Extended Play*

Spencer Christian, Weathercaster, KGO-TV San Francisco. Former Weathercaster, ABC's *Good Morning America*

Vernon Glenn, Weekend Sports Anchor and Sports Reporter, KRON, San Francisco

Vickie Jenkins, Media Consultant, Performance Power

Lori Hillman, Former Producer, *The CBS Evening News with Dan Rather*

Gayle Lederman, Makeup and Fashion Consultant

Steve Perez Schill, Weathercaster, WFLD Fox-TV, Chicago

Craig Miller, Host, HGTV, Former Reporter, CNN, KDKA-TV Pittsburgh, and KPIX San Francisco

George Maguire, Commercial Performer

Joyce Tudryn, President, International Radio and Television Society Foundation, New York, New York

All of the above are not only good at their jobs, they are good people willing to share their knowledge with others.

Credit goes to Kathy Kerchner for information on soundbites and to Don Fitzpatrick for his information on resume tapes and other employment information. Thanks to Jo Laverde at Nielsen Media Research for providing Designated Market Area information.

Mike Rehmus, video and cinema technician at Solano College, was responsible for many of the photographs and other graphics in this textbook. Mike contributed invaluable artistic expertise.

Writers need good editors. Pat Perry was invaluable with her copyediting before the manuscript went to the publisher. Allyn and Bacon's Molly Taylor provided outstanding feedback and morale support. Michael Kish assisted with advice and kept this project on track.

A huge thank you goes to Karon Bowers, acquisitions editor at Allyn and Bacon, for having the faith in this project to move it forward.

The following educators reviewed this book:

Clayland H. Waite, Radford University

Ralph E. Carmode, Jacksonville State University

John MacKerron, Towson University

Robert M. Jacobs, Bradley University

Finally, thanks to all my students. They provided excellent feedback during the formative stages of this text.

Gary Dreibelbis
San Anselmo, CA

CHAPTER ONE

The Video Performer: The Impact of Video, the Players, and Defining Performance

"Television is the most awesome force in the whole Godless world."
—Peter Finch as the character Howard Beale
in the 1976 film *Network*.

Anyone who has seen *Network* probably has strong opinions of Howard Beale's assessment of the power of television. The fact remains that no 20th-century medium has had as much social impact on society as television. If you doubt television's influence, consider the following:

- Watching television is the dominant leisure activity of Americans, consuming 40 percent of the average person's free time.

- In the average American household, the television set is on for over seven hours a day.

- Children between the ages of two and five watch an average of 31 hours of television per week.

We could continue with the evidence regarding television's impact on our lives while debating whether or not this influence is in decline due to the Internet and other technologies. However, it's obvious that many people spend a significant amount of time in front of a screen of some kind.

For nearly 30 years following the advent of television, viewers had limited television viewing choices, with most sets being able to receive only three to six channels. Cable television expanded the video landscape in the 1970s and 1980s, providing more viewer options (often at a cost) and programs aimed at specific audiences (called *narrowcasting*). Direct broadcast satellites and Internet video streaming technologies have added even more choices while also providing interactive elements for viewers.

There is some evidence that viewers, especially younger ones, are less concerned with the technology or sources of their program viewing than with viewer gratification, or what they are getting from various media. Research from MTV claims that younger viewers are more democratic about their use of media, mixing television, VCRs, the Internet, and so on, depending on the task at hand, from receiving entertainment to doing school-related research to buying products online. Indeed, teenagers and young adults seldom distinguish between traditional broadcast stations and cable services, and most people are no longer loyal to a particular television network or station.

Traditional television executives, other executives involved in "new media" such as Internet companies, and Wall Street investors are debating the future of television as we now know it. What will be the nature of the screen providing us with entertainment and information? One thing seems certain, however; despite new technologies and the ability to provide content in new and different ways, human video performers will still be an important element of what we see on the present and future screen. The ability to communicate information, entertain, and connect with an audience will continue to be vital as it has been in the past. In some ways the task of the video performer will become more demanding, as performers and technicians alike determine the best ways of presenting content on various screens.

The video performers of today and tomorrow are not only news anchors, reporters, interviewers, commercial spokespersons, and so on. Many professionals have appeared on screen for news interviews, corporate videos, or even employment interviews. Almost any professional may be seen on a screen of some kind during his or her career. These opportunities will continue to increase as delivery systems become more common and less expensive. As the artist Andy Warhol predicted, "Everyone will have his [or her] 15 minutes of fame."

This book provides advice on how to be an effective communicator in front of the camera lens and information concerning how the screen mediates your performance. Much of the information can be used in a variety of performance contexts. In other cases advice is focused on specific performance situations such as news interviews or commercials. Whether you want to be a news anchor or perform better for your next corporate training video, this book has information you can use.

Viewers' Changing Perceptions of the Video Performer

During the first few decades of television viewers were often in awe of the people they saw onscreen; seeing anything on the television screen was of course a novelty during the medium's early years. As television matured, certain individuals who were effective communicators became household names and were held in high public esteem.

Even today, certain television performers are popular icons. For example, during any edition of NBC's *Today* show dozens of people crowd on the street outside the studio watching the production and attempting to make contact with current hosts Katie Couric, Matt Lauer, and Al Roker. Granted, much of the enthusiasm comes from people carrying signs and wanting to be seen on television by friends and family at home; but in addition, the *Today* hosts connect with the audience and the audience wants to have personal contact with them. Other programs have imitated *Today* in using street-level "fishbowl" studios where people can watch their favorite performers and the production process.

RATINGS POINTER

Ask yourself and your friends: Who are some of the performers you admire most on television (news anchors, interviewers, talk show hosts, etc.)? Why do you like *them* (don't focus as much on the show as on the performer)?

What verbal and nonverbal aspects of the performers do you see as positive? Do they present information in a clear manner? How do they use emotional appeals such as humor? ★ ★ ★ ★

A different perspective on audience perception of the video performer is that with so many channels, choices, and opportunities for people to appear on television, appearing on television is somehow less special than it used to be. With public access television, cable programs, and many other opportunities to appear onscreen, the experience of performing is no longer the rarity it once was.

The truth is probably in the middle. Even though there are more channels and technology provides more opportunities than ever for people to be seen on a video or computer screen, there is still something unique about the screen experience for both performer and viewer. Also, viewers have certain expectations of what they see onscreen, whether they are watching a network production or a college distance learning presentation.

Our culture has become more and more visually literate as a result of ongoing exposure to various media. Viewers quickly turn off or tune out a production if the performer is not dynamic or engaging or if the visual elements are unclear or unsophisticated. In most cases even the most dynamic public speaker must adapt his or her performance to the video medium.

Much has been made of shortening attention spans, particularly among "the MTV generation," that is, those who have become accustomed to rapid visual stimuli on the screen. Evidence indicates that people can process information faster now than in previous generations and that they can pay attention to multiple images on the screen. Internet technology is providing **streaming video** with multiple images and interactive capability. The challenge for the video performer is how to use these technologies to communicate messages while remaining the focus of the production.

Why Do We Use the Terms Performer and Performance?

This book uses the words *performer* and *performance*. Other books use the word *announcer* when referring to those who speak on television and radio; in fact, several books combine radio and television announcing into one subject.

Performer is in many ways the more comprehensive term for what a person does when appearing on television. There are times when the person reads from a prepared script and fulfills the traditional function of an announcer, but most news anchors and reporters would not refer to themselves as announcers. Many performers prefer to be called by their specific area or function—news reporter, talk show host, business reporter, and so on. No matter what a person's title or function, certain skills and principles are universal to almost any video performance situation.

The term *performers* also indicates that they may present themselves and their information on the spot. They will not always have a prepared script; they may have to work with limited notes or an outline. Knowledge of a particular person or subject matter becomes important in situations that demand performance because it is impractical or impossible to script the production's content fully.

Interview or panel shows are examples of semiscripted situations in which the host must think quickly while keeping the show within its time limits. In these situations the show's introduction, conclusion, and a few questions may be the only items that appear in a script, along with time cues for each individual segment. Similarly, an interviewee may have some idea of questions and areas to be covered but has to respond to questions and provide information spontaneously.

Several television production books distinguish between performers, who appear onscreen as themselves, and actors, who portray fictional characters. This book focuses on the performer rather than the actor, although a number of principles clearly apply to both performance and dramatic situations. It also discusses techniques that video performers can learn from actors.

Some television professionals and educators may take issue with the use of the words *performer* or *performance* in context, arguing that the terms connote an insincere, inauthentic, or self-serving presentation. However, it is interesting to note that *performance* comes from the old French *par + fournir* and literally means "carry through to completion." Whatever the production situation, it is the responsibility of the person we see onscreen to "to carry through to completion" the intent of the production by maximizing the meaning and connecting with the audience.

While performers generally have high levels of self-confidence, the best are successful because they keep their audience in mind and present themselves not just for self-gratification but for the audience's benefit. Ease of manner, conversational style, and believability are equated with high-quality performance. Consider for a moment some television performers you admire. Do they look as if they are working hard? Do they seem to be enjoying what they are doing? Are they interested in communicating important information to you? Do they seem to be just talking to you, as opposed to lecturing at you? In most cases the performers we enjoy and admire the most are the ones who seem to communicate most naturally no matter what the program may be. Your goal as an aspiring performer should be to develop your own natural style and appear believable, no matter what the performance situation.

A Thumbnail History of Video Performance

Video performers have evolved over the past half century from people just trying to survive the conditions of the studio to get a program on the air to people who project a natural style and work with sophisticated equipment and experienced professionals. Early performers working at the few television stations in existence prior to World War II had to work under extremely bright, hot lights and wear green, blue, or red makeup because of the limitations of early video systems.

In Jeff Kisselhoff's book *The Box: An Oral History of Television 1920–1961*, Hugh Downs of ABC's *20/20* described one of his first experiences in television as a newscaster for a Chicago television station in 1945: The lights in the studio were so hot that the perspiration dripped from his face onto his script and he sweated through his suit jacket (Downs went on to say that this was probably a good thing because it kept his jacket from catching fire).

Many early video performers came to television from radio, and some had difficulty making the transition to a visual medium. Most early television programs were "radio with sight" with stiff "talking head" announcers and few visual enhancements. Early television performers often seemed overly formal and stilted, but production techniques and performance styles changed within a few years of the advent of network television in 1946.

CBS's Don Hewitt (now executive producer of the CBS newsmagazine *60 Minutes*) was one of the first to emphasize visual elements such as maps, graphics, and use of film for a network newscast. News anchors and other performers quickly learned that (1) television needed to incorporate such visual elements and production values in order to survive and (2) television was an intimate medium requiring natural delivery styles.

Production techniques and performers would continue to evolve throughout the 1950s and 1960s. New genres of programs such as game shows made their way to the screen, and many local stations produced late afternoon children's shows featuring cartoons, films, and a live emcee (usually dressed as some type of character such as a cowboy or astronaut). These local children's shows gave way to less expensive syndicated cartoon packages that stations could purchase.

As network newscasts expanded from 15 to 30 minutes in the early 1960s, local stations also began to invest more time and resources in their newscasts. And the 1960s saw the first women and ethnic performers appear on network and local newscasts, bringing some diversity to the television screen.

After remaining the only female network news correspondent for 12 years after she was hired in 1948, ABC's Pauline Frederick was eventually joined by women such as Barbara Walters and Nancy Dickerson, who were hired in the 1960s and 1970s. Mal Goode, also of ABC, was the first African American hired as a network news correspondent in the early 1960s. Local stations began to hire more ethnic Americans as news anchors and reporters later in the decade.

The 1970s saw the development of more portable **ENG** (electronic newsgathering) cameras and VCRs for newsgathering and **EFP** (electronic field production) purposes. Networks and local stations made the transition from shooting news stories, commercials, and other productions on film to using videotape, which was faster to edit and less expensive. ENG and EFP meant that news operations could cover more stories in the field and cover

In the 1960s ABC's Mal Goode was one of the first reporters to come from a minority group. Here Goode interviews another famous first, Jackie Robinson, the first African American major league baseball player

them faster. More reporters and production personnel were hired at a number of stations to cover field stories.

Cable television also began offering more opportunities for video performers in the 1970s, while public access television provided opportunities for those who wanted to produce as well as perform in programs. Although there were questions about the overall quality of these productions and whether anyone was watching, many local politicians and government officials did their first video performances over public access television and thus learned to adapt their delivery styles to video.

Other for-profit cable services were developed in the 1970s and early 1980s as the television industry imitated radio in seeking out niche or specific audiences. Experts in specialized areas became video performers for a myriad of new cable services, a trend that continues today with cable services such as Home and Garden TV (HGTV) and CNBC.

News came to viewers from a different source in the 1980s with the advent of Ted Turner's **CNN** (Cable News Network). Following the format and structure of 24-hour, all-news radio stations for his new cable television service, Turner believed that in this way he could present stories in more depth as well as cover breaking news.

CNN got off to a rocky start (established television personnel said that CNN stood for "Chicken Noodle News"), but it offered opportunities to many younger reporters and performers while also providing a springboard for promising reporters from networks and local stations. CNN eventually established itself as a credible television news operation, especially following its coverage of the Gulf War in 1991. CNN's development and growth came during a decade when the traditional networks (ABC, CBS, and NBC) were cutting back their news operations by closing national and international news bureaus and laying off reporters and production personnel. Much of this downsizing resulted from takeovers of these networks in the mid-1980s by corporations determined to cut costs.

The CNN concept was soon adopted by local cable news channels such as News Channel 8 in Washington, D.C., and Bay TV in San Francisco. These local cable news services provided further opportunities for younger reporters, with many moving on after only a year or two to local on-air news departments (more about these services and opportunities for employment later in this book).

With the advent of ESPN in the late 1970s, and later ESPN 2 in the early 1990s, the all-sports format also made the transition from radio to television. Fox Sports Network, too, now provides coverage of local sports events, creating a need for more performers as play-by-play announcers and analysts (although many sports analysts are former athletes).

We've seen more choices of news and programming formats during the past 10 to 15 years as additional cable channels have become available and the traditional networks have developed cable services of their own (for example, NBC with MSNBC and CNBC). Stop and consider the different types of programs and cable formats we now see (home shopping, health, financial, home and garden, high tech, nature, etc.). Many of these programs and formats did not exist just a few years ago.

People with specialized expertise are in growing demand as video performers in a variety of situations. The following list is only a starting point for the various video performer opportunities:

Television News
Anchor

Field reporter or correspondent

Specialized reporter in health, business, technology, consumer affairs, traffic, and so on

Arts and entertainment or film critic

Weathercaster

Sports anchor

Sports reporter

Public Affairs
Host and interviewer (these people often come from the news division)

Moderator for panels or debates (also often from news division)

Special Events
Parades or other special events host

Sports Coverage (aside from within a newscast)

Play-by-play announcer

Game analyst (often former athletes)

Hosts of sports interview show, weekend sports wrap-up shows, and shows produced for a particular sports team

On-site and sideline reporter

Pregame show host

Specialized Programs

Interview or talk show host

Host on special-interest show such as business, home and garden, nature

Reporter or host on documentaries

Emcee on game shows

Emcee on children's shows

Host of concert, film, or other arts event on television

Veejay or host of show profiling musicians

Commercials

Product demonstration performer

Performer in "slice of life" or "mini-drama" commercial

Infomercial performer (often a well-known personality or person who developed the product or service)

Telesales person on shopping channels such as QVC or Home Shopping Network

Voiceover Talent

Narrators can perform any of a number of video productions, including commercials, station promotional announcements, and documentaries.

This list is by no means comprehensive. As you look at the various headings and positions, you may be able to add to the list. As you "channel surf," see how many other performers and formats you can find. The fact remains that there are numerous opportunities for hardworking people who want to be video performers.

Many aspiring performers have been discouraged on hearing that there is tremendous competition for video performance work and that there are no jobs available. Certainly, there is intense competition for video performance work; however, you can see that opportunities exist for a wide variety of video performers.

When you consider that new cable services seem to appear almost weekly and that more and more programs are geared to special interests, aspiring to be a video performer is a realistic goal for dedicated and knowledgeable individuals. The convergence of Internet and video technologies will also surely provide new types of programs and opportunities. (More information concerning educational training and self-presentation through internships, resumes, and resume tapes is provided in Chapter 12 of this book.)

What if you don't want to make your living as a video performer but instead want to develop video performance skills because in your chosen profession you may appear or are already appearing onscreen? First consider the list of professions and situations in which video is now used in some form:

>   Corporate training or salesperson
>   Educational video and distance learning instructor
>   Religious leader
>   Law (in court trials and advance preparation of clients and witnesses)
>   Politics
>   Service organizations
>   Political activism
>   Medicine
>   Public relations
>   Video conferencing
>   Employment interviews via teleconferencing

Obviously these are just a few of the many professions and situations which call for video skills. As stated earlier, virtually any professional will probably appear on a screen of some kind in the next decade. The career success of individuals may be determined in part by how they are perceived during their onscreen performances. It has long been said that those possessing good communication skills can advance faster in their respective jobs. Good video performance skills are a subset of overall communication skills.

Getting Started: The Equipment You Need and How to Practice

Whether you are a student currently enrolled in a video production or performance course or a professional seeking to develop or improve your video performance skills, you will find that regular practice will help you develop your skills. Having the right equipment is important. You don't need a full studio in order to have individual practice sessions; basic consumer equipment will help you outside studio or more formal practice situations.

Regular practice will help you discern both positive and negative verbal and nonverbal aspects of your performance skills. Videotape doesn't lie, and you may well become aware of previously unnoticed poor vocal habits or distracting mannerisms. Those who already have jobs as television performers often view videotapes of themselves to help them improve their performance.

A small camcorder is one of the best investments you can make. Your instructor or a friend who knows about consumer electronics can assist you in making your choice if you're unsure what to buy. Your budget will probably dictate your purchase, but most consumer camcorders provide adequate video quality under the proper lighting conditions. (*Consumer Reports* magazine is an excellent source if you're unsure which camcorder is best for you. *CR* also gives quality rankings for video products.)

A small tripod is also a good investment. This allows you to mount your camcorder for steadier shots and hold it in place when you don't have a camera operator.

Whether you spend several thousand dollars for the latest digital camcorder or a couple of hundred dollars on a "closeout" model, you should look for a machine with an external microphone jack that can accept an external microphone. Most camcorders now have built-in microphones that may be used in a variety of situations to record ambient sound; however, these microphones do not give you the quality you will need for serious practice and critique sessions. If you are any distance from the camcorder microphone, your voice will lack *presence* (the degree to which you sound as if you are speaking into the microphone). When figuring out your budget, aim to save a few dollars on the camcorder while investing in a good external microphone. Having good audio is an important element for your critique sessions in determining poor speech habits and mispronunciations. Later in this book you will see that audio is one of the most neglected elements of video production.

If your budget does not permit you to buy a camcorder, you may be able to borrow one from your college, university, or workplace (many businesses now have basic video equipment of some kind). Large corporations have professional video facilities where they produce in-house video productions such as sales and training tapes. The personnel in these facilities usually have very demanding schedules but they may be able to give you some studio time for practice (especially if you are task oriented and have specific things you want to accomplish during a practice or rehearsal session). Libraries will sometimes lend video equipment, and video rental stores often rent camcorders.

If all else fails, you can practice delivery in front of a mirror to observe gestures and other nonverbal mannerisms. The mirror has its limitations because it differs in the way the video medium mediates our perception of the performer (more about this in Chapter 2).

If you lack access to video equipment, invest in a quality audiocassette recorder. You should find a recorder that provides excellent voice reproduction and allows you to use an external microphone. Microrecorders may be useful for recording meetings or class lectures, but they will not provide the fidelity you need for your practice sessions. Professors, audiovisual experts, and those who work at radio stations recording news and sports interviews can be good purchase consultants.

After you have purchased your equipment, keep several things in mind as you practice:

■ **Always practice the way you will perform.** In other words, maintain the same level of energy and concentration during a practice session as you do during a real production or classroom production assignment. Practicing any other way will produce limited results and improvement for you. You should treat each practice session as if it were a real performance or production. As corny as it sounds, practice really does make perfect.

■ **Pretend you are someone else.** As much as possible, when you play back a tape in a practice session try to divorce yourself from the fact that what you're seeing and hearing is you on tape. Try to imagine that you're seeing, hearing, and critiquing someone else so that you can be more objec-

Practice and critique will help speed your progress as a video performer.

tive about your performance and not obsess over some elements that are insignificant in the big picture of your development as a video performer. We've all heard people say, "I don't sound like that" after hearing themselves on audiotape or videotape. The fact is that audiotapes and videotapes provide accurate representations of the way you really sound (in other words the way you sound to everyone else who hears you).

You hear your own voice as it is muffled along your jawbone and transmitted to your inner ear. Don't worry about the fact that you don't sound the way you think you do. Work on maximizing your vocal potential and controlling the things that you can control in regard to vocal aspects such as projection and proper pronunciation of words. It has been said that voices are like instruments in an orchestra; we need all types in order to ensure audience interest.

■ **Find a person you can work with (colleague, fellow student, etc.) during practice sessions.** Give each other honest critiques about what you see and hear on tape. You'll also find that having another person present to operate equipment allows both of you to concentrate on your performance while you are being recorded. The support from another person can help energize you and assist with the overall quality of practice sessions.

■ **Keep a log of your practice sessions and the improvement you are making.** Work on isolating certain elements during a session, such as maintaining proper vocal projection or avoiding distracting gestures. Note your progress and what still needs attention. This advice may sound like unnecessary extra work, but you will find that this process actually speeds your progress. There's a saying among video performers and those who teach performance: "Tape is cheap!" Try to keep at least one tape that represents various stages of your development as a video performer. If you are a student performing in various class assignments or a business professional who has been videotaped for any reason, try to get a copy of the tape and keep it for future reference. If you're a student trying to break into the industry as a video performer, you may be able to use the assignment as part of a resume tape.

■ **Be a "creative borrower."** Get into the habit of watching other performers and determining what they do well with their performances. Are there things they do that you could incorporate into your own performance style? Make sure, however, that you don't steal catchphrases or mannerisms that are unique to a particular person (for example, most people would laugh at another sports announcer yelling John Madden's "Boom!" to accentuate a hard-hitting football tackle). There is a difference between creative borrowing and stealing.

■ **"Take your work seriously, but don't take yourself too seriously."** This excellent advice from at least one video performer later in this book extends from your first practice sessions until you're an accomplished video professional.

Channel Surfing Ahead: What You Will Learn in This Book

The nature of the video medium and how it shapes the perception of performers is covered in Chapter 2. You will see how the screen differentiates the way we view the video performer from the way we view a public speaker.

Chapter 3 discusses your appearance and credibility on the screen. You will see that a number of principles from traditional communication theory also apply to video performance. This chapter also considers what to wear and avoid wearing, as well as makeup.

Chapter 4 deals with nonverbal communication, including facial expressiveness, gestures, and movement; Chapter 5 covers vocal aspects such as voice production, phrasing, and emphasis.

Chapter 6 explores the production environment and video personnel, while Chapter 7 looks at the equipment you'll be working with.

Specific performance situations such as interviews (with you as both interviewer and interviewee), news, weather, sports, and commercial talent are covered in Chapters 8 to 11. Chapter 12 provides information on how to get started in the industry through resumes, resume tapes, and internships, as well as discussing the possible future of the industry.

Interviews with a variety of video performers and production personnel appear throughout the book. You will notice that they do not always agree with one another; it is up to you to assimilate the perspectives of each interviewee and discover what seems to work for you and your unique style as a performer.

After addressing issues such as the impact of video on society, the importance of developing performance skills, the evolving nature of video performance and performance roles, and some beginning practice techniques, it is time to start your development as a performer by learning the unique aspects of the video medium and how they shape any performance, ranging from reading copy on *The Six O'Clock News* to doing a training video for your company.

Exercises

1 Keep a log of your viewing habits and how you use television over two weeks. What percentage of your viewing is for entertainment? Do you watch news or informational programs? How does your use of television affect your perception of video performers in various contexts?

2 Note how you relate to video performers in situations such as training sessions, distance learning, and other types of video instruction. Do the performers meet the same standards as those you would see on network or local television? What do they do well, and how could they improve their performances?

3 Review videotapes of past video performers and note the differences between past and present performers. You can find these tapes at video stores, broadcasting museums, or from college instructors and libraries.

4 Develop a budget, and determine what type of video and audio equipment you can afford to purchase to help you with your practice sessions and development as a video performer. Also find out what is available to you through your educational institution or place of employment. In many cases you will be able to use this equipment at little or no cost.

INTERVIEW

Kate Botello

Host of Tech TV's *Extended Play*

Kate Botello, former host of ZDTV's *Screensavers* and *Gamespot,* and current host of Tech TV's *Exended Play,* is one of cable television's rising stars and an example of the emerging role of the video performer in the 21st century. *Screensavers*, cohosted with Leo Laporte, is a show that helps viewers with their computer problems. *Gamespot* highlights developments in computer games. Both have been instant hits due in large part to Kate. Kate was trained in theater, got a "real job" in Ziff Davis's information services department, and was recruited by Laporte to cohost *Screensavers* when he caught her doing a Judy Garland impression while fixing a laser printer.

Question: What was the biggest transition for you from your theater experience to performing on television?

Kate Botello: The back row. In the theater you play to the back row. I played everything big, and when I saw myself on video for the first time I thought, "Oh no! Huge! Everything is too overdone! Anything you think you're doing right on video is probably way too much. So take it down to where you think you're being really tiny, and then take it down further. You have to realize that instead of being seen by someone with two good eyes at a decent distance, you have one big eye that's right in your face. Normally, when you're talking to people there's an environment involved and they're looking at your gestures and there are lots of other things going on. But if it's just you and a lens, it's very quiet and very focused in; so even the tiniest blink reads. You have to really learn how to be as one on one as you possibly can; you don't have to present. The more you present the worse you look. You have to try and be just you and me at the coffee table explaining how the computer works. It's very difficult.

Q: What aspects from stage acting can you transfer to video performance?

KB: Energy and creativity are big ones; because you don't want to be bland either. You're having a conversation, but you want to keep people interested in what you're saying. So, you have to find a creative way to do that. You still want to take people to a *place*, which is the same thing you do in theater. In video, especially with the show we were doing, you try to get people to an understanding place. So you still have a goal. When you're doing a scene in theater you still have to say "What do I want in the scene? What do I want to get?" What I want in video is I want you to understand me. So I have to come up with creative ways to get you to understand me.

I also try to understand the audience as a real live connection; that's the other important thing from theater. In theater, you know there are humans in the audience and you're working for them. In television, you're on the set and you look up and you're looking at a big glass lens. You can't overwhelm yourself by thinking, "There are 17 million pairs of feet up on the coffee table who are looking at me!" But you still have to remember there are humans out there that you're talking to.

I found that when I first started, I would talk to the camera person. So I started small by imagining I was talking to Deb (the camera operator). So I would try to deliver my information to Deb, because she was standing behind the lens. After I got to meet our viewers, I would imagine two or three every day. I'd say to myself, "I wonder how Danielle feels about this segment?" So I'd do the next segment for Danielle. You always have to think about who you're talking to.

Q: What are some of the challenges you face when you're demonstrating a computer or game and trying to relate to the viewers at home?

KB: The thing that I always felt was the most difficult to do was "Vanatizing," holding up a product—especially computer pieces, because they are shiny. The lights hit them wrong. So you have to learn all these different things.

You have to learn to hold up a product and hold it steady. My hands shake all the time whether I'm nervous or not because I'm one of these really hyper people. So I have to set things down on the table; tilt them up to the camera. You have to look in the monitor; you have to multitask. So I'm looking at the monitor, making sure the computer is held at the right angle, making sure my nails are out of the way, that I'm pointing to the specific part of the equipment I'm talking about. Meanwhile, making sure I'm hitting all the technical points and being conversational; because you never know when the director is going to call for a close-up and you don't want to be there starring blankly and reading the cue card. You have to be present in those three places at once.

Netcams are another challenge when you're talking to callers on the phone. Where is the caller? The caller is air. You can't look up. When you hear a voice over a PA system you look up and tilt your head sideways and listen to what the person on the PA system is saying. But when you're watching on television, in theory, that caller is supposed to be right there and you're answering the question to the lens. You have to remember that you're hearing out here, but you're talking to the lens. Netcams help, because you can look at the monitor and see who you're talking to; but you can't get caught by the director looking sideways because it always looks terrible. You have to learn to keep all the same action and focus toward the camera; remember, that's where your audience is. You have to lock eyes with them.

Another challenge is when you have a live audience. There was one time when we had hundreds of people screaming and clapping. Here we are on headsets and we're playing to the live audience, but in that situation we're not supposed to play to the live audience; we're still on the lens. So we're still projecting vocally, which is what you do for the live audience, even though we are miked. Our actual audio is going out to the lens, which is right in front of us. It comes out like we're way too hyped, and over the top, yelling and looking in the wrong place. When it comes to the show, you have to focus in and keep it small.

You acknowledge your live audience when you can in between thoughts as long as you let your at home audience know that there are a lot of people that you're talking to in front of you. It's just like when you talk to two people at once. You can zoom in on one as your primary contact and turn to look just a little at the other person.

Q: Talk about why you use humor on the show.

KB: Because computers can be boring, really boring. You can lose people. It's the same thing as in a lecture; you've got to keep people's attention, especially when it's something they fear. So you have to keep it light so you can remove those barriers in order to say, "This isn't just about science, and hardware, and '1's and 0's.'" This is part of life, and life is funny. So you have to try to find something that is funny to throw in.

We found, generally speaking, that planned schtick, any time we decided that "This is where something funny will happen," is very rarely as funny as when it happens by accident. You can find things that are funny—a frustration you have with the computer, something that can go wrong. Technology can be funny. It's a challenge, but you can find funny things that frustrate you.

Also, find things that have happened to you, because they have probably happened to the audience and they can identify with you.

Q: How do you take technical information on the show and make it user friendly?

KB: A great way to do that is to think about what is a real world application. We do a lot of analogies. If you're talking about "packets," someone might ask, "What's a packet?" and you respond by saying, "It's an envelope." The way you come up with an analogy depends on who is your audience.

Q: How do you think television is going to look in ten years?

KB: That's going to be really interesting! First, there's the advent of high-definition television (HDTV), that is going to be the nightmare of performers everywhere because it is going to amplify your skin down to the pore. So the days of the heavy pancake makeup anchor are going to be gone once everyone gets HDTV.

At the same time convergence is becoming huge by bringing enhanced television and the Web. The "pipes" are getting bigger. Soon, everyone is going to have broadband. It used to be that broadband was just for people who wanted to surf the Web fast, or play games fast. But now there's streaming video over the Web. It doesn't look great right now, but in the future as the "pipes" get fatter, there will be more and more choices. There will be endless hours; you can stream any time you want, and anyone can surf from their living room. What will happen is that there will be thousands of opportunities for anyone who wants to talk, teach, or offer a show over the Internet.

Q: So do you think it is a valid premise that in the 21st century anyone can be on television?

KB: I think it's an absolutely valid premise, because anyone and their dog can have a videoconferencing session right now. We have people calling up our shows on the net cam. We have some people who figure out that you have to look at the net cam and others who turn to wood because they are facing a camera.

Q: What are some of the problems the performer faces with streaming video? What do performers need to do to adjust to that medium?

KB: That is the biggest challenge that we have. We always ask, "Oh, that's going to be streaming?" And it changes what we do. The way the technology works today on an average connection is that if you so much as wink, the whole thing locks up and there is a smear in front of your face.

You want to always work for your lowest common denominator, because you can't assume that your whole audience is broadband. Some people still stream over a 56K or a 28.8K. What they are getting on that is a series of quick pictures. So you pretty much have to stand as still as you can and make sure your voice is getting across what you need to say. If you're holding a product, imagine that you have to slow down as if you are being seen frame by frame.

Q: So what is your advice concerning movement?

KB: It's better if you gesture to the camera instead of to your sides. Anything more that you put in the background that has to get streamed is difficult. You've increased your range as to what needs to be fed. When you stick your arms out to your sides, your background has changed. Keeping movement forward will help, but limiting gestures is the best thing. Small movement and gestures don't work. Another tip is the same kind of thing that you do after coming back from a videotaped story or package. The first thing you want to do is to get their attention, so don't use gestures. When you come back you want to be eye to eye; I want to bring you back to me.

Another example is a teleconference job interview. You have to imagine that everything is focused in. Cross your arms out of the frame so your arms and hands don't flutter and stare into that lens, making contact like you would in a regular job interview.

Q: What are the differences you face between doing a live show versus a taped show like *Extended Play*?

KB: There are huge differences. With a live show, the camera tally light is on and I can keep my energy up for an hour. *Extended Play* is taped, so you have to keep your energy up over multiple takes. Now we're moving out to location shoots, so it's even more difficult because I have all these distractions going on around me. In those situations, I have to envision that I'm at a party, and I'm talking to one person at a party.

I think that the additional thing that is going to be useful is that I have to produce. Now what I have to do is put a videotaped story or package together, which means that I have to know what I'm talking about, learn how to talk about the subject in a conversational manner, learn how to write for a voiceover so it sounds conversational as opposed to print. That's very important, because nine times out of ten people will write a script for a voiceover and it sounds like a magazine article or an essay. You have to write to speech. Read it out loud before you do it.

After that we have to take the whole piece in and edit it and come up with pieces of video that convey what I've already said in the voiceover, which is another challenge. Once you know the whole process of what's involved in putting these spots together, you still have to keep the focus to you. You have to get people's attention and have them focus on you.

Q: Discuss what you do in creating a profile of the audience.

KB: On my last show, *Screensavers,* we were talking to technology enthusiasts who generally already knew a lot about technology. These are people who love technology and don't so much want to know the "what'" to do but the "why" behind what they are doing. It's an educational thing and they want to feel smarter.

Gamespot is all about entertainment— what the audience wants to learn. "Is the game fun? Where should I spend my money?" Gamers are passionate about games, and they are younger. You can't patronize, but you have to use different language. You have to keep their attention a little more. People who are there to learn are more likely to give you their undivided attention. But a "gamer" watches a show the same way they watch a game. A game can be very "ADD" [attention deficit disorder]. There are explosions going on over here and something else going on over there.

But a game can also be hugely immersive, to [the point] where you are sucked in and you don't see anything else but that game. So you have to realize that there has to be a way to keep things immersive and the way that they do that is to put things in the first-person perspective. You are the one experiencing these things; so a great challenge is to make those who are watching the show feel like they are playing the game, which is a huge challenge, but it can be done. Viewers are watching for fun and they want to see action. They want to see those screen shots to see how pretty the game looks, they want to see the monsters, and they want to see the special effects because they are going to spend their money. People want to know if this is going to be exciting and cool.

You don't want to show people walking down a path, even though the graphic may be pretty, if the real fun of the game is the "Slime Beast" at the end of the path. You're going to have to show the "Slime Beast" to get people to want to go down the path with you.

Q: So you have to be organized as to when you show various elements.

KB: Yes! It's like on *Beavis and Butthead;* whenever something blows up, Beavis says, "Explosions are cool!" Well, people think explosions are cool; that's the reason why action movies have explosions every five minutes. Sometimes you have to put explosions in your package; that's why people are playing the games and watching the show.

Q: Is part of the challenge of the show that younger people can process information faster than older people?

KB: Younger people can handle a lot more stimuli at once than people in my generation. There are people who are used to seeing a million things going on at once and others who like to focus in. You have to find a happy medium. You can't just make the show for those who are avid, obsessed gamers who are used to seeing a lot. There's one game out now where there are so many things going on at once that I can't even find my character on the screen—but they can.

If I want other people to learn how to play games, I can't just talk to people who are already into it; you have to get new people. I have to come up with some kind of compromise; I have to show the noise and the silence. I have to make both of those work because I want to get the attention of people who are new and keep the attention of people who are already into it.

Q: Finally, if you were to list what you consider to be the most important elements of video performance, what would they be?

KB: First, always consider your audience. Talk to them and figure out who they are. Even if you only have surveys, read them. That is your job as the talent; you've got to find out who you're talking to. Tailor yourself accordingly. It doesn't mean that you completely change your personality depending on who you are talking to, because people will sniff you out as a fake. It's more like if you're at a party, and your best friend is in one corner and the CEO is

in the other, you're going to talk to them a little differently.

Identify with your audience and find something you can identify with; be as normal and conversational as possible. Remember that this is real life, especially if you're teaching or explaining something. You have to be as straightforward as you possibly can; don't rely on the magic of television. You can say, "The camera's on a weird angle now." On the *Screensavers* show we never pretended there wasn't a crew there or that we were not making a television show, because the whole purpose was demystifying technology. You can't demystify technology and allow the magic of television to hide all the flaws at the same time. Be yourself, be patient, and come up with real-world examples for what you're talking about. Think, "What else works this way?" You learned to do that back in kindergarten when the teacher asked, "What else is big and red and bouncy?"

Be aware of your eyes and who you are talking to. Remember that the understanding is more important than the explanation. People understanding you is more important than you coming up with a lovely way to explain it. Have a beginning, a middle, and an end to an explanation. If you are meandering, your audience will meander as well. Tell them what you're going to tell them, tell them, and then tell them what you told them.

When I was in theater, I had an instructor who said that the nonverbal behavior for understanding was when you walked up to someone and put your hands on his or her face. In television, you have to find a way to reach out and take the viewer by the face, and eye-to-eye make them understand.

CHAPTER TWO

The Impact of the Screen on Your Performance and Your Responsibilities as Performer

Four decades ago media theorist Marshall McLuhan made the now famous statement that the medium is the message. McLuhan emphasized that each medium has different ways of shaping our perceptions of messages. Nowhere is this truer than in television. Early video performers, ranging from Hollywood celebrities to politicians, had to learn to adapt their performances to television. For some performers this transition took years. Others vanished from public view because they were unable to adapt.

Understanding the characteristics of the video medium will give you a major advantage as a performer and will help you become an effective on-screen communicator. These concepts are universal, applying across the board to a variety of situations. This chapter discusses how people watch television; how the unique aspects of the video screen impact your performance; your responsibilities as a performer; and how to control nervousness while performing.

The Unique Aspects of Video

Video as an Intimate Medium Consider for a moment how you watch television. In most cases you're watching in your home, either alone or with a few family members or friends. With exceptions such as bars, airports, and a few other public places, it is seldom that you watch television in a public area or in a crowd.

Video convergence with the Internet means that television becomes even more personal when viewers sit at computer screens and interact with programs. Educational institutions and numerous corporations now have carrels and rows of screens capable of showing various video formats. Even though there may be dozens of people viewing the content simultaneously, people in the room are often isolated because of the configuration of viewing stations.

Another aspect of intimacy is that video performers often appear repeatedly on a nightly newscast or daily talk show. Viewers feel that they know the performer and form viewing preferences accordingly. A piece of advice that has proved helpful for both radio and television performers over the years is for them to visualize one or two people listening in a car or at home watching their performance.

The major principle to remember is that most successful performers are audience-centered, that is, they always have their audiences as the priority when performing. Knowledge of the following aspects of video will help you connect with your audience.

Screen Size   You will read several times in this book that video is a close-up medium. For years, television screens were relatively small, requiring directors to use close-ups of performers so that they seemed closer to the audience. Screens have gotten bigger and the resolution (picture clarity) has improved. **High-definition television (HDTV)** makes video images appear as if they are high-resolution photography that moves. Conversely, as more people watch video on computer screens, their screen size will be relatively small.

No matter what the screen size, watching video will continue to be a close-up experience. Directors like to fill the frame with a subject during newscasts and talk shows so that the viewer feels a closer connection with the performer. Many of the shots a director will use are called **head shots** that approximate life size interaction.

It is important for you to remember that you must scale your performance to the close-up nature of video. Some people who are effective public speakers have difficulty making the transition to video because their gestures are too big or seem staged. Others may overproject their voices instead of allowing the microphone to do the work.

In most cases, you should treat television performance as an interpersonal communication experience in which you connect with other performers in the studio and with viewers watching you at home. This is often difficult because you are in a large studio space with people behind cameras and other equipment, in a situation not conducive to intimate communication. You will learn specific techniques on how to achieve this interpersonal style in the chapters on nonverbal and vocal aspects.

RATINGS POINTER

We've discussed video as an interpersonal medium, but what about television situations in which the performer is talking to a large in-house audience, such as a late night talk show monologue or an infomercial production demonstration? Note what the performer has to do in order to talk to the audience while maintaining contact with viewers at home. Note when performers look into the camera lens and how they limit movement even if they are in a large space. ★ ★ ★ ★

■ **Aspect Ratio**   Aspect ratio refers to the proportional dimensions of the video screen, which is three units high and four units wide (the bottom and top of the screen are longer than the sides). It is important to remember that video is a horizontal medium, because this dictates which objects look best on the screen, how subjects and objects are shot, and how performers must hold or position objects.

A musician playing a guitar is an easy shot for directors to compose, because guitars are held horizontally. The musician and guitar fill the frame, providing pleasing composition for the viewer. A golfer putting on a green provides more of a compositional challenge, however, because there is more empty space around long narrow objects.

The regular screen aspect ratio is 3 × 4.

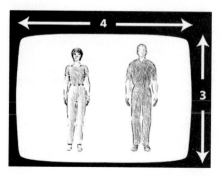

The HDTV screen aspect ratio is 9 × 16, similar to a movie screen.

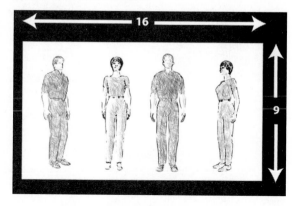

Commercial performers sometimes have to hold products in unnatural positions to allow viewers to see the products and for the sake of better screen composition. For example, how many times have you seen a commercial spokesperson holding a small product package next to his or her head parallel to the chin? We will see in later chapters how aspect ratio impacts your nonverbal communication.

Depth of Field   You've probably heard this term with regard to still photography. **Depth of field** is the area in front of the camera that appears in good focus. Once a camera focuses on you, be careful that you don't move too close to or too far away from the camera; you might step out of focus. Work with your director, camera operators, and other personnel so you know your use of space and movement limitations.

Image Size   Objects closer to the camera will appear larger than objects in the background. Performers near the camera will usually use more subtle facial expressions and gestures than those farther away from the camera. You should try to adjust your mannerisms along with your position in relationship to the camera.

Screen Space Versus Real Space   One of the first things that new video performers note is that **screen space** is very different from real space. Physically, they have to work closely with other performers, and furniture

Performers often have to hold objects close to the head for good composition.

Foreground and background size relationships.

These objects are placed too far apart for proper composition.

and props are very close together. What seems to be close in the television studio appears normal on the video screen because the screen exaggerates distance.

When you're standing in a video studio watching an interview being shot, you will notice that the interviewer and interviewee are sitting very close together and their knees may be close to touching. View the same two people on the screen and the distance looks normal. Some performers feel uncomfortable at first because of the lack of interpersonal space between people on the set, but most are able to make the adjustment with time and practice. After you have become more experienced, you may need to give newer performers some orientation concerning screen space.

Besides working close together, performers also need to control gestures and other movements to keep them somewhat slower and smaller than they would use in normal conversation (more about this in the chapter on nonverbal and vocal aspects).

Another consideration regarding space is object placement. If you have a table in front of you with several objects you'll be using in the production, you should move the objects closer together. This will make them appear at a normal distance from one another on the screen.

■ **Audio Presence**   The nature of the video screen also impacts audio. You may be tempted to overproject your voice in a large studio or space. Remember that while you may be performing in a physically large space, you're being viewed in the tight box of the video screen. Work for a consistent voice level, and let the microphone and audio engineer do the work of making sure you can be heard. Work on phrasing, emphasis, and rate to communicate emotion. Take a tip from actors and stage directors who say that volume does not always equal emotion or intensity.

■ **Video Decreases Your Dynamism**   One thing you may notice after watching yourself on videotape is that you appear to lack energy. You probably thought that you were enthusiastic in your performance, but somehow it seems flat on screen. Video is a flat medium, and the loss of depth tends to diminish your energy level or dynamism.

Video performers often have to force a bit more energy into their performances than they would use during normal conversation. Finding the balance between energizing your performance and overdoing it can be challenging, but working with videotape and friendly critics can help you find the right level. What seems overdone or "over the top" for you may be the proper energy level for your video performance.

■ **Video Exaggerates Movement**   We have already mentioned that you should control gestures and other movement. Keep in mind that television exaggerates all movement and that you can appear nervous or distracting to viewers if you do not limit it.

Perhaps you've seen a performer standing in front of the camera swaying back and forth and moving out of the frame. This makes it difficult for the camera operator to keep the performer in the frame and is annoying for the viewer to watch.

Equally annoying to watch is a performer who sits in a swivel chair and moves back and forth or side to side. Learn to sit in chairs without making distracting movements, and alert guests to do the same.

Walking on a set or on location must also be controlled. You should walk a little more slowly than your normal pace. We will discuss movement in more detail in the chapter on nonverbal communication.

The difference between the experienced and novice video performer is that the former understands these universal aspects of the video medium and they become second nature when performing. Experienced performers also understand their responsibilities in a variety of contexts.

Your Responsibilities in the Production Process

Novice video performers are often surprised by the fast pace of the video production process. People who have performed in theater or film sometimes find it difficult to adjust to the faster pace of video production. If you have watched a theatrical film being shot on location, you probably noticed that there were numerous "takes" and that it took a great deal of time to shoot individual sequences. You may have been involved in a high school, college, or community theater production that took weeks of rehearsal before the public performances.

Video productions are usually fast-paced with strict deadlines and budgets. Performers need to adapt to this quicker pace. The tasks discussed below are your responsibility during preparation for and implementation of the actual performance.

■ **Preparation** It is important for you to realize early in your career that preparation is one of the most important aspects of performance. Video performers who are well prepared for their productions are highly prized in the industry. Performers who have their scripts memorized, remember the backgrounds of guests they are interviewing, and know what visual elements they will be using in productions are far more successful than those who haven't prepared in advance.

There is an expectation in the industry that if you are a performer, you will be prepared to the best of your ability. If you are in a video performance or production class, you should treat each production assignment as if you were doing an actual production in the video industry. Take each assignment seriously and practice the way you will perform. Instructors have designed assignments with specific purposes and goals in mind, so try to understand the intended outcomes of assignments and prepare accordingly. Talk to your instructor if you are unsure what he or she expects.

If you're a professional doing a video performance, use practice time wisely and know your content. Watch rehearsals of your performances in advance of the real production. You should strive for the same level of preparation as industry professionals.

RATINGS POINTER

In production and performance classes you should try to perform so well that you can save your performance on tape to create a resume tape. A resume tape shows brief excerpts of your performances in a variety of situations and is a prerequisite of your being hired in the industry.

If you're in the private sector doing any type of video performance, you should save all your tapes. You never know when you'll be asked to give another video presentation, and your ability to communicate via video may make you more marketable (many corporations are looking for people with some form of on-camera experience). ★ ★ ★ ★

■ **Working with a Script** Trying to memorize a **script** may seem difficult. However, here are some hints to make it easier. First, you should try to work without a full script whenever possible. If you don't have a **teleprompter** (a device that projects your script in front of the camera lens for you to read) and you have to read a script word for word, it can limit your contact with the audience (especially if you have to spend a large portion of the time looking at the script). In many cases you can give the necessary information to viewers without reading a script word for word.

In cases where there is too much information or a need for exact word choice, you may use several preparation techniques to aid memorization or greater familiarity with the script:

- **Write your own material.** Information is usually easier to remember if you created it, and if you can write it yourself, the script will also be written in your speaking style, making it easier for you to deliver.

- **Practice the script out loud.** Don't sit in a chair and read the script silently to yourself or mumble through the reading. Any time you perform a motor skill such as speaking or typing your script, it will assist you in the memorization process; also, you will begin to recognize the cadence, along with other vocal aspects, and you will memorize the way you are "saying" the material.

- **Prepare a mental outline of the script.** Do this before trying word-for-word memorization. Know the key concepts, or "skeleton," of the script before trying to memorize the details. If you know the progression of the script's main ideas, it will be much easier to remember individual words.

- **Record your reading.** Make an audiotape and then listen to yourself. After doing this several times, you'll begin to remember the vocal patterns and the rhythm you hear. The great thing about this technique is that you can listen to the tape while driving in your car or doing other activities.

- **Do a picture outline of the script.** Draw small pictures that visualize the script's concepts in the margin or on another piece of paper. Many people find that they are able to remember visual imagery better than words.

- **Print your script on colored paper.** You may have watched television news anchors and noticed that their scripts are on pink, blue, or some other colored paper. This is because white paper reflects studio light, making it difficult for the camera's contrast range and quality reproduction. Performers also find it difficult to read a script on white paper with so much studio light reflecting off the script.

- **Make the fonts as large as you need for easy reading.** Use your computer's word-processing capabilities to do this. You can boldface words that you want to emphasize and type other cues that will help you with your reading, such as phonetic spellings of difficult names and places.

- ***Use notes instead of a script when possible.*** You can use the script as an outline, but use notes to aid you in being more spontaneous. Make sure you write out introductions, transitions, and conclusions, because these are crucial for observing time limitations and serve as cues to the director.

- ***Mark your script to indicate when important cues are coming.*** For example, note when to go to a videotape or other production elements, when to move, or what words to emphasize (again, you can do some of this on your word processor in advance so that your script is easier to read and not filled with pencil markings).

- ***Number each page.*** Write the numbers on one of the top corners and don't clip or staple your pages together. Follow the practice of news anchors and slip the page you've just completed under the rest of the script.

Teleprompters and cue cards are used in a variety of fully scripted situations, but since you never know when you will have to perform without the aid of these devices, knowing how to work with a script or "hard copy" is essential.

After considering how video shapes your performance and the numerous responsibilities you have as a performer, you may be thinking, "I have trouble enough speaking in public or performing under basic circumstances. Now I have to worry about a new set of issues and technical aspects. How do I stay calm in this new situation?"

You have one final responsibility as a performer, and that is to give the impression of being at ease and in control of the situation. Few things are worse for viewers than watching a nervous performer; in fact, nervous performers often make viewers nervous. There are several techniques you can borrow from public speaking and other types of performance situations to help you manage stress as a video performer.

Minimizing Performance Anxiety

Whether you call it performance anxiety, stage fright, or fear of public speaking, the stress involved in performing in public is real. Results from some public opinion polls indicate that speaking in public is our number one fear (worse than the fear of death). One can easily list ten or more stress factors in public performance. Years of polling students and professionals have revealed several major elements contributing to performance anxiety:

■ **Reluctance to be the center of attention.** As strange as this may sound, many performers are shy and fear the first few seconds of any public communication event. There is a feeling that all eyes are on the performer and that any mistakes will be readily visible to the audience. This type of thinking puts the performer at an immediate disadvantage in communicating his or her message effectively.

■ **Unfamiliarity with the studio or performance environment.** Television has been around for many years, but for some people the television studio or performance area is still a novelty. Suddenly the performer is faced with an unnatural environment in front of the camera(s) and lights with people moving around in the background while he or she tries to maintain concentration. Such a situation is disconcerting and hardly conducive to trying to connect with an unseen audience.

■ **Fear of making mistakes.** Most novice public speakers are afraid of stumbling over words, forgetting where they are in the presentation, or misspeaking in some other way. This fear is heightened in the video performance environment for many of the reasons mentioned earlier and because the performer is often asked to do things in rapid succession while maintaining concentration. For example, television news anchors must speak to the audience in a natural manner and maintain concentration while they are receiving information through an earpiece (called an **interruptible foldback** or **IFB**). Think about the person who is doing a demonstration on a home and garden show who must not only complete the project at hand but also talk to the camera and project a warm and friendly personality.

■ **Anxiety concerning whether the audience will like the performer.** This is the question all performers, especially beginners, ask most often. Your performance appears onscreen for the audience to enjoy or reject. You may be discouraged if someone gives a negative critique of your performance in a live public speaking situation, and this feeling is often intensified when you hear a critique of your televised performance. The stakes are higher for the performer in a local television station or network situation, as thousands of people are viewing at a given time (consider that in some major cities—also known as markets—a program getting just one Nielsen rating point is attracting an audience of 40,000 people).

■ **Personal appearance.** We've already discussed how we usually don't like the way we sound when we hear our voices on audio- or videotape. The same feelings often surface when we look at ourselves on the television screen. Video flattens our appearance while also showing us in profile or at other angles that seem strange to us. The screen also tends to make us look heavier than we do in real life. Any or all of these factors are sometimes discouraging for beginning performers, causing them to be overly critical when viewing their tapes.

There are probably other concerns you have or that you have heard from others regarding public performance, and specifically video performance. Compare notes with your fellow students, instructors, and colleagues about your performance concerns and how to deal with them. Following are some suggestions for minimizing the five previously mentioned fears, along with some ways to deal with general stress you may experience as a performer.

Performers who have information they believe in and want to share with audiences usually want to be the center of attention. There's an old saying in public communication that you should either be sincere or fake sincerity. Faking sincerity is incredibly difficult, so don't talk about things you don't believe in or can't get excited about.

In many ways performance is like a video soapbox for you to express your knowledge, share information, entertain, or introduce interesting people to an audience. See your performance as an opportunity instead of an obstacle to connecting with an audience. Put yourself in the position of the audience: They want to be entertained or informed, and they want to connect with you as a performer even though the chance for them to establish this connection may be relatively brief because of their short attention spans or use of remote controls to change channels.

Content and organization can affect your delivery. If you know what you're going to say and it is well organized, you start to do natural positive things that energize your delivery (think about the way you use your voice and gestures while telling a friend an interesting story). Don't forget that while there may be many viewers, the fact remains that video is an intimate medium and what you're really trying to do is visualize and connect with one or two people in a room watching you.

In most cases you can control familiarity with your video performance environment. As in any public performance situation, you should be familiar with your space and the objects in that space. Try sitting or standing on the set you will be using. Practice in front of the cameras and lights, and be familiar with as much of the production process as you can. If you are demonstrating objects during your performance, try working with the objects in advance, and find out which cameras will be shooting each object. See if you can find production personnel who are available and willing to speak with you about what to expect.

Try taking a tour of the studio well before your scheduled production so that you can observe what is going on under less pressure. This advance trip to the studio will help you with another practical matter: knowing how to get there. Nothing increases your stress level more than getting lost, and then trying to calm down so that you can perform.

Everybody makes mistakes. Even the most seasoned performer may misspeak, stumble over words, or look at the wrong camera. The key concepts here are to keep mistakes to a minimum, not draw too much attention to them, and move on.

We discussed the importance of preparation earlier in this chapter. Preparation not only helps you become familiar with material, it increases your confidence level and helps in minimizing mistakes. If you do make a mistake there are catchphrases such as "or rather," "I misspoke, what I mean is . . ." and others that you may use to get back on track. Make sure you have several of these catchlines in mind so that you will seem natural and in control if mistakes do happen.

Sometimes you may get caught looking at the wrong camera. Your floor manager will try to get you to look at the right camera and you can try to see which camera has its **tally light** shining (the tally light is the red light on top of the camera that indicates which camera is "taking" or "on"). Turn your head and body smoothly toward the camera that is on and don't draw attention to the mistake. Watch how news anchors handle the situation if they are caught looking at the wrong camera. In most cases they are excellent models.

Don't dwell on a mistake once you've made it. This disrupts your concentration and increases the possibility that you will make more mistakes. A good analogy is a football fumble. A good running back who fumbles the ball doesn't dwell on the fumble but instead thinks about what he will do the next time he gets the ball (most good running backs want the ball given to them again as soon as possible). Obviously, once you've made a mistake in a live video production, you can't return and do a "retake." Videotaped productions allow you to do multiple takes so that mistakes can be edited out; the best "take" is used for the final version of the production.

Videotaping and post-production work (editing, adding graphics and video segments, etc.) help to increase the overall quality of a production and video performance, but video performers should not be less prepared during a videotaped production. Treat videotaped productions as if you are performing live, preparing at the same level and intensity as if you had to get it right the first time.

If you do make a mistake, try to regain your composure immediately, because the director and crew will want to restart the production as soon as possible (in many cases the director may keep the tape rolling and restart within a few seconds). Listen to and focus on the director, producer, and crew so that you won't repeat the mistake.

Above all, don't make mistakes worse by making negative facial expressions or verbal comments. Rolling your eyes or shaking your head makes the situation worse and is not something that professional performers do. Be careful not to show verbal or nonverbal displeasure concerning your performance at the end of a production, because you may still be on air or the tape still rolling. Never make negative comments about another performer or guest. Too often these comments are either heard in the control room or captured on tape, with embarrassing results.

One final thought about mistakes: The mistake always seems ten times worse to you than to the audience. You know what you want to say and how you should say it, but if it doesn't come out quite right the audience is often unaware that you made an error (watch yourself on videotape after a performance and in many cases your response will be, "That's not nearly as bad as I thought it was.").

The question of whether or not the audience will like you is one that performers repeatedly ask. You can increase the likelihood that audiences will like you by following many of the steps previously mentioned in this chapter. Preparation, sincerity, and a polished performance will all create a positive foundation for the audience's perception of you.

Keep in mind that you have unique knowledge and abilities. Television viewing would be dull if everyone performed the same way and had the same style. Work on isolating what you do well in performance (there will be tasks you do well even as a novice performer) and try to enhance these. Try to be objective about the skills that need improvement and to get feedback from others you trust.

Watch what other performers do well, but don't try to copy them. As noted earlier, there's a difference between watching performers for general techniques you may want to use in your performance and stealing another performer's style, which will damage your credibility.

Audience analysis, discussed in detail in Chapter 3, is another tool to help you understand how the audience perceives you. If you know what is important to the audience, you are more likely to understand how to relate to them and elicit a positive audience response.

RATINGS POINTER

You may have heard about a local television performer who moves to a different city and fails to connect with the audience. The performer probably isn't doing anything different than what he or she did in the previous location. Different geographic regions have varying preferences concerning content and style. Performers often have to make adjustments to their individual styles in order to be successful in a different location. ★ ★ ★ ★

Chapter 3 offers tips to help you improve your clothing, makeup, and other aspects of your personal appearance. Again, when critiquing videotape of your performances, try to distance yourself a bit from the fact that you're watching *yourself* onscreen. Some performers make a conscious attempt to review their performances as if they were watching someone else. When you watch yourself on tape, you're usually surprised by the way you look and sound, but others will see how you look on tape as a close reproduction of how you look and sound in real life.

One final thought on appearance. Even the most attractive performers would like to change something about themselves. How many times have you cringed when you've heard an attractive person say things such as, "I wish I could lose a few pounds" or "I wish my nose was smaller." Control what you can control and try not to worry about the things you can't.

Your clothing, grooming, and other related factors will all help you look better. Work on controlling these and you will make significant progress in improving your on-screen appearance.

Additional Tips to Minimize Performance Anxiety

We've discussed some of the main reasons for performance anxiety and how we can minimize it. The following additional tips may also help you manage your stress:

■ **Know your body.** What makes you feel energized, and what makes you feel more stressed? Everyone has different eating and sleeping habits, and for some people exercise provides positive energy whereas for others it results in hyperactivity. Take note of what you can eat or drink before you perform.

Many speech and voice coaches will tell you to avoid caffeinated drinks because of irritation to your throat. Others claim that a cup of coffee or hot tea helps to clear the throat (while also providing some energy). Some performers can drink carbonated beverages before performing and others can't. Some people have problems with dairy products because they coat the throat. After several practice performance sessions, you will know what works for you (the same goes for what you can eat before performing).

Some people like to exercise or take a brisk walk to relax before performing, while others avoid physical activity. You will find a ritual that works for you, but one thing is certain: Regular exercise will improve your energy level, your breathing, and probably also your overall appearance.

Avoid smoking, and if you use alcohol, use it sparingly. Yes, we've often seen video or photographs of well-known performers smoking, but we now know the harmful effects of smoking to throat and lungs. Smoking is similar to "running with weights" in regard to your vocal care. Overuse of alcohol can also irritate your throat.

■ **Warm up your voice before you start.** Practice reading your script or talk to crew members before your performance. This helps keep your voice from cracking and sounding raspy (some vocal warm-up exercises are provided in Chapter 4).

■ **Yawn.** It may sound strange (and you may look strange doing them), but exaggerated yawning exercises help to relax your throat and neck muscles while giving you more oxygen. Some of the best performers swear by these exercises.

■ **Be familiar with the beginning of your script.** Know the first few words to the point that you could recite them at a moment's notice. You should be familiar with your entire script, but the first few seconds are extremely important in building confidence and establishing positive momentum. If you get through these first moments, you will increase your confidence level and, therefore, the probability of having a successful overall performance.

■ **Check your appearance.** This sounds pretty basic, but do look in a mirror before you go on the set to see if your tie is straight, blouse or shirt buttoned, and everything is zipped. Performers often waste production time (and cause embarrassment to themselves) because they have not taken care of these details before walking on the set.

■ **Channel your nervous energy.** You can do this by pressing your thumb against your fingers as hard as you can. This piece of advice comes from speech consultant Ron Hoff in his book *I Can See You Naked* (the title comes from that old piece of public speaking advice that you can minimize your nervousness by visualizing your audience naked or in their underwear). You can channel nervous energy down your arm and into your hands and thumb, then release it through pressing your thumb against your fingers. In most cases, no one will be aware that you are doing this. Transferring much of the nervous energy in your arms and shoulders to your fingers will give you better control of it.

■ **Have some water nearby.** Keep it just out of view of the camera (if you're doing an interview from a desk or if there is a coffee table on the set you can keep your water in view). This will help keep you from getting a dry mouth and throat and prevent you from being dehydrated under hot studio lights. Try to take sips of water between takes if you are in a longer production. This is especially important if you are shooting a field production on a hot day. You'll often see news reporters and other performers carrying water bottles with them on location.

Feeling at least a little nervous before you perform is natural and can actually assist you. There's an old saying used by performance coaches: "It's perfectly natural for you to have butterflies in your stomach. What you want to do is to get them flying in formation." Using the tips we've discussed in this chapter will help you keep your butterflies "flying in formation."

Rewind and Fade to Black

Knowing how the screen mediates your performance, understanding your responsibilities as a performer, and learning how to minimize your stress can give you a good foundation for becoming a successful video performer. The principles outlined in this chapter are universal and apply to a wide variety of situations.

While practicing, work on developing rapport with classmates, colleagues, and friendly critics to see how you're progressing as a performer. The more eyes and feedback you can get from people the faster your learning curve and the greater the likelihood of your success.

Chapter 3 extends and builds on some of the items touched on in this chapter concerning appearance while also helping to build your credibility as a performer.

Exercises

1 Videotape yourself, and study your gestures and movement. See if your movement is adjusted to the video or if you need to work for more overall control.

2 Try at least two of the memorization techniques mentioned in this chapter. Is there one that seems to work best for your learning style? Remember that people learn and retain information in different ways; some are better with imagery, whereas others are better auditory learners.

3 Talk with at least one other person about what causes you stress in public performance. Do you agree with the analysis presented in this chapter? Are there other things that make you anxious as a performer?

4 Develop a pre-performance ritual that works to reduce your stress. What tips have you included from this chapter? Have you developed some advice of your own? Compare what you do with what others are doing in pre-performance. Once you find a ritual that works for you, make sure you re-peat it every time you perform.

INTERVIEW

Fran Andrews

Client Coordinator, Golden Gate Productions

As a client coordinator, Fran Andrews prepares clients for a variety of productions at the Golden Gate Productions studios, located just north of San Francisco. Fran works with clients such as ABC's *Good Morning America*, Fox Sports, ESPN, Chevron, Bank of America, Toyota, and the San Francisco Giants baseball team. In this interview she talks about how television mediates one's performance.

Question: What do you see as being the major difference(s) between a live and video performance?

Fran Andrews: The most important thing to keep in mind when doing a television versus public performance is that television is very unforgiving and very specific. You're in focus and we see your entire face and every expression. If you try to cheat a look off to the side to see what is going on, everybody's going to see that. When you're doing a public performance, you can often get by with a cheated glance or with an offhand gesture. With television, you can't get away with much of anything.

Q: Compare energy levels between public and video performance.

Fran Andrews (center) confers with crew members before
a production at Golden Gate Productions.

FA: Because of the distance between you and the audience, if you're too hyper the audience may not see all of that. If you're too low energy, that's a problem in both situations, but more of a problem with television because it dulls your energy level. If you speak clearly, you can get away with having a higher energy level; but that's only if you speak clearly. If you don't speak clearly, you get this whirlwind blur and people's attention gets lost because they are not hearing what you're saying. On the other side, if you're too low with your energy, people watch you and they just want to take a nap or change the station.

Q: What about the lack of depth you get with the television screen?

FA: There are some things you can do to compensate for this. If you're concerned about how you are perceived, you can cheat to one side or another in television where that is more difficult to do in person; people are wondering why you're tilting your head to the side. That does work as an advantage. Again, energy is that key thing here because television is a flat medium. If you're energetic, you help solve the lack-of-depth problem.

Credibility and Appearance

As we watch television on a daily basis, we are bombarded with hundreds of persuasive messages. Often, we make judgments about these messages based upon who is delivering them, ranging from which political candidate to vote for to which athletic shoes to buy.

The concept that the person presenting the message is important in the art of persuasion is not a new one. Over 2,300 years ago Aristotle said that a speaker's character "may almost be called the most effective means of persuasion he possesses." During the centuries since, scholars have tried to isolate the principles that assist in building a speaker's or performer's character or credibility.

Credibility is a term we often hear applied to public officials and performers, and there are numerous definitions for the word. For our purposes, credibility is defined as why people ought to listen to, remember, and act upon what you are saying. Your credibility will determine whether or not you are able to maintain audience interest while providing informative or persuasive messages.

People used to think in terms of status or rank when considering source credibility. In light of political events over the past twenty-five years or so, we know that a person's high rank doesn't necessarily make him or her credible. Credibility is something that an individual must earn no matter what his or her status may be.

Credibility is situational and is determined by the audience. There is an old joke about three baseball umpires who discuss how they call balls and strikes. Umpire 1 says, "I call them what they are." Umpire 2 counters with, "I call them as I see them." Umpire 3 tops the other two by stating, "They ain't nothing until I call them."

In many ways the determination of whether or not you are a credible performer is made in much the same way Umpire 3 calls balls and strikes: You aren't credible until the audience says you are. A person may seem credible in one situation but not another. A former professional athlete may be asked to be a color analyst for a game because of his or her expertise and understanding of strategy of that sport. The same athlete would probably not be asked to give his or her opinion about the stock market on a cable financial network.

The Building Blocks of Credibility

Many elements contribute to your credibility. These may be grouped into four major areas: trustworthiness, expertise, dynamism, and identification.

Trustworthiness   Trustworthiness is the audience's perception of you as honest, fair, sincere, and friendly. Viewers make judgments as to whether they would like to meet you, if given the chance, and whether they perceive you as liking your job.

In situations such as television journalism, trustworthiness becomes a key component in viewers' decisions to watch and listen to particular news anchors, interviewers, and reporters. Audiences *value* broadcast journalists who have established records of accuracy and honesty and usually perceive them as trustworthy; for example, in 1976 opinion polls determined that CBS anchorperson Walter Cronkite was perceived as one of the most credible people in the nation. Journalists who are inaccurate in their reporting or jump to conclusions when covering an event damage their trustworthiness and often shorten their careers.

We live in an age of what might be called the "antiperformer," in which some television performers draw attention to themselves and their shows by loud, fast talking, and outrageous behavior. Networks, local stations, and cable channels fill the airways with talk shows featuring bizarre hosts and guests in an effort to attract ratings at a low production cost. Some use questionable language or outright profanities on air.

This type of "antiperformer" behavior may be attractive to some breaking into the industry, but they should ask the question, "Is this really what I want to do and how I want to be perceived in the long term?" In most cases, the answer is no.

Those who tend to have the longest performance careers and be most admired by the audience and their industry peers are performers respectful of their audiences. Ask yourself how you want to be perceived by people months or years from now concerning your personal and performance reputation. Remember, too, that it may take a long time for you to establish a positive reputation and that just one unethical or questionable act may permanently damage it.

Building a reputation for trustworthiness extends beyond the studio and television screen. Many local and national television personalities are involved in community and public service work, hosting various special events and giving speeches, often without pay. Some give tours of their stations to various visiting groups. Giving back to the community can have a major positive impact on public perception of performers and their stations.

Expertise   Performers who are knowledgeable, qualified, and informed have expertise. Television stations and networks hire professionals in other fields to appear in specialized programs and segments because of their areas of expertise. Doctors now appear on local news health segments, stock market analysts in business segments, and experts from other professions and specialists in their areas of expertise.

Preparation can be a key element in whether or not the audience perceives you as an expert in a certain area. Have you done your homework when researching a particular news issue or guest on an interview show? Do you seem to understand all sides of an issue? If you are performing in a corporate training video, do you seem to know your subject matter and do you present the information in an engaging manner? The best performers spend time in preparation and research no matter how familiar they already are with the guest or subject matter.

Delivery can also contribute to the audience's perception of your expertise. A performer who can maintain eye contact with the camera and deliver information without notes is usually perceived as one with high expertise. Ability to avoid excessive pauses, vocalized pauses ("you know," "and ah," "well") and mispronounced words also contributes to positive perception.

Performers who can humanize complex or technical information are among the most effective experts onscreen. Audiences appreciate those who can talk about the technical aspects of computers or clearly explain a new medical procedure, especially when they demonstrate their knowledge in a warm, uncondescending manner.

If you are presenting complex information to the audience, don't make the assumption that they know what you know; look for ways to simplify the concepts with the help of visual aids, analogies, and other forms of imagery.

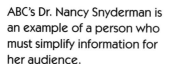
ABC's Dr. Nancy Snyderman is an example of a person who must simplify information for her audience.

Research by psychologist Alan Pavio determined that people remember words paired with pictures better than words alone. Pavio's research demonstrates the importance of visual imagery in viewer comprehension and retention.

In Chapter 7 you will learn about some of the technical tools available to you to add visual elements to your production.

Dynamism   Audiences perceive as a dynamic performer someone who appears to be energetic, strong, assertive, and involved with his or her material. We seem drawn to those who exhibit conviction and energy. Dynamism is even more important on television than in other types of public performance because, as mentioned earlier, television diminishes one's apparent energy. Performers who do not look dynamic in live interactions face an even more difficult task when appearing on the television screen.

Vocal and rate variety, facial expressions, and gestures are a few of the ways in which you can achieve dynamism. Conveying a high level of interest and desire in presenting your information can also make you a dynamic performer. These techniques are discussed in Chapters 4 and 5.

Identification   Basically, identification is how the performer demonstrates common ground and connects with an audience. Performers often try to show that "My ways are your ways" and give hints about their interests and concerns. This approach is as simple as a weather forecaster saying that the next day's rain or snow may cause problems for travelers.

Good performers do basic audience analysis before their productions, trying to predict what the audience's attitudes may be toward the subject matter and how to appeal to them in presenting the information. Marketing surveys and other research can give some knowledge of the audience. In short, performers attempt to meet audience needs. Many television programs fail to meet these needs and are canceled after a short period of time. There is no guarantee that a program will run for a long time if it is addressing the needs and wants of the audience, but it has a greater probability of success if all involved with a program are audience centered.

Audience analysis is important in all public communication, but its importance is even greater with regard to communicating on television. Video performers usually address voluntary, not captive, audiences. Even in televised corporate training sessions, audiences usually tune out a video trainer faster than an in-person trainer, and numerous studies point to the resultant failure of video instruction and distance learning attempts by colleges and universities.

Performers should conduct a basic **demographic analysis** before performances that includes information regarding age, gender, race, and so on. Geographic or regional information is also important, because what succeeds in one region of the country may not "play" in another. For example, some regions prefer sportscasters who seem to cheer for the home team (often referred to as "homers"), whereas other regions prefer more objective sportscasters.

Psychographic analysis involves determining people's attitudes toward certain issues. Knowing the issues that are important to your audience and how they feel about them can give you a major advantage.

You may be thinking that it is a difficult task to analyze a mass audience watching a local station or national network, because you are not dealing with a set of homogeneous eyeballs. There are unifying characteristics of audience analysis in almost any performance situation, however, so try to create in your mind's eye the profile of a typical viewer watching you.

Trustworthiness, expertise, dynamism, and identification will assist you in establishing credibility. One more practical element that contributes to credibility (and one you can control in most cases) is how you are introduced.

Introductions

When you are going to be introduced by another person, it is important to provide that person with as much positive information as possible. If you are going to be a guest on an interview show, make sure you provide the host or producer with information regarding your past accomplishments and items that may help you identify with the audience.

Scholars of persuasive theory often call this the **primary tuning effect** that sets up the audience to be positively predisposed to the performer. The audience will in fact form perceptions of you even before you speak. You never get a second chance to make a first impression.

The Unselfish Performer

Unselfish performers are those who are audience centered rather than those who perform only for personal gratification. Those who consider the needs and desires of the audience will usually succeed in making a positive impression on that audience. Unselfish performers feel a sense of accomplishment when they know that they have maximized the meaning of their messages for viewers.

In his book *The Director as Interpreter,* Colby Lewis writes, "Preserve the nature of your material as faithfully as you can despite its being obliged to pass through your cameras and microphones in order to reach its audience." In this statement Lewis is referring to the obligation of the television director to translate information for the viewer at home; however, the video performer has the same obligation.

In addition to the conceptual elements of credibility, practical elements such as clothing and makeup can significantly enhance your standing.

■ **Clothing and Makeup**   Clothing contributes to one's credibility in any public speaking situation and is extremely important for the video performer who must take into consideration the technical limitations of video as well as style, color, and other factors. Keep three general principles in mind when choosing your clothing.

■ **Select clothing and accessories that attract and don't distract.** You want to draw attention to yourself, not your clothing, when you appear on television. Clothing and accessories that draw too much attention can distract the audience from you and your message.

In most situations it is better to err on the side of conservatism than to be a little too trendy. Be careful of styles and colors that may be too extreme for your performance situation and may be better suited to a weekend party or MTV video. Despite what you see at awards shows, where the focus seems to be on fashion, you and not your clothes should be the center of attention.

■ **Select clothing that fits the performance situation or context.** Obviously you need to match your clothing to the performance situation. News anchors and reporters almost always wear professional styles. In field or remote locations, it is not uncommon to see news reporters in ski parkas, jackets, rain gear, or other outdoor clothing, especially when they are reporting on severe weather conditions or doing other types of on-location stories.

Sports anchors sometimes dress less formally and may wear a sports jacket over a sports shirt or mock turtleneck. In Hawaii, it is not uncommon to see sports anchors and weather forecasters wearing Hawaiian shirts. Performers on early morning news shows may wear less formal clothing than performers appearing later in the day. Those doing demonstration shows will wear what is appropriate to the task they are doing: gardening, auto repair, or building a deck. A travel show host will wear comfortable clothes appropriate to the locale or destination.

No matter what the performance context, you want your clothes to be stylish, clean and pressed, and the best match for the situation. Watch

"When in Honolulu . . ." KGMB's Jade Moon and
Jim Mendonza wear Hawaiian shirts on Aloha Fridays.
Dress can be situational or regional.

performers in various program formats and see how they dress. Notice that even in less formal situations the clothing usually complements the performer and his or her message. When in doubt, you should dress up, not down. Some situations can be ambiguous; for example, you will see a wide variety of fashion on late night sport interview programs. Sometimes you will see athletes professionally dressed; at other times they will be wearing sweatshirts, jackets, or party clothes.

Ultimately, the issue is audience perception. Consider your long-term record of success, not just a short-term shock impression. Your choice of clothing can communicate respect for the audience, increasing the probability that the audience will show respect and admiration for you in return.

An excellent practitioner of this philosophy is basketball great Michael Jordan. Jordan typically wore a suit and tie when walking through a hotel lobby to catch the team bus. His reasoning was that for many of his fans this might be their only glimpse of him in person and he wanted to create a positive impression during those brief moments. He transferred this thinking to his television appearances, always wearing clothing appropriate to the program.

■ **When you are practicing, try to wear what you will be wearing during the performance.** Make your practice sessions true dress rehearsals by wearing the same clothes during these sessions that you will wear when you do the live or on-tape performance. Some people think this is unnecessary, but there are benefits to practicing in your performance clothes.

First, you and the production staff will see how your clothing and accessories look on camera before the actual production. Are your color choices the right ones for video? Do your clothes seem to blend into the set? Will you have to make some changes to correct these problems?

Second, you get to see how you feel in your clothes, and they will almost certainly be more comfortable when you wear them on production day. If you're not used to walking in a certain type of shoe or wearing certain types of clothing, rehearsing in them will help you become accustomed to the clothing choices you've made.

Another consideration is that when you look good, you will also feel good about yourself and be more confident about your performance, so start cultivating this feeling during your rehearsal sessions. You don't need to wait until the real performance to start building your overall confidence level.

One of the "ratings pointers" in Chapter 2 mentioned that you should treat practice sessions and in-class assignments as if you were doing a real production and that you should practice as you perform. It is amazing how many times students in class production situations (video production or performance classes) attempting to be credible performers (news anchors, interview show hosts, etc.) come dressed in T-shirts or sweatshirts. Look at each production situation as another chance to improve your credibility and skills as well as possible material for a resume videotape.

RATINGS POINTER

You may want to bring a couple of outfits to the studio before your dress rehearsal to see which clothes contrast most effectively with the set and look best on camera. Your producer and director will appreciate this, and you will look your best on production day. ★ ★ ★ ★

Performers who remember these general principles of selecting clothing that attracts and fits the performance situation and practicing in their performance clothes will have an advantage over the person who knows only about clothing colors and styles.

Clothing and accessories contribute to your overall attitude and credibility, boosting your confidence as you perform. If you want to be a serious video performer, be prepared to invest some money in your wardrobe. The additional benefit of having a professional wardrobe is that you can wear these same clothes when you go to television stations or production houses for employment interviews.

■ **Specific Clothing Considerations** Use the following checklist when selecting your clothing for video performance:

■ **Textured clothing looks better on camera than clothing with a flat or shiny finish.** Be careful with silk blouses and ties (you may want to bring these to the studio and check them out on camera before the production).

■ **Avoid detailed patterns.** Checks, herringbone, plaids, stripes that are thin or close together, and highly contrasting patterns may look good to *our* eyes, but the video system doesn't "see" the way we do. You may have noticed performers on television who haven't followed this advice; their clothing seems to vibrate on the air, giving the impression of generating heat or radioactivity. This is sometimes called a **moire effect.**

■ **Colors are a relative concept when considering clothing choices.**
Fashion trends dictate which colors are in vogue or are considered "power
colors." On the other hand, some colors look better on television than others, because the video reproduces colors in a slightly different way from how
we see them.

Medium blue or gray suits and blazers tend to look best for both men
and women. Women have a wider choice of colors, but they should try to
stay with middle tones and not choose extremely dark or light colors. The
television system translates colors into what is called the **gray scale** (black,
navy blue, and other dark colors are at one end of the scale, pastels are in
the middle, and white and lighter colors are at the other end of the scale).
Try to choose colors in the middle of the gray scale.

Blue is a good color for video performance. The video system accentu-
ates blue, and it often looks better on the screen than in person. However,
avoid blue or green if you are working with a chroma-key set. **Chroma-key**
is a special effect whereby a color, usually green or blue, is canceled by the
video system and other visual information appears on the blue or green surface. Most chroma-key sets are green because people tend to wear less
green than blue.

Perhaps the most common example of chroma-key use is a weather
forecaster performing in front of a blue or green set on which the weather
map and other visuals appear. The only way the weather forecaster can see
the visuals is via monitors on the set. (We will discuss how to perform with
chroma-key in a later chapter.) If the forecaster wears the same color clothing as the color of the chroma-key set, the visual information will appear on
his or her clothing. For example, part of a weather map could appear on a
green tie. Test clothing items that appear close to the same color of the
chroma-key set so that you won't have this problem.

The video system has some problems with certain shades of red that
can bleed or glow on camera, sometimes causing a neon effect. Red is also
somewhat muted when seen onscreen.

Colors and how they translate into the gray scale.

Black	Brown Dark Green Dark Blue	Red Medium Blue Medium Green	Light Blue Orange	Light Gray Tan Pastels	White

If you are a performer with darker skin, you may want to avoid wearing a starched white shirt with a dark jacket. Try an off-white shirt or blouse and a jacket color more in the middle of the gray scale.

■ **Avoid clothing that makes you look heavier.** Television tends to add a few pounds to your appearance, but there are several steps you can take to counteract this effect. If you wear clothing with stripes, avoid horizontal stripes and select vertical stripes, which have a slimming effect. Wear colors toward the darker end of the gray scale. Avoid wearing loose-fitting clothes, opting instead for clothes that are more tailored and cut to a slim silhouette.

Colors will look different under various studio and outdoor conditions, so it's best to have options and be flexible. What looks great in one situation may cause problems in another facility or location.

RATINGS POINTER

You may have seen the following tip in the film *Broadcast News.* Just before sitting down, tug your coattails downward and then try to sit on them. This will give your suit coat or blazer a nicer line and help keep it from hunching up around your shoulders. ★ ★ ★ ★

■ **Limit your use of jewelry.** Avoid shiny items that reflect light and bloom on camera. Subtle earrings are fine, but large earrings can distract the viewer and draw attention away from you. Necklaces may rub against clip-on (lavaliere) microphones and cause distracting clanking sounds. Accessories enhance your appearance as long as they are not too detailed or distracting. Bring jewelry and accessories into the studio and test them on camera before the performance.

As with clothing, you should take an understated approach toward jewelry and accessories so that you remain the focus of the production. If you have "piercing" in nontraditional areas (nose, eyebrows, etc.) you should probably remove the jewelry from those areas before your performance.

Eyeglasses may cause problems in studio situations due to light reflected by the frames or lenses. Plastic frames reduce glare best and should be treated with antiglare coating. Choose conservative frames rather than ones that might draw attention away from you and your message.

You may want to consider wearing contact lenses if you need vision correction. At least a few youthful-looking performers wear contact lenses while also wearing eyeglass frames without lenses to make themselves appear older.

You can eliminate problems with lighting and eyeglasses by getting to the studio early so that the production crew can see how the lights reflect off your glasses. In some cases, a minor lighting adjustment corrects the problem.

RATINGS POINTER

If you are on location, you need to be prepared for any kind of weather. Make sure you carry rain gear and weatherproof boots if there is the possibility of wet weather. Many reporters and other performers have had to deal with snow or rain without proper clothing and footwear, contributing to miserable experiences. ★ ★ ★ ★

■ **Makeup**   Many performance situations require some type of **makeup** to enhance and accentuate certain features. The bright lights of the studio give skin tones a washed-out or unnatural look, and the close-up nature of television highlights skin imperfections.

For men, makeup can eliminate shine from the upper lip, nose, cheeks, and forehead. Some men with high foreheads also use a bit of powder to reduce shine. Shaving before the production and using makeup help reduce five o'clock shadow.

Women can often use their normal makeup base. Media consultants advise women to pay particular attention to the eyes so that the viewer's attention is drawn to them. Use eyeshadow in gray and brown shades and avoid blue, which the camera distorts in such a way that the person can look ghostly. Women should also avoid lipsticks that contain bluish tones.

In general, women and men should use warmer makeup with reddish tones rather than cooler makeup with bluish tones. Makeup should be natural and subtle. If you have dark skin, you will face many of the same problems in regard to bluish tones. Experiment with a good foundation that eliminates shine while highlighting your features. Test makeup in the studio whenever you can.

When working outdoors on hot days, make sure you have a towel or tissue to blot your face. You may also want to take along some powder to eliminate shiny spots and glare.

You can find most if not all performance makeup at your neighborhood drug or department store. Basic pancake makeup from the Krylon series (CTV-1W through CTV-12W) will work for a variety of skin tones. Make sure you put foundation on your neck as well as your face if there is a big difference between the two areas. Many salons provide special makeup products and advice on how to use them.

> **RATINGS POINTER**
>
> Emerging video technology will introduce new issues with regard to makeup and appearance. As HDTV brings clearer, more detailed images into homes, performers will need to pay more attention to skin imperfections—that's the bad news.
>
> The good news is that there are now camera lenses that eliminate lines and wrinkles from the face, making the performer appear more youthful. Unfortunately, these cameras are not in use in all production facilities, so basic makeup techniques are still the best way for a performer to improve his or her appearance. ★ ★ ★ ★

Rewind and Fade to Black

Due to the intimate nature of video, television audiences often notice a performer's credibility and appearance more than live audiences would. The four major elements of credibility—trustworthiness, expertise, dynamism, and identification—and specifics concerning appearance will all help you make a favorable impression on viewers.

Some performers disregard the suggestions made in this chapter; but all performers need to assess how they want to be perceived and remembered by viewers in the long term. Get feedback from fellow performers, colleagues, instructors, and others concerning how they perceive you onscreen. Your style and persona will evolve over time, so frequent perception checks will assist you with your progress. Keep in mind that you are unique and you will do some things well that others will find difficult to do. Continue to develop your strengths while working on the areas that need improvement.

Finally, most people don't recognize how good they are. Accept positive feedback from others, and enjoy the outcomes when you work hard and do a good job.

Exercises

1 Develop a list of television performers you perceive as credible. Compare this list with your friends' and colleagues' perceptions. Include performers from a variety of programs (news, talk shows, interviews, etc.). Do these performers possess the four elements of credibility (trustworthiness, expertise, dynamism, and identification) discussed earlier in this chapter?

2 Create a performance context in which you are an authority on a specific subject being interviewed on a talk show. Prepare information that you would give to the producer or talk show host for your introduction on that program. Be careful not to be overly modest about your accomplishments and expertise as long as you can verify what you've done.

3 Make an inventory of your clothing and accessories that are appropriate for video performance. Look for clothing that is suitable for a variety of program types. What do you have that you can wear, and what do you need to buy to fill in wardrobe gaps? If you're a student or young professional on a budget, don't be afraid to check out thrift stores. You may be amazed at what you find and how little it costs.

4 View at least three videotapes of your performances over a series of weeks. What changes and improvements do you note? Where do you still need to improve?

5 Suppose you've been offered a position as a news reporter in St. Louis, Missouri. How would you familiarize yourself with the following data?

a. Type of city government.

b. Most important issue to the general public.

c. Favorite foods.

d. Favorite sports team.

e. Population demographics.

f. Popular leisure activities.

INTERVIEW

Gayle Lederman
Makeup and Fashion Consultant

Several years ago Gayle Lederman went from appearing in front of the camera to becoming one of the top television and film makeup and fashion consultants on the West Coast. She does performer makeup for a variety of productions, including those seen on Discovery Channel, Animal Planet, and PBS. Here she gives advice concerning makeup and clothes.

Question: Why do people need to wear makeup when performing on television?

Gayle Lederman: The reason is to even the skin tone. Also, if there are any blotches or imperfections on the skin, the camera will exaggerate them. As a makeup person I feel that it is necessary to have the person look their best so that their message gets across and viewers are not stopping to take a moment to look at the imperfections and miss the message. The face can look good in person but off balance for the camera. If there is a slight off-balance, and most faces are not even, I have to make the face look more balanced. My eye tries to translate into what the camera is going to see.

Q: Aren't there technical factors to consider as well, such as lighting?

GL: Lighting is really important. Lighting, camera, and makeup are a synergistic process that can help a person look his or her best. I decided that I would learn as much about lighting as I could. Today, if I see something that doesn't look good on the monitor and I know it's a lighting problem, I'll go up to the lighting person and say something to them. People who are willing to work together can correct things, and they can also come to me with suggestions on how a person should look.

Q: What are some of the most common problems you encounter with men when doing their makeup.

GL: Shine. I don't like a face to look like a corpse, but shine is a big one. Dark circles under the eyes. Imperfections on the skin. Men will often complain about their receding hairlines and that they are uncomfortable with them. I have a technique to fill in certain areas or I will see it and fill in whether or not they have asked for it. Lines around the mouth and nose, especially if they are deep. I also look at eyebrows and I can fill them in. If a person has fair skin, I will darken the tone.

Q: What about some common problems for women?

GL: Women are different because more detail is needed. Some women want to look natural, while others want to look as if they are wearing makeup. If a woman wants to look as if she's wearing makeup, there has to be a way of toning that down so that she doesn't look clownish. Cheekbones. Women always want to look as if they have high cheekbones if they don't already have them. Shading the nose. Also, looking as if you have smooth skin. There is a way of doing this so that the person doesn't look as if she is wearing a lot of makeup. The camera is sensitive to this and will pick it up if a woman is wearing too much makeup.

Lips. Women today want to look as if they have big lips. There is a way of emphasizing them to make them look a little larger. I have a theory that if someone is communicating through the mouth, and women have the ability to emphasize their mouths, men don't, women can have an advantage because they wear lipstick.

Q: What types of makeup tones look best on camera?

GL: My eye likes to look at a warmer tone. There are some women that if I go to a warmer tone, it doesn't look good so I may have to go to a bluish tone, but generally I stay away from the bluish tones.

Q: The best thing is for performers to have someone like you do their makeup, but can a performer do his or her own makeup application?

GL: You're right. The best thing is to have a makeup artist do your makeup application. Most people don't see themselves in an objective way on camera whereas a professional will. They need to know how they are appearing on camera objectively; then I can come in and teach them how to do their makeup. They need to have the correct eyeshadow and eyeliners, blush, foundation, lipstick, and powder. Those are the basics that they need and the correct application. I can teach that, but it has taken me years to develop what looks best on camera. The feedback I get is that people like how I make them look on camera.

Q: What about makeup for HDTV?

GL: The feedback I've gotten from technicians involved with HDTV [is] that makeup is going to be crucial in the next few years and that the stations' budgets will be increased for makeup and makeup artists. Today, with many productions, the first place they cut in the budget is with makeup. I think that's absurd because this is an image business and if they don't look good on camera with makeup and hair it's distracting to viewers. You would be amazed at the amount of people who watch and will e-mail, call, or write in, and say, "You look terrible! What about that hair! What a lousy makeup job!" When I was working at KPIX Channel 5, San Francisco, they were always watching their main anchors and sometimes there was awful e-mail. People like to criticize.

Q: Did you ever work with a news consulting firm where they came in and said, "Change the look of that anchorperson?"

GL: I have. They will often come in and want the person's image changed. In many cases it is not with the person's makeup but with their clothing. I can help with that. Consulting firms will call me in and say "We want a new look on that person."

Q: Where do you start with clothing choices?

GL: We start with both color and style. I'll go to the anchor's home and see what he or she has in their wardrobe. I'll also watch video of them to see how he or she looks on the screen.

There are certain colors that look good on camera and with a person's skin tone. I'll tell them, "This looks good with your skin tone." If they don't have the clothing they need to look good on camera, we go out and buy. . . . By changing the clothing I will know what to do in adjusting the person's makeup. I find it to be an exciting creative process, much like putting the pieces of a puzzle together when they all fit. It's exciting to see the finished product on camera and to see a face and a person come alive.

CHAPTER FOUR

Vocal Aspects of Performance

We tend to take our voices for granted until we suffer a sore throat or laryngitis. Speaking is accepted as something that anyone can do, and many educators (including those teaching video performance courses) give little attention to vocal production or how to improve **vocal quality.** As mentioned earlier, some beginning performers hear themselves on audio- or videotape and dislike their vocal quality, but resign themselves to believing that they can't improve their voices.

There is less emphasis today on performers having an announcer's voice or "pear shaped tones"; we hear a variety of voices on television. Still, the fact remains that optimal vocal production is an important aspect of the total package of you as performer. Performers who understand the importance of voice and how to improve and preserve it will continue to be effective communicators for years.

Almost anyone can improve his or her voice; even if you've been blessed with a pleasing voice appropriate for video performance, you can still improve and protect it. This chapter explores vocal production; some specific aspects of your voice such as pitch, rate, and volume; vocal problems and how to solve or minimize them; phrasing and emphasis; and commonly mispronounced words and pronunciation guides.

Your Physical Voice

■ **Breathing**   If we take our voices for granted, how much more do we take breathing for granted! Breathing is the foundation of vocal production, since proper breath support contributes to good vocal production and inattention to breathing contributes to less than pleasing vocal quality, with possible vocal damage.

Most people think of breathing as a function of the only the chest area, that is lungs and rib cage. Performers who use only chest breathing are limiting their vocal potential and may have a "breathy," less full vocal quality. In situations in which the performer is feeling some stress, he or she may feel a sense of running out of air, causing even more stress.

Even if you have never taken speech or voice lessons, you have probably heard of "breathing from the diaphragm." **Diaphragmatic breathing,** or deep breathing, takes place in the large shelflike muscle that forms a wall between the chest and abdominal cavities. This type of breathing allows you to take deeper and fewer breaths, contributing to relaxation while speaking. Another advantage of diaphragmatic breathing is that it is a great way to lower your pitch naturally without putting strain on your vocal cords.

Concentrate on where you are getting your breath support and how often you need to take breaths. One way to do this is to place your fist a couple of inches above your waist and watch its movement as you breathe. Does your fist move in a controlled way, or does it move too fast? This is a good visual indication of whether or not your breathing is controlled. Some speech and voice coaches have the performer lie flat on his or her back with a book on the stomach to monitor the movement and control of breathing. Try breathing "from the gut" when you're speaking in day-to-day conversation so that you are able to make the transfer to diaphragmatic breathing when performing.

■ **Pitch and Resonance**   Simply defined, **pitch** is how high or low your voice sounds and **resonance** is how your voice is amplified by vibrations through bones in your chest and face. You can think of these areas as mini concert band shells that reinforce sound.

Most broadcast performers pitch their voices at a level that is mid to low range and seems pleasing to most ears. Don't force your pitch lower through your throat but instead concentrate on deeper breathing and discovering your pitch range. Most people use only a small part of their range.

Resonance can help determine your optimal pitch, with most resonance being achieved in the nose, mouth, and throat. Try placing your palms along the sides of your nose and read a short text. You will feel the vibrations as a result of resonance, and you can often determine your best pitch through this feeling.

Most people have no trouble recognizing positive nasal resonance and two nasal resonance problems: **hyponasality** and **hypernasality.** Hyponasality sounds as if you have a stopped-up nose. Hypernasality produces higher, pinched pitch and is often associated with certain East Coast accents (the stereotypical New York or New Jersey accents). Put your fingers on the bridge of your nose and, keeping your mouth closed, run through the sounds *mmmm, nnn,* and *ng.* This provides you with an excellent example of nasal resonance. Good nasal resonance is often a function of clear and healthy nasal passages. If you have problems with nasal resonance, you may need to seek medical attention to correct the problem.

RATINGS POINTER

Sometime in your performance career you will have to speak when you have a cold and your nasal passages are blocked. You can help this problem by repeating the words "guns and drums" at least a dozen times and forcing the words through your nasal cavity and head.

Focus on the *m*'s and *n*'s and say the words in a loud voice. This helps clear your head and nose while helping you to focus upon nasal resonance under less than ideal conditions. Many performers also drink hot fluids before performance to help clear the head. ★ ★ ★ ★

There are things you can do to modify to what is called **assimilative nasality.** Try saying "Amanda and Dan were fond of meandering in the garden." Focus on the *a*'s—do they sound tight or pinched? Does it sound like a Brooklyn accent? This is a characteristic of assimilative nasality, a condition in which the soft palate in the back of your mouth lowers into position for the *m* in Amanda and remains there for the following *a,* or the soft palate anticipates the *n* in Dan and carries over a nasal sound into the *a.* In both examples, the nasal sound *m* or *n* ruins the adjacent vowel sound.

Assimilative nasality can be controlled by focusing on your soft palate (the portion of your mouth in front of the uvula, which you raise when you yawn). The most common cause of excessive nasality is the palate's laziness or slowness to rise. When saying the word *man,* try lengthening the *m* two or three times its normal length before pronouncing the *a.* Repeat the word several times and gradually shorten the *m* to its normal length. When the vowel precedes the nasal consonant, as in *am,* try focusing on the mouth movement necessary to produce the vowel *a.* Lengthen the sound and exaggerate the movement until you can produce a clean *a.*

You can improve resonance by focusing attention on lip and tongue activity and "forward placement" of vocal tones. Bring sound forward in your mouth; concentrate on how you move your lips and tongue and how you drop and close your jaw.

Other Vocal Aspects You Can Control

No matter what kind of voice you were born with, there are things you can do to sound better. Performers often compensate for not having deep resonant voices by paying attention to the following items:

■ **Articulation** Years ago speech coaches made a distinction between **articulation** (the production of consonants) and enunciation (the production of vowels). Today, most people combine the two into the category of articulation, the process of how sounds of speech are broken into recognizable words. The three agents most observable in this process are the lips, tongue, and palate.

There are numerous issues we could discuss in regard to articulation; for our purposes here is an overview of common articulation problems:

■ **Laziness versus overpreciseness.** Lazy speakers often have articulation problems with consonants such as *p, b, v,* and *f.* Improper tongue placement causes problems with consonants such as *t, d, k,* and *g.* Lack of forward placement and failure to open the mouth cause problems with vowel sounds. Dropping *g*'s off words with -*ing* endings makes for obvious, sloppy articulation.

On the flip side, some people articulate too precisely in public performance situations, sounding phony or affected. Performers will work on consonants such as *b, v, d, z,* and *w,* developing popping hard consonants and ignoring everything else. Be careful of overprecise *t*'s in words like *water.* These *t*'s should be softened to make something close to but not entirely a *d* sound.

■ **Sound substitutions and omissions.** Consider some of the following words and the potential for misunderstanding: "lig" for *leg,* "jist" for *just,* and "sinator" for *senator.* This is another easily corrected form of lazy speech. Be careful of dropping the final consonants in words such as *word* (not "wor") or *deed* (not "dee").

■ **Lack of breath support and tension.** Lack of breath support and tension in the throat can cause you to cut words off before they are completed. Follow the advice given earlier concerning diaphragmatic breathing, yawning exercises, and voice warm-up exercises. Also avoid being lazy with your lips, tongue, and jaw.

Get feedback concerning articulation problems from instructors, colleagues, and others you trust. Try not to be defensive, because most of these difficulties can be corrected with a little work.

Articulation is often contextual in the sense that we become less formal with our friends and fall into certain patterns. Obviously, the way we speak in casual conversation can differ from more formal situations, but make sure you are able to adjust and adapt to the more formal way of presenting yourself in performance.

■ Volume

Volume is often a problem for public speakers who do not breathe properly and need to fill the room with their voices (especially if they don't have the benefit of a microphone). It is less of a problem in television production because the microphone and the audio engineer do much of the work to assure adequate vocal volume. There are some differences you should consider regarding video volume versus "public volume."

Use your conversational volume, as if you are talking to one or two friends. Avoid the temptation to overproject just because you're in a large studio or speaking for people you see in the studio such as floor managers or production assistants. Volume variety can be used to indicate excitement or intensity, but you should try to establish a controlled range of volume so that you don't sound as if you're shouting. Establish contrast by using a softer volume when appropriate. Lowering your volume is an effective means of drawing viewer attention to you and your message at strategic moments.

A basic question in mic use is how far the mic should be from your mouth. When using a handheld mic or other nonclip-on or lavaliere mics, you should place the mic about 6 to 8 inches from your mouth. You can judge

Performers should talk across the microphone instead of directly into it.

this distance by making a fist in front of your mouth and putting your thumb on your lower lip and stretching out your pinky finger. Put the microphone at the end of the pinky finger; this should be about the right distance for mic placement (you will learn more mic techniques later in this text).

Instead of speaking directly into the face of the microphone, try turning it slightly to the side and speaking across it. This will help eliminate problems such as hissing on *s* and *sh* words (called **sibilance**) and **popping** on words beginning with *p, b, t, d, k,* and *g.* These are called **plosives,** with the biggest culprits being *p*'s and *b*'s. How many times have you listened to someone speaking "popping his or her *p*'s and *b*'s" into a microphone until it sounds as if it will explode? Talking across the mic also helps eliminate breathiness, when a small puff of air precedes words.

In remote situations where traffic or crowd noise is a problem, you will have to speak louder, adjusting your volume to fluctuating conditions. Sometimes you can actually move the mic closer to your mouth and reduce your volume. Experiment with these techniques and get feedback from your production crew as to which technique sounds best given the particular situation.

■ **Rate**   Most of us have a delivery rate of 100 to 150 words per minute. Media consultants often urge performers to speak at a slightly faster rate of 160 words a minute or higher. This helps to promote dynamism and energy while also compressing more information into less time. Performers who are able to speak comfortably at a faster rate are able to say more during a 30-second commercial or read more news stories per block of newscast.

When you watch videotapes of your early performances, take note of your speaking rate—do you sound too slow? Many new performers speak too slowly, diminishing their dynamism as well as causing listeners to stop paying attention. Force yourself to speak and read a little faster when reading or giving information extemporaneously.

If you are performing with another person, you should try to match delivery rates so that neither of you sounds too fast or slow in comparison to the other. News anchors try to have rates that are similar and consistent with each other when reading their stories.

Rate variety helps maintain audience interest, and the strategic use of pauses creates not only interest but anticipation, although the overuse of pauses can be unpleasant for listeners and make you sound overly dramatic or unnatural. One speech consultant says, "There's power and poise in pause." You should be careful that you don't fall into the habit of using vocalized pauses ("ah" and "er" being two of the most common ones). These cause you to sound less prepared and less polished in your delivery.

Increase your speaking rate, but don't imitate the announcers reading disclaimers at the end of car commercials. Work for a rate that makes you sound energetic and interesting. Some performers who do speak more slowly find other ways to sound interesting to viewers. Bill Moyers and David Brinkley have slower rates but use inflection, phrasing, emphasis, and natural storyteller styles to make them effective communicators.

■ Pronunciation

Correct **pronunciation** of words is certainly something you can and should control, as listeners expect performers to pronounce words correctly. Knowing some of the reasons for mispronunciations will help you deal with this problem.

Not knowing the correct pronunciation is one of the most common contributors to mispronunciation. Sometimes we see an unfamiliar word, name, or place and simply take a stab at the pronunciation or, worse yet, slur the word hoping that no one will notice. Sometimes, we mispronounce words because we have learned the wrong pronunciation (in some cases, from well known television performers and politicians who should know better).

Consult pronunciation guides such as newswire service guides (produced by television news services on a daily basis to include pronunciation of names and places in the news), and announcer's guides such as the *NBC Handbook of Pronunciation*. Another excellent guide is *The Big Book of Beastly Mispronunciations* by Charles Harrington Elster. After looking at his guide you may be amazed how many words you are mispronouncing in everyday conversation. Some commonly mispronounced words are listed at the end of this chapter.

Some performers misread words that look similar to one another. Familiarity with the script or cue cards can correct this problem. Take note of potential problem words, and practice them before your rehearsal and performance.

Some performers are sloppy with pronunciation or have developed bad habits over the years. They omit syllables or add an extra syllable to monosyllabic words. Listen to the way established performers pronounce words. Check pronunciation guides, and start working on correct pronunciation not only in performance but also in everyday conversation.

RATINGS POINTER

One of the most common pronunciation errors is the letter *w* pronounced as "dubba ya" instead of "double u." You hear this often in announcements of station call letters and website addresses. Don't make this common mistake. ★ ★ ★ ★

Common Vocal Problems
and How to Correct Them

The section on resonance addressed the problem of nasality. Several other vocal problems can impair the vocal aspects of performance. In most cases, these can be corrected through awareness and work during practice sessions. Following are descriptions of seven of the most common problems with performance voices.

■ **Fading Volume**   Many untrained speakers and performers drop volume at the ends of sentences, causing listeners to lose the last few words. You may need to work on deeper breathing and better overall breath control if you have this problem. Simply talking louder is not enough, because there is a tendency to overproject at the beginning of the sentence and still trail off at the end.

Remember that the ends of sentences are just as important as the beginnings. Even though the microphone is doing most of the work, you must have consistent volume throughout the sentence. A related bad habit is speeding up at the ends of sentences as if in a hurry to complete them. Maintain consistent rate throughout the entire sentence unless there is some interpretive reason for a rate change.

■ **Rising Inflection at the End of a Sentence**   The habit of **rising inflection** makes statements sound as if they are questions because the inflection or pitch rises at the end of the sentence. Some people do this on a regular basis, creating a vocal pattern that is both repetitive and annoying. This pattern also sends a metamessage that the performer lacks confidence. Again, awareness of the problem and practice are often the keys to improvement.

■ **Mouth as Slit**   As you might imagine, this refers to performers who don't open their mouths wide enough, causing garbled sounds, sluggish consonants, and retracted vowels. Volume may also be a problem, even with the benefit of a microphone. Speech trainers have noted that men who have mustaches or beards are prone to this habit. Dropping the jaw can help, as can practicing vowel sounds with the mouth open wide enough to insert two fingers.

Retracted Voice   In "valley girl" and cockney dialects many sounds remain in the back of the throat and get swallowed. This problem of **retracted voice** causes very hollow vocal quality and difficulty in projecting vowel sounds. Dropping the jaw and working on forward placement of sounds can often help with this problem, as can better breath control. Exaggerated movement of the lips and tongue may also help.

Pinched or Tight Voice   Performers with pinched or tight voices are often difficult to listen to because of strident or thin vocal quality. This fault is often caused by a tightening of the throat muscles or glottis due to nervousness or an attempt to overproject without proper breath support.

Some of the vocal relaxation techniques mentioned in Chapter 2, such as warming up the voice and excessive yawning exercises, help reduce the excessive glottal tension that causes a thin voice. Converting nervousness to positive performance energy can also create a fuller voice. Some performers visualize a large ball in the back of their throat to assist in opening the throat.

Hissing s Sounds   It's not uncommon for performers to have some problems with s sounds. Often the s comes out as a hissing noise (excessive sibilance) that sounds even worse with certain types of microphones. This problem is often caused by the imperfect meeting of the top and bottom teeth. Compensate for this problem by bringing your jaw forward and getting the top and bottom teeth in better alignment. Another hint is to make a t sound as in *take*, then try saying the word *steak* without moving your teeth, keeping them in the t position. For many people the t position is the best one to use for s's.

Hoarseness   Some people have deep, somewhat raspy voices that may be attractive for certain performance situations. However, if someone's voice is too hoarse or husky, it can be unpleasant for the listener and may indicate vocal damage. As mentioned earlier, smoking and overuse of alcohol can contribute to a hoarse or raspy voice; so can misuse of the voice.

Many people overproject by overworking their throats and not using deep breathing. The result can be damage to the vocal folds in the form of **vocal nodules.** Some public speakers such as politicians who have overused their voices have required corrective surgery and a period of vocal rest for up to six weeks. If you experience hoarseness on a regular basis, you should seek medical attention.

You may have developed bad habits that are relatively easy to correct. If you need additional help, don't be afraid to contact a speech trainer or pathologist to assist you with speech problems. Your goal as a performer should not be to change your natural voice but to maximize its potential. Once you are aware of the technical aspects of your voice and how to correct vocal problems, you can turn your attention to some of the more artistic aspects of using your voice.

The Video Performer as Interpreter

When reading prepared scripts, whether news copy or commercials, you become an interpreter of the words on the page. Interpretation has a number of definitions, but two that will work for our purposes are "maximizing the meaning of the message" and "bringing the words on the page to life." Performers who have the ability to interpret a script or even a prepared introduction during an interview segment seem more involved in the production and present themselves in a natural and conversational manner.

Novice performers often read scripts in a neutral tone with little regard for bringing the copy to life. They are like reading machines whose eyes pick up the words off the page and speak them with no emotion or interest. The following are general principles of interpretation that a performer should consider in a wide variety of situations.

Internalization   Scripts often communicate various moods and messages. **Internalization** is a term often used in acting when the actor attempts to take the script and make it a part of him- or herself (this is also true of the character role the actor will play). Internalization includes close analysis of the script regarding the emotions and moods one is attempting to communicate. Chapters 10 and 11 discuss specific contexts such as news and commercial copy, but you can use internalization when reading prepared material for any performance.

Before you read the script in performance, make sure you understand its message and central idea(s). What **mood** are you trying to create (urgency, a need to know, this is fun, etc.)? Allow the mood to be heard in your voice. Listen to different types of commercials: Which ones are lighter, and which ones attempt a more serious tone? Note the difference in tone that news anchors use in reading a tragic story about a house fire as opposed to a "puppies and babies" story. If the viewer believes that you are feeling what you are reading, you are more likely to convey your message.

■ **Believability**   In theater, films, and television dramas we see actors playing various character roles. Believability is the actor's skill in making us think that he or she is not on stage, but rather the character being portrayed. In Chapter 1, we made the distinction between actors and performers that actors portray characters, while performers are "themselves" during a production; still, performers should borrow the concept of believability from actors.

Believability is closely linked to internalization and credibility. The believable performer feels and is connected to the material, as well as projecting an image of trust and concern for the viewer. The performer must have some connection to the content and be familiar with the message it is trying to communicate. Research regarding an interview guest, topic, or commercial product can help you to sound more believable on screen.

■ **Concentration**   Performers should also borrow the actor's concept of concentration. Acting textbooks list several elements that make up the concept of concentration, including eliminating distractions and being absorbed and focused on a task. Actors must remain "in character" during theater productions even when there are distractions from the audience, such as audience members in the first few rows of the theater attempting to talk to the actors while the play is in progress.

Television performers must communicate meaning and emotions while facing different distractions in the studio or in the field. In the studio, cameras and people move about while you are speaking; in the field people in a crowd wave behind you and shout. Concentration requires that you be focused to the point of being able to ignore distractions.

The special challenge for the television performer is that a small portion of your concentration must be devoted to distinguishing between ambient distractions and meaningful distractions while you're reading (obviously this is true when you're reading nonscripted material as well). Ambient distractions are those that seem to happen in continual patterns (cameras moving about a studio, crowd noise, etc.). Meaningful distractions are production personnel trying to get your attention to communicate necessary information (a floor manager signaling where you should move, or a crew member indicating that something out of the ordinary has happened).

Beginning performers often feel challenged by the fact that they must concentrate on interpreting the script while being aware of distractions. As with any new skill, practice will help you develop concentration skills and anticipate potential production distractions.

▧ Word Color   Descriptive words or basic objects may be *colored* in tone to sound like the word or object. The word *cool* may be colored in such a way that you extend the *oo* vowel sound to suggest the feeling of cool. The same is true for a word such as *rock:* you can hit the final consonant harder to suggest the hardness of *rock.*

Word color is often used in commercials to add interest and variety. Check your script in advance and look for opportunities to color words. This may be difficult if you're using cue cards or teleprompters, but you should be familiar enough with the script to remember some opportunities as you see them on the prompter or cue card. If you prepare your script on computer disk to feed the teleprompter, you can underline key words you wish to color.

Be careful that you don't overdo or overuse word color, because you may sound unnatural or insincere. Listen to yourself on tape to see if you are using word color in a natural way.

▧ Visualization of Imagery   Visualization of imagery is a term often used in oral interpretation of literature. If you've ever watched someone give a dramatic reading of a short story or play, you may have noticed that the reader seems to see the imagery and reflect it in his or her eyes. In other words, if the reader is talking about seeing someone in the distance coming over a hill, his or her eye placement and concentration suggest that the reader actually sees the person in the distance.

Video performers may use a modified version of visualization, although obviously in most cases you can't look off camera to suggest various images. Try using "your mind's eye" to visualize script content while you're reading. If you're reading commercial copy, visualize the audience or yourself using the product.

In other situations try converting conceptual or technical information into imagery or word pictures. For example, when explaining technical or abstract information, use analogies to help simplify the material for the audience. We convert most of the information we process in daily life to some type of image, so use this ability to your advantage when you read.

■ **Phrasing** A phrase is a group of words that express a thought, image, or movement. Singers are familiar with **phrasing** in music, but many speakers have difficulty in phrasing when they are reading prepared material. The goal of phrasing is to group related thoughts together. Some of the most common bad habits readers have developed in regard to phrasing include the following:

■ **Don't be a respecter of commas and other punctuation.** Be careful that you don't let punctuation dictate how you phrase and when you pause. Punctuation assists with meaning for the person reading information silently, but it is not always the best indicator of meaning for the oral reader. Performers should keep the ear instead of the eye of the listener in mind.

You don't have to pause at every comma; not every period needs an extended pause. Some of the best-placed pauses occur where there is no punctuation mark. Think in terms of grouping words for meaning and not how they are grouped together on the page.

■ **Never pause at the opening of quotation marks.** When reading a quotation, you may have a tendency to pause right before the quotation. Pausing at this point throws the listener's attention back to the word preceding the pause (which is usually *said* or *saying;* not very exciting words to highlight). When you see quotation marks in copy tell yourself, "Do not pause."

■ **Avoid overuse of pause.** We've mentioned the strategic use of pause and how it adds interest to your reading. Beginning performers often use too many pauses, causing predictable vocal patterns and a practical problem of not being able to finish all the copy in the specified time (for example, a 30-second commercial).

Look for moments where a pause will create the most meaning and anticipation for the listener. An old commercial for Jell-O is one of the best examples of anticipation: The jingle went "J-E-L-L-pause-O." Listeners anticipated the pause and filled in the "O" before it was spoken.

■ **Emphasis** The highlighting or prioritizing of words is called **emphasis.** When you emphasize a word, you bring it to the attention of the listener, the message being that this word is important. Mistakes in emphasis are common errors made by performers reading scripts, and even veterans are not immune to such errors.

One general rule concerning emphasis is to accentuate the word that carries the meaning of the sentence forward. Two common ways to carry meaning forward are to introduce something new or to introduce something being contrasted. Some other guidelines regarding emphasis include the following:

■ **Emphasize people's names, product names, and places.** Key names and places are obvious words to emphasize. After establishing the name of the person or place, you may put a little less emphasis on these words as you repeat them throughout the copy or script, although product names are often emphasized or "punched" throughout a commercial script.

■ **Be careful of overemphasis of common adjectives and adverbs.** Certain words such as *really, very, big,* and *all* should not be emphasized as if the performer was reading a fairy tale to a small child. Look for a variety of descriptive words to emphasize, and avoid repeatedly emphasizing common adjectives and adverbs.

■ **Don't emphasize most prepositions.** For some reason people love to emphasize prepositions when they are reading and this tendency is another common mistake made by news anchors and other performers. Prepositions usually do little to carry forward meaning in what you are reading.

We hear this bad habit not only when listening to television and radio performers but also in a variety of public communication situations. How many times have you heard a flight attendant announcing over the intercom "We will be landing *in* Chicago in 20 minutes." The listener might be tempted to ask, "As opposed to *under* Chicago?"

While emphasis is an art and there are times to break the emphasis rules, these guidelines provide you with a good start in deciding which words deserve the most attention from the audience.

Rewind and Fade to Black

There are performers who have had little or no vocal training but have still been successful through natural talent or style. Nevertheless, the more you know about your voice and how to preserve it, the more likely you are to be successful as a video performer. Knowing basic guidelines for interpreting words from a script, teleprompter, or cue card will give you a blueprint for the decisions you make in reading your material during the preparation and rehearsal process.

You will also be aware of some of the most common mistakes made by beginning and more experienced performers and how to avoid them. Knowing these principles may help you compensate for not having the ideal television performer voice. Your ability to convey meaning can be more important than vocal perfection.

Keep in mind that few of us really like the way we sound, but the central question in performance is, "Do others like the way I sound?" Chapter 5 will help you to look good as well as sound good.

Exercises

1 Video- or audiotape yourself reading at least three to five minutes of copy. Find three things you like about the way you are reading the script. Do you hear any vocal problems? Check with an instructor or other friendly critic.

2 Watch a variety of television performers (newscasters, interview and talk show hosts, commercial spokespersons, etc.) and note their phrasing and emphasis when reading or speaking extemporaneously. What do they do well? Do you notice any mistakes?

3 Choose a short story from literature (ten minutes or less) and try reading it as a storyteller with mood shifts, internalization of emotions, word color, and visualization of imagery. Speculate on how your reading of the story differs now from the way you might have read the story before reading this chapter.

4 Try the following concentration exercises:

a. Note as many details of someone's clothes as you can in ten seconds.

b. Have someone do at least three distracting things in the background while you're reading a script.

c. Concentrate on a tune in your head while listening to different music on CD or the radio.

d. Select one sound out of a confusion of sounds and concentrate on it.

e. Some "just for fun" (and borderline silly) concentration exercises:

Sit in a rocking chair without rocking.

Listen to the "William Tell Overture" without thinking of the Lone Ranger.

Watch a commercial and focus only on the people in the commercial while ignoring the product.

5 Try some of the following to improve breath support, saying each with a single breath:

a. Amanda's voice expressed her humility.

b. Italy is in the southern part of Europe.

c. The afternoon was cooled by a gentle breeze.

d. Those who learn nothing have nothing to forget.

e. When we persuade others, we often convince ourselves.

f. There is little that is new except that which is forgotten.

Recite the alphabet, and try to inhale only at the marked places. Pause at the marks even if you don't need to inhale:

a-b-c-d-e-f-g-h // i-j-k-l-m-n-o-p-q // r-s-t-u-v-w-x-y-z

6 Try saying the following words without exaggerating the *t* or *d:*

bottle, kettle, settle, metal, little, rattle, written, bitten, button, kitten, mountain

ladle, paddle, saddle, hidden, sudden

7 Make clear distinctions between the vowel sounds for the words in the following sentences:

a. The *pen* was placed next to the *pin.*

b. The *men* are *lean* and *mean.*

c. *Fred* was seldom *afraid.*

d. *Ben,* where have you *been?*

e. She *said* that she found the *seed.*

f. *Ed* called for *aid.*

g. *Fred* fought to be *freed.*

8 Record yourself saying the following words without "popping your *p*'s." Work for proper microphone placement by talking across the mic instead of speaking directly into it:

pea, person, poor, pill, put, pack, pit, pull, power, path, pot, powder, pay, pile, pick, pitch, pool, pound, peel, pole, perfume

9 Practice speaking these sentences while changing your pitch as indicated by the direction of the arrow:

a. Winter came, ↑ wind, freeze, and snow.

b. He stopped suddenly, ↑ then turned to the right.

c. Why Tom did it, ↓ he could not tell

d. Our team lost, ↓ but the game was close.

e. Will you, ↑ or won't you?

f. It can't be done, ↑ no matter how you beg.

g. Hey there, ↓ that's enough.

h. We're tired, ↑ much too tired.

10 Here is a list of commonly mispronounced words; a correct and incorrect rhyme-word is shown in each case.

Word	Correct Rhyme-Word	Incorrect Rhyme-Word
1. assume	fume	doom
2. because	pause	buzz
3. been	bin	den
4. begin	tin	ten
5. blew	moo	mew
6. bury	berry	hurry
7. blue	moo	mew
8. catch	patch	fetch
9. chew	moo	mew
10. corps	store	corpse
11. creek	week	wick
12. de luxe	looks	spooks
13. drought	out	mouth
14. duty	beauty	snooty
15. err	burr	air
16. feat	feet	fate
17. flew	moo	mew
18. from	Tom	sum
19. get	bet	bit
20. gross	dose	toss
21. hundred	Mildred	thundered
22. inquiry	wiry	bleary
23. June	spoon	hewn
24. just	must	mist
25. new	mew	moo
26. our	sour	are
27. poor	tour	sore
28. pour	sore	tour
29. pretty	witty	Betty
30. program	telegram	glum
31. room	whom	fume
32. student	cue	moo
33. water	daughter	after

11 Now check out some of these commonly mispronounced words. Can you think of others?

1. across (a-CROSS) not (a-CROST)
2. athlete (ATH-leet) not (ATH-uh-leet)
3. comfortable (COM-fort-a-ble, or COMF-ta-ble) not (COMF-ter-ble)
4. electoral (eh-LEK-tor-al) not (eh-lek-TOR-al)
5. espresso (ess-PRESS-oh) not (ex-PRESS-oh)
6. February (FEB-roo-air-y) not (FEB-yoo-air-y)
7. figure (FIG-yer) not (FIG-er)
8. library (LIBE-rare-ee) not (LIBE-air-ee)
9. minuscule (MIN-uh-skyool) not (MIN-ih-skyool)
10. nuclear (NUKE-lee-ar) not (NUKE-yoo-lar)
11. often (OFF-en) not (OFT-en)
12. probably (PRAH-bab-ly) not (PRAH-bal-ly or PRAHB-ly)
13. pronunciation (pro-NUN-see-A-shun) not (pro-NOUN-see-a-shun)
14. sophomore (SOPH-a-more or SOPH-more) not (SOPHT-more)
15. supposedly (sup-POSE-ed-ly) not (sup-POSE-ab-ly)
16. toward (TOW-ward) not (TOR-ward)

INTERVIEW

Spencer Christian

Former ABC, now KGO San Francisco, Weathercaster

Spencer Christian is well known to viewers of ABC's *Good Morning America* as the weather forecaster they woke up to with the national weather picture. Christian now presents weather for ABC affiliate KGO in San Francisco. He continues to score high in public opinion polls on credibility.

Question: What do you consider to be the important elements of establishing credibility as a video performer?

Spencer Christian: There are certain things that are givens. Obviously, any performer in order to establish credibility needs to demonstrate knowledge of the subject matter. I think it's also important

that the viewers perceive you have an interest in the subject matter and that you are interested in what you are reporting. Some people seem knowledgeable, but they don't really seem interested in the subject.

In my case, I think it comes across to the viewers that I really want to connect with them. That's not something you can teach. I don't know how to put that in textbook terms to pass on to students. I consider myself not to be a reporter in a narrowly defined category such as a weather person or a general assignment reporter; I consider myself a communicator in the broad sense of the word. I think that a good communicator wants to connect with his/her audience, and I think that has come across to most viewers who watch me on the air. So if they perceive that I have knowledge of the subject matter, I'm interested in the subject, and I want to connect with them, they feel that I'm talking to them one on one. That's a personal communication, not some guy on television broadcasting to millions.

Q: You were a teacher for a while. How does that translate into doing the weather?

SC: It is helpful, but I don't think of myself as a former teacher because I only taught for one year. . . . When I was a teacher I would look at the faces of the students and I could tell if I was losing someone's interest. Obviously, you can't do that on television. But I think if you are employing all of the tools of a communicator, meaning command of the information, the ability to use language that allows you to reach a broad base of people, if you are animated and can use nonverbal communication to get your message across, all those tools help. I used those in the classroom and now on television.

Q: There are times as a weathercaster that you are wrong with the forecast. Given this, how do you maintain credibility with viewers when you know there are times when you will be wrong?

SC: As a weatherperson it is important to remind your audience that it is an inexact science and that you are striving for the highest level of accuracy that you can

attain, but that it is an inexact science and that there are going to be inaccurate forecasts. In the San Francisco Bay area, where you have all these microclimates, it is particularly important to remind the audience that weather patterns can be dramatically different from location to location within a relatively limited area. When we do have an inaccurate forecast, I like to explain what happened. I like to go to the map and show the viewers on what basis we issued the forecast we gave the previous day, what the alignment of systems was, and what factors we took into consideration. I then tell them how the systems moved differently from what we expected: we show them the changes that occurred to make the forecast be inaccurate. If you can explain what happened, people are forgiving.

Beyond that, I think they are forgiving if they like you. I don't know how you can make people like you. Probably, you do this by seeming not to try and make them like you. One thing that allows people to like you is your ability to not take yourself too seriously. When you take yourself too seriously and that comes across, people are looking for the chance to say, "Oh, he's wrong! He made a mistake." When you take yourself too seriously you invite critical examination. If you can demonstrate in your style and personality that you don't take yourself too seriously, people are forgiving, they forget about it, and the next day you still have 100 percent credibility rating.

Q: Are there stylistic differences between doing a national forecast like *Good Morning America* and a local forecast?

SC: I don't think there are any stylistic differences. There are format differences. When I was doing national weather, I had a shorter period of time than now when I'm doing local weather. The only time when we went into detail was when there was severe or unusual weather. When you're doing local weather, especially when you're in a place like the Bay area where the weather is so dramatically different from point to point, people want much more detailed information. . . . Stylistically, I don't think there are any major differences. I haven't changed my personality, or the way I prepare, or the way I connect with my viewers.

Q: Do you try to create a profile of a typical viewer in the San Francisco Bay area in comparison to a viewer in the national audience?

SC: That's a good point. There is that difference. I think early in the mornings a national audience didn't expect a very detailed localized presentation of weather. They wanted something pretty general for people who traveled, or were planning with their families, or their kids were away at school. I know that viewers want something different in my report when I'm doing local weather. I do have that in mind. But I don't know if there is a big difference in the way people respond to my style of communication on national or local telecasts.

I know they want more information and when I began my stint here at KGO-7, it was important for me to get across to the viewers that I knew the geography of the area, that I had been here before and was not a total stranger, and that I had some understanding of the microclimates. I was concerned about credibility and about communicating to the viewers that I was knowledgeable about Bay area weather. I don't think that concern altered my style or presentation.

It was important for me to be conscious of the fact that I needed to focus first on the information here and let the entertainment value come later, whereas at *Good Morning America* I had to fine-tune my presentation so I could stroll in there with very little preparation on some days and still present a credible, informative, and entertaining report. Here, I gave much more attention to the substance and content of my report without thinking much about being "Mr. Entertainment." Once I was comfortable with my knowledge of Bay area weather, I let more of that entertainment side of my personality come across.

Q: Of all the television performers you've seen, who is the person you most admire?

SC: There are many that I admire, but two stand out. The only person I looked to as a hero in my youth, as a role model, was David Brinkley. There are so many things about him I admire, but in a nutshell, I love the fact that he is really intelligent, knowledgeable, and very well informed. He took his job seriously, but made it clear that he didn't take himself too seriously. That always came across.

He always had a little bit of an offbeat sense of humor when he was reporting on political conventions or election coverage. He would give you the important information and analysis, but he would give you a humorous story or observation, that not only communicated to the viewer that he didn't take himself too seriously, but that he didn't take too seriously this whole political theater he was covering. I always liked that about him. He never injected humor at the expense of the content and the serious informational value of his reporting. It always seemed to be appropriate humor and it always seemed to fit. It was a part of the package. That's why I've always admired David Brinkley; he was one of my heroes and maybe one of my only heroes as a youngster.

In later years, there was Tom Snyder who I think was the best interviewer I've ever seen. Tom always seems interested in every topic he's discussing and always seems genuinely interested in every guest. He never seems like he's forcing it or trying too hard. No matter how guarded the guest may have been on Tom's show, he was able to open that guest up and bring out something that made him or her interesting to the viewer. It always seemed to be that he was able to do it not because he was working hard, it was because he really wanted to get to know this person and he was interested in what he or she had to say. I just love that style.

Q: What advice do you give to people starting their careers as video performers?

SC: The best piece of advice I can give is to be yourself and be brave enough, courageous enough to expose your vulnerabilities, flaws, warts, and blemishes on the air. What I mean by that is, don't try to be someone you're not. Don't try to assume another personality. Have a good command of the language and be well informed, well read, and develop all those textbook communication skills. It is important if you're going to set yourself apart as a video performer to recognize what distinguishes you from others—what is it that defines your personality, is interesting, unique, and compelling—and cultivate that. Make it part of your style.

Don't be afraid to let people see who you really are. I think that has been a large part of whatever success I've enjoyed. People say when they meet me in person, "Well, you seem just like you are when you're on the air." Well, I should. I think it's good if I have that kind of consistency with my personality. There's so many people I've worked with who are so different on the air because they assume another posture or personality, and then when you meet them off the air they seem so different. I think people can tell when

you are a real person. If you are not afraid to expose the real person you are, you stand a much better chance of allowing viewers to make a personal connection with you. This is going to make you more popular, probably better respected, give you a chance to develop a larger following; that's really what it's all about.

You can have all of the most important information in the world to report and you can be the most widely read individual in the business, but if you don't have anybody listening or following, you're not going to be an effective communicator because you're not going to be reaching anyone.

Q: Is there a question that should have been asked and wasn't?

SC: I have a greater appreciation of what wasn't asked. A question wasn't asked concerning how I define my role as a communicator based on my ethnicity. People will often ask, "As an African American reporter . . . ," and I say "No. I'm not an African American reporter, I'm a reporter who happens to be black." My racial-ethnic background has nothing to do with how effective a communicator I am. It doesn't define my role as a journalist or limit me any way as a communicator. It doesn't mean that I have to be given certain assignments.

So often these days when we are talking to Asians, or women, or people of color, we begin to define these individuals on the basis of their gender, skin color, or cultural heritage. . . . I would like aspiring journalists to know that if you define yourself in those narrow ways, then it makes it easier for the larger society to define you narrowly and expect certain things of you only because of the color of your skin or cultural background. If you can liberate yourself from that narrow self-definition, in an unspoken way you will communicate to society that you will not be defined that way. You are an individual first, and that's the way you want to be viewed. You don't have to say it or wear it on your sleeve, it just comes across. It doesn't mean that you have to lose any part of who you are, it just means that you don't have to define yourself so narrowly.

On another issue, I do have a pet peeve. This is not coming from some "aging guy" who is down on all the young people in the business. There is a whole generation of people who have entered broadcast journalism who have taken lots of courses in mass communication but who haven't had much of an education in history, literature, philosophy, things that truly give you knowledge. They come in with backgrounds where they don't know much. I see so many people in the business today who don't know much about history, even recent history. They know all about how to put a story together, how to write a good lead sentence, how to posture when they are on camera so they have that serious compelling look on their faces. But if you ask them about an event that takes place at a major party convention and ask them to put it in historical perspective, going back to the 1960s, they have little knowledge of that. They ask, "Who ran in 1968? That was before I was born." Well, Abe Lincoln was before I was born too, but I know he freed the slaves.

I'm disappointed in the lack of knowledge so many people coming into the business seem to have.

I'm also disappointed in the lack of writing skills, even with people at the network level. . . . There are people at the networks who write in fragments, run-ons, and poor sentence construction and you wonder, "Where did these people go to school and what qualifies them for the jobs they are doing?" Apparently, the people who are hiring them don't feel it is important to have good writing skills. I guess they want them to write in the language of the common person. I feel that as professional communicators, it is important to set the standard and raise the bar and not cater to what we think is the lowest common denominator. I don't think that is the way you reach people. I think we're here to not only to inform but to stimulate people to think, broaden their thinking, increase their awareness, to inspire and elevate their level of understanding and curiosity. We should give them information that is interesting and encourage them to want to know more.

I encourage people coming into the business to read more and learn something about current events, not just about the style of presentation. Read history, especially recent history, know about where we have been socially and politically, where we have been and where we are now.

CHAPTER FIVE

Nonverbal Communication and the Video Performer

It is no secret to anyone that the nonverbal aspects of communication contribute to our perception of the messenger. Most people have heard the expression "It's not what you say, it's how you say it," without realizing how much of the meaning of any message reaches the receiver nonverbally. Often, we form impressions of people through "gut instinct" without analyzing why we feel as we do about people we meet on the street or news anchors we see on television each evening. Before we discuss the importance of **nonverbal communication** on television, we need to consider the general importance of nonverbal communication in shaping meaning.

Mehrabian's Research in Nonverbal Communication

During the 1960s, Stanford University psychologist Albert Mehrabian did significant research in the area of nonverbal communication. Mehrabian had long been fascinated by the importance of nonverbal communication in a variety of contexts. After much research he determined that the meaning of a message could be divided into three means of communication and that percentages of meaning could be assigned to each means. These means and percentages are facial expression/body language (55 percent), vocal intonation (38 percent), and word choice (7 percent).

Facial expression is self-explanatory. Body language includes such aspects as posture, use of hand gestures, and movement.

Vocal intonation refers to how a person uses his or her voice to communicate emotion; for example, is the person laughing or using a happy tone of voice? Does he or she sound angry or harsh? Is there a lack of vocal variety?

Word choice refers to the exact words being used, in other words, the speaker's selection of particular words and phrases rather than others.

You may disagree with Mehrabian's percentages (some think that he attributes too much importance to facial expression and body language and not enough to word choice), but it's difficult to argue with the general principle that nonverbal aspects play a major role in communication.

Consider everyday communication events such as reading a letter or office memo. When only word choice is involved, there are often misunderstandings of intent or emotions. The reader may be uncertain whether the writer is being sarcastic or describing true feelings. Some written correspondence may be interpreted more harshly than intended. With the advent of e-mail, new "indicators" have been developed to communicate the emotions of the writer. For example the symbol " :) " can show that the writer is happy or just joking, whereas typing a message in all uppercase letters can convey the effect that the writer is shouting

Talking on the telephone incorporates two of Mehrabian's elements, word choice and vocal intonation, but such conversations still leave room for misinterpretation. A listener may, for example, misread a pause as anger. In reality, the pause may occur merely because the other person is thinking about what to say next.

Classic examples of how hearing only the verbal cues may skew our perception of the communicator are the 1960 presidential debates between Richard Nixon and John F. Kennedy. Those who saw the debates remember that Nixon was perspiring, unshaven, and pale while Kennedy looked tanned, rested, and more energetic. Kennedy also wore a suit that con-

The Kennedy-Nixon debates demonstrated the importance of nonverbal communication for political candidates appearing on television.

trasted with the set background; Nixon wore a suit color that made him appear to blend into the set. Most viewers were watching on black and white sets, so contrast was a problem.

The result was quite different on radio, though. Those who only heard Nixon thought that he won the debates, whereas those who both heard and saw Kennedy on television thought that he was the clear winner. The 1960 presidential debates were defining moments not only for politicians but for anyone attempting to communicate effectively via video.

One thing about Mehrabian's findings is certain: when the nonverbal and verbal cues contradict one another, we believe the nonverbal cues. A performer's nonverbal and verbal expressions should be consistent. Conflicting verbal and nonverbal cues give rise to problems in the minds of viewers. For example, a former senate candidate in a midwestern state created a negative impression by punctuating most statements she made, even serious statements, with a smile:

> There will be an increase of unemployment to 10 percent in our
> state this year due to plant closings (smile). This will mean we will
> have less money for our public school system (smile).

The constant smiling led voters to believe that the candidate was not taking these issues seriously and that unemployment and public education were not important to her. She lost the election by a landslide. There were other reasons for her defeat; but her onscreen image did not enhance her appeal to voters.

Another famous example of conflicting nonverbal cues in the political video arena took place during one of the 1992 presidential debates between President George Bush, Bill Clinton, and Ross Perot. President Bush told the American people that he wanted to be president for a second term; however, on a wide angle shot, the television cameras caught him looking at his watch while Bill Clinton was speaking. This gave many the impression that Bush was wondering how much time was left in the debate and that he would rather be somewhere else.

RATINGS POINTER

Don't assume that you can't be seen by the camera and home viewer even though you are not speaking or you think you are off camera. The director may decide to take a cover shot (a wider angle shot of the individuals on the set) or a reaction shot of you while someone else is speaking. Like President Bush, you may find yourself communicating a negative message to viewers. ★ ★ ★ ★

As noted in Chapter 2, the unique aspects of video shape how the message is perceived. It is important to note that there is no guarantee that a person who is an effective communicator when seen during a live event will necessarily be successful when viewed on the screen.

For example, many would regard Reverend Jesse Jackson as one of the great public orators in American politics. In live speeches Jackson has energy that is effective in large auditoriums and plays well to huge crowds. After watching him speak on television, however, some critics observed that he was "too hot" or too energetic for the medium, meaning that his large gestures and strong voice did not transfer well to the television audience. Rev. Jackson has done much in recent years to adjust his nonverbal communication to the video medium to make himself more effective in the more intimate television context (especially on television news interview shows).

It is also important to remember that because video is a two-dimensional medium, there is a loss of depth in the video performance. The performer must therefore do more to project energy to compensate for this loss. Effective communicators know how to tailor their nonverbal behavior to video. What follows is a head-to-toe guide to nonverbal communication on television.

Head Movements

Most people don't think about their head movements when speaking in interpersonal or public speaking situations. Sometimes head movement in live situations is not a distracting problem and is barely noticed. But on the video screen excessive movement can make your head your worst enemy. Video is a close-up medium that exaggerates movement. Usually, a performer is shot at close or medium range. Viewers probably give little thought to the composition of these shots or to what the camera operator or director must do in order to achieve them, but knowledge of close-up and medium shots and the limitations of both may help the performer avoid distracting movements (shot composition is discussed in Chapter 7). Following are some general guidelines regarding head movement.

How much movement is acceptable on the video screen, and what type of movement shows the performer in a positive light? First, it is important to consider the position of your head. In most cases you should tilt your head slightly toward the camera if you are addressing viewers at home or slightly toward the other person(s) on the set if doing an interview. This head tilt can aid in giving the impression that you are interested in the viewers at home or the people you are talking to in the studio.

In general, you should look comfortable and not appear as if you have a stick tied to the back of your neck, while still limiting excessive head bobbing or back-and-forth movement. It is important to remember that such movement will look exaggerated to the viewer. It can also cause problems for the technical crew as they attempt to keep you in the frame.

Controlled head movement is the key. Movements should be a little slower and not as "big" as in live communication encounters. Another tip is to visualize a "movement zone" of about three to four inches for each side of the head. This allows for movement to the front, back, and sides without apparent lack of control or moving out of the frame. Such controlled and purposeful movement can be a major aid in creating a credible performer.

RATINGS POINTER

Once during a video training session at a *Fortune 500* corporation, a consultant was invited to discuss communication skills in the workplace. The session included teleconference call-in questions during a live telecast. In an effort to give positive reinforcement and appear friendly, the consultant continually nodded during the question-and-answer session. Viewers soon started snickering because his head movements seemed so exaggerated that they lacked sincerity. The head movements drew the most frequent comments on the evaluation of the training session. ★ ★ ★ ★

Your Eyes

You may have heard the eyes referred to as "the windows to the soul." Nowhere is this truer than in video performance. Acting and speech coaches often say, "If I don't believe your eyes I don't believe you." The video performer has the special challenge of trying to connect with the viewer by looking into the camera lens. There are other issues: where to look, how to read teleprompters and cue cards, and how to relate to other performers on the set in a natural way through eye contact (issues discussed in later chapters). In short, your eyes affect your credibility and attractiveness to the audience. Several key considerations will assist you with eye contact:

■ **Eye-to-Lens Contact**   When speaking to the viewer, you should look directly into the camera lens as if it were the viewer's eyes. Making this **eye-to-lens contact** is especially difficult because the camera is an intimidating piece of hardware hardly resembling human eyes. The old piece of advice practiced by numerous successful video performers over the years of "visualizing the eyes of a friend superimposed over the camera lens" can minimize the stress of looking at the camera. Practice and critique of your videotapes will also help.

If you don't look directly at the camera lens, you will not be looking into the eyes of the viewer.

Often in everyday conversation we look off to the side to think about what we are going to say next. This behavior is very distracting when you are onscreen and may cause the viewer to doubt your credibility. If you need to break contact with the lens (or with another person if you're looking at them during an interview) you should look downward slightly instead of off to the side.

It is important to remember that any type of eye movement will be exaggerated, especially during close-up shots. Sometimes you will be tempted to glance slightly off camera or look at the floor manager, production assistants, or other human beings in the studio. Resist the temptation and use the camera lens as the target when you are talking to the viewer.

Learn to develop your peripheral vision to see floor managers giving you signals or cues. Floor managers should stand as close to the camera as possible when giving you cues and signals so that you will be less likely to look off camera.

■ **Using Studio Monitors**   Another temptation is to look at yourself in the studio **monitors**—a high-quality video receiver—during production. You should not do this unless some other program material or videotape is being included in the program. For example, a news anchor may read the lead-in to a previously videotaped and edited news story (often referred to as a **package**) looking directly into the camera lens. As the videotape story "rolls," the anchor will probably look down at the monitor to watch the story.

During **b-roll** video (video that is rolled into the production while performers are talking in the studio or on remote) the performer may also look at the studio monitor. In an interview, the interviewee may have videotape to show. In this case the interviewer must watch the tape while it is running on the studio monitor and may describe the action or ask questions about the tape. Other images seen on the studio monitor may come from slides or a **still storage** system. If you are curious about your performance—and you should be—watch tapes of yourself following the performance when you may give them your undivided attention.

RATINGS POINTER

When using a monitor to view videotape during a performance, it is a good idea to hold eye contact with the camera lens until you are certain that the videotape segment is rolling and being seen by viewers. Don't rush to look at the monitor until you are certain you are clear of the camera. The red tally light on the camera and the floor manager can help you here. ★ ★ ★ ★

■ **Distracting Eye Movements**   Eye movement while trying to maintain eye-to-lens contact is another potential problem for the performer. Eyes looking up or down when you are thinking about what to say next, or eyes shifting back and forth, are very distracting to viewers, as is excessive blinking. You should tape yourself to see if you are unconsciously making any of these distracting eye movements. Awareness and practice may help eliminate them.

To avoid excessive blinking, you should arrive on the fully lighted set well before the production begins, because it may take several minutes for your eyes to adjust to the lights. If you arrive on the set at the last second and don't allow your eyes to adjust, you are bound to blink.

Eyeglasses may also cause problems when the studio lights reflect off the lenses and produce glare. In some cases, technicians can adjust the lighting positions to eliminate the problem. If you wear glasses but can see relatively well without them, you may want to try taking them off before the performance.

■ **Energy through Your Eyes**   Your eyes must communicate that you are involved with your subject matter and that you want to share the information with the viewer. Try to channel excess energy through your eyes. The late NBC news anchor Jessica Savitch, one of the first women to anchor a local or network newscast, would visualize a "fiery energy ball" behind her eyes, then try to project the energy. This approach may sound extreme, but always be aware that you need to appear energetic and involved through dynamic eye contact.

Chapter 7 explores the use of prompting devices such as cue cards and teleprompters.

Your Mouth

The video medium can give the impression that a performer is unhappy or harsh due to the loss of depth on the screen. A neutral facial expression in real life may look harsh and unfriendly on the video screen. This is why it is important to smile, when appropriate, while speaking on camera. Smiling makes the performer look energetic and eager to communicate with viewers.

Obviously, you must consider the message content before deciding whether to smile; it is important to keep the verbal and nonverbal elements of the performance consistent.

RATINGS POINTER

Try reading a piece of copy or text and videotape yourself looking into the camera lens, speaking with a slight frown. Then try reading the same copy with what you consider to be a neutral expression. Finally, try reading the copy again with a smile. When you play back the video-tape, see which reading you like the best. ★ ★ ★ ★

Unless your copy covered a serious subject, you probably most liked the reading when you were smiling. For some people, smiling while on camera is natural; others need to practice smiling while speaking. In any event, a smile can give the impression that the performer enjoys being part of the program and can strengthen his or her connection with the viewer.

Your Hands

Effective use of hand gestures can do much to improve your performance and help you maintain a high energy level. Many beginning performers fail to use hand gestures and keep their hands folded in front of them, sometimes in a tight, "white knuckled" manner, creating an uncomfortable and unnatural look.

As many public speakers know, hands can reveal nervousness. Performers are often seen making distracting gestures such as tapping their fingers or wringing their hands. To avoid this you should videotape yourself and monitor these movements. When sitting down, rest one hand over the other; when standing up, press your thumb against your forefingers. These techniques look natural and also guard against unwanted hand movement.

Hand gestures are a natural part of human communication, and recent research indicates that we would have difficulty regulating our verbal communication if we didn't gesture. Consider the way in which you use hand gestures in everyday conversation. Usually, when the palms of our hands point downward, we are using gestures for emphasis. Gestures with the hands pointing upward tend to be friendlier or warmer. When you think about the purpose of your gestures instead of merely "talking with your hands," you usually communicate more meaning.

It is important for video performers to adapt their gestures to the close-up medium. Gestures that look normal in real life may be too wide for the video screen and give the impression that the performer is out of control.

To prevent this problem, you should imagine a "gesture box" in front of your body. Visualize the edges of the box extending from your shoulders to your waist, from top to bottom, and from the left side to the right side of your torso. The "gesture box" is similar to the strike zone in baseball; you need to keep your gestures in the frame. Notice experienced performers and politicians on television; they seldom gesture beyond this box.

As with any movement on television, hand gestures should be controlled and not too fast or jerky. Imagining that you have small weights on your arms and hands will aid control and help minimize wild-looking gestures.

You may ask, "If the camera is shooting me in a close-up and my hands are seldom on the screen, do I need to gesture?" The answer is yes, because even unseen gestures will help you communicate more energy through your eyes and face, as well as enabling the director to go to a wider angle shot in which your hands are visible in the frame. Seen or unseen, gestures also help you to seem more natural. You may have heard about or seen film of actors in radio dramas who used their hands while performing even though they could not be seen by the home audience. Gesturing and other expressive behaviors helped these actors to communicate emotion and believability.

Hands and arms should always be relaxed and should not provide a barrier between the performer and the audience. Avoid body language that

Make your gestures smaller than you would in normal conversation and keep them in the gesture box.

makes you appear to be interpersonally closed, such as clenching your fists or folding your arms in front of you; opt instead for nonverbal behaviors that make you look more open and relaxed.

Your Posture

One of the major problems for beginning performers is that they do not know how to sit or stand in front of a television camera. While these activities are second nature to us in day-to-day communication, we suddenly lose the ability to appear natural on the video screen. The following suggestions will help you attain a more comfortable on-camera appearance.

Sitting   Many beginning performers look stiff or uncomfortable when on camera, either due to stress or because they perceive the television performance as formal. Whatever the reason, the performer often looks like a child who is sitting in a corner as punishment. This appearance of being ill at ease creates a nonverbal barrier between the performer and the audience.

To avoid looking uncomfortable, try sitting in a chair with your back straight against the chair's back. Then lean forward a bit with your shoulders and head. Immediately, you will look at ease but not too casual; you will seem more interested in the guest on the set; or if you are looking directly into the camera lens, you will seem more interested in the viewer.

On the other hand, performers sometimes look too relaxed on camera. Some lean back in their chairs with their stomachs out and legs spread like fans watching a football game on television; they should have a drink in one hand and a remote control. You often see athletes appearing like this on sports interview shows. It is important to remember that being too relaxed or sloppy creates a less than flattering appearance.

Be comfortable but not too casual when sitting in chairs.

■ **Standing**   Performers often wonder how to stand on camera. Some appear too stiff or rigid, as if they were in a military drill, while others tend to shift their weight from side to side or onto one foot. Still others use unnatural arm and hand positions that they would never use in everyday conversation.

■ **Standing too straight/stiff.** New performers often feel (standing or sitting) that they must have a rigid posture with their legs straight and locked into position. This is very uncomfortable for the viewer as well as the performer. The proper upright posture for video is to stand straight with shoulders back slightly. One way to do this is to visualize a small hook in the center of your back fastened to a string pulling you back.

Bend your knees a bit without locking them. Locking the knees not only makes you look stiff but also limits blood circulation, making you feel uncomfortable. You can cheat a bit by putting one foot slightly in front of the other. This will give you a better base, making you feel more relaxed and less shaky in the knees. Keep about 12 to 18 inches of space between your feet when you are standing so that you have a sturdy base.

Remember that any nervous movement such as swaying back and forth or shifting weight from one foot to another will be exaggerated on camera and may put you outside the frame.

Correct posture improves your overall appearance while also making you look slimmer. This is an added benefit for those who are concerned with the fact that video makes a person look somewhat heavier.

■ **Arms and hands while standing.** Your arms and hands may also contribute to the impression that you are uncomfortable while standing. Two distracting positions that performers adopt with their arms and hands while standing are the "fig leaf" and putting their arms behind their backs. The "fig leaf" position is holding your arms in a V shape in front of your body and folding your hands in front of you below the waist (we'll leave it to your imagination why this is called the "fig leaf"). Other performers put their arms behind their backs and clasp them in what might be called a "reverse fig leaf."

Besides making you look uncomfortable, both of these positions limit your ability to use gestures naturally because your hands are clasped. Often you see people using either the "fig leaf" or "reverse fig leaf" twitch their shoulders or hands because they want to gesture but think they can't. This creates a distracting, if not comical, impression.

All the positive gesturing techniques discussed earlier can also be used when standing; remember to keep all gestures above the waist and below the armpits, in the gesture box in front of your body. Gestures below the waist look tentative and weak, while gestures above your shoulders make you look out of control.

The best way to use gestures while standing is to remember "the three Ls—*lift, level,* and *lay. Lift* reminds you always to lift your arms and to gesture above the waist. *Level* reminds you to keep your arms and gestures level and not gesture with one arm higher than the other. *Lay* helps you to control your gestures by reminding you to lay your arms gently down by your sides without slapping the sides of your legs.

■ **Your Feet and Legs**   According to some experts in nonverbal communication, your feet and legs are the most honest parts of your body. People who can conceal their feelings by controlling their facial expressions and gestures, will nevertheless often allow nervous energy to be channeled through the feet and legs. Some people may smile but move their legs or jiggle their feet in a distracting manner. Many beginning performers don't know what to do with their feet and legs during interviews and often create distractions when the director takes a "two shot" or "cover shot." There are several things you can do to control feet and leg movements:

■ **Keep your legs together when sitting.** While this may be second nature for women, it is not always so for men. How many times have you seen a male athlete being interviewed on a talk show sitting in a chair with his legs wide apart? It is as if he thinks he is being shot only in close-up. Remember that the director may want to take a wider angle shot that includes your whole body.

Both men and women can cross their legs at the knee. Women may also cross their legs at the ankles. Women and men can keep their legs

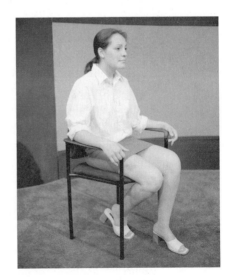

Performer demonstrates
the runner's position.

together and put one foot in front of the other in what is called the "runner's position," like a runner coming out of the starting blocks. Women wearing short skirts or shorter women may prefer the runner's position.

■ **Be aware that your feet can show nervous energy.** We can often correct nervous habits once we are aware of them. Monitor what your feet are doing and make sure they are not jiggling or making circles. Tape practice sessions to see if your feet are under control.

■ **When you get ready to stand up, make sure both feet are on the floor for a few seconds before you stand.** This may seem obvious, but many performers have experienced the awkward feeling of trying to stand after sitting with their legs crossed for several minutes. Make sure you give yourself contact by having your feet touch the floor for a least a few seconds near the end of the time you will be sitting. This will make you less inclined to appear nervous when you leave your chair.

Movement and Walking

Again, it is important to remember that since video exaggerates movement, you must control it when you are walking. In most cases there will be designated areas where you will walk to or "marks" that you will have to hit (more about hitting your marks in Chapter 7). You will often walk to areas that have been lighted for you. If, however, you are permitted to move freely and lighting is not a consideration, you should walk or move with a sense of purpose. The performer who paces back and forth is distracting to the viewer and creates a problem for the production crew.

Walking should be controlled and slower than your normal pace. Also, any type of movement within the frame—such as turning around to show a different area of the weather map—should be controlled and executed at a slightly slower speed than regular movement (we will discuss how to work with chroma-key maps and other visuals in more detail in Chapter 10).

When you are moving from one area of the set to the other, you can give visual warning cues to the director and camera operators so that they know what you are doing (make your first step a little slower than the other steps to let the production crew know that you are moving). Sometimes you can give basic verbal cues to the crew to alert them that you are about to move ("Let's go over here and see what's happening in the kitchen"). The production crew usually appreciates any type of visual or verbal warning.

Try to warn the production crew if you are sitting and about to stand; this helps the camera operator keep you in the frame and may also help a microphone boom operator keep the microphone out of view. Many shows now use wireless or lavaliere mics but the boom mic is still in use. Some-

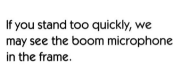
If you stand too quickly, we may see the boom microphone in the frame.

times a guest on a talk show suddenly stands up and the microphone and boom are visible at the top of the screen. The boom operator then has to move the mic and boom quickly out of the frame. This problem will not arise if the performer moves more carefully when standing.

Another problem with standing up too quickly is that if the camera operator does not anticipate your move, your head and upper body may go off camera, leaving your waist in the center of the shot.

Rewind and Fade to Black

The more you understand the importance of nonverbal communication, the greater your chance of being an effective video communicator. After reading this chapter, you may think that there are so many nonverbal behaviors to consider that you will never remember to pay attention to all of them. Practice and increased comfort level in performance will help make the principles covered in the chapter second nature.

During practice sessions, try working on one or two elements at a time. For example, try working first on your eye contact and communicating energy and expressiveness through your eyes; then practice facial expressiveness, then other nonverbal behaviors. If you divide the overall task into components, it becomes more manageable. Although most of these suggestions also apply to field production situations, the unique aspects of nonverbal communication in those situations will be dealt with in later chapters.

At the end of a performance, don't make the assumption that you are off screen or inaudible just because you think the show is over. Looking disgusted with yourself or other negative nonverbal and verbal behaviors may still be visible to the viewer during the closing seconds. Classic stories from both television and radio have been circulated around the industry by people who have seen or heard performers do or say things that they would not like viewers to see or hear. Wait until you get an "all clear" from the director, floor director, or producer before making the assumption that you are off camera and off mic, or you may be a candidate for a bloopers show.

RATINGS POINTER

Too often both experienced and novice performers make the assumption that they are not on camera and then suddenly appear on screen, in some cases much to their embarrassment. Even though someone else is speaking during the production, you should not make the assumption that you will not be seen.

The director may decide to do a reaction shot, or human error may occur (a director calling for the wrong shot or a technical director activating a wrong camera). You should also anticipate being seen on screen before showtime (your floor manager should alert you to the approaching air or tape time).

Too many performers have been caught off guard by appearing on screen sooner than they had expected. During the early days of CNN, a reporter appeared on the air picking his nose because he thought his story had not started. ★ ★ ★ ★

Exercises

1. Watch five different types of television performers (for example, news anchor, interviewer, talk show host, sportscaster, weather forecaster). Are there differences in their nonverbal behaviors? Which elements of their nonverbal performances do you like the best? Which do you like the least?

2. Notice differences in nonverbal performances when performers are sitting down as opposed to standing up.

3. While watching television, pay attention to nonverbal performance mistakes (legs spread apart, poor use of gestures, standing up too quickly, etc.). Keep a log of these for two weeks.

4. Watch political leaders to see if they use "the gesture box" even when they are not talking directly to the camera.

5. Videotape yourself interviewing a friend on a subject of interest. Observe your nonverbal behaviors when you play back the tape.

INTERVIEW

Vernon Glenn

Weekend Sports Anchor and Sports Reporter, KRON San Francisco

San Francisco television viewers call Vernon Glenn "Mr. Involvement" because of his energy and "up close" approach to his sports feature stories. He has taken batting practice with the Oakland As, been thrown from a bull, and has taken blows from a professional boxer. Glenn's "Mr. Involvement" features are seen throughout the week, and local television critics have called them the best features on local television. He also anchors KRON's weekend sportscasts and can be heard on KNEW and KNBR radio in San Francisco.

Before joining KRON, Glenn, a graduate of the University of Virginia, worked at WBAL-TV in Baltimore as weekend sports anchor and at WXEX-TV Richmond as a sports anchor and reporter. His energy and personable style make him an ideal subject for discussing the nonverbal aspects of video performance and other topics.

Question: It seems as if you're having fun when reporting sports. We get all the information, and you also seem to be enjoying yourself. How hard was it for you to develop this style, or did it come naturally to you?

Vernon Glenn: Just like with anything else, as you do things over time, you become comfortable with them. Sports had always been fun for me, but to relate that to television and to project and give a nice presentation is an on-the-job, learn-by-doing repetition kind of thing. I want people at home to think, this guy is having a good time. It's been a lot of years of evolution, but once I felt comfortable in what I was saying, doing, and talking about, I was able to ease into my style a little bit.

When you see me now I'm bubbly, I'm hopping around and interacting with the anchors. It's hard for me to sit still. I'm gesturing and talking with my hands a lot, and I'm smiling and telling people, "You've got to see this play; isn't this play something!" Hopefully my enthusiasm through my smile, laugh, and gesturing will translate to, "Hey, this guy is having a good time!"

I started in April of 1985 and it probably took me (in this market) until 1993 or 1994 to really feel comfortable with what I was doing. I got to San Francisco in 1990 and I had the "deer in the headlights" look: stiff, mechanical . . . look at the camera, read the teleprompter. If you looked at my eyes close enough, you could see the pupils going left to right as I read the teleprompter. But now it's a whole comfort zone.

There's confidence in the voice and you can tell by the nonverbal presentation that this guy is relaxed, this guy knows it, and he's telling me a story. He's not just giving me the facts. Some people are comfortable in doing that but that's not my style. I don't even write out everything I say any more. Eighty-five percent of what I say is ad lib. The other 15 percent of what I say I've scripted only so the director and the producer can follow along and will know when I want them to roll the videotape.

Once that tape rolls, I'm in the living room with you and I'm watching the highlights just like you.

I have what's called a "shot sheet" that gives me the situation, what happened, and what the result was. How I fill in the blanks is up to me, and I don't even know what I'm going to say before the highlight rolls. The spontaneity and excitement of getting up there and giving that presentation and having a high level of energy, unscripted and fly by the seat of your pants and still be able to get your point across, and tell them the "who, what, when, where, why" is satisfying to me.

I guess the key words are confidence and comfort zone and being able to intertwine those two with the knowledge that you have. You mesh those things together, and when you go on the air and that bright red light comes on, have a good time.

Q: What was the most valuable piece of advice given to you concerning the nonverbal aspects of performance?

VG: I'm reminded of what Larry King told me before I started a job in Baltimore. I was with my dad in a restaurant in Washington, D.C., and I said "Hey, there's Larry King over there; I've got to get up and say something to him."

So I went over to him and said, "I'm Vern Glenn, someone who's just getting going in the business and about to go work in Baltimore. I'm wondering is there any kind of advice you can give me that would kind of help me along?" So I'm waiting for this prose to come out and he just looks up from his drink and says two words; "Be yourself." And that was about it.

But you know what? He's right! If you try to be somebody else, sooner or later someone's going to figure it out and ultimately you won't be comfortable with whatever you're doing or whomever you're imitating.

You should concentrate on being yourself and not take yourself seriously.

Take your job seriously, and not yourself seriously.

Q: What do you focus on when you look at videotapes of yourself?

VG: It always helps to look at your past shows. I should do it more than I do now; I don't take the time to do it as much as I used to. In looking at those shows you are your own worst critic. If you look at tapes over and over again sometimes it's just the little things, a little tweak here and there, that can improve the overall package. What I look for is, was it clear, concise, and entertaining? Were all the facts straight, or did I talk as if I had marbles in my mouth? I'm looking to see if I had a good rhythm going—a good sense of flow, good sense of presentation.

Then I get picky on some of the other things. When I look at what I said over the highlights, I want to make sure that I referenced the highlights not only clearly but well. If there was a shot of Boy Scouts in the stands edited in between plays, did I say, "On Boy Scout Day at Candlestick Park where there were 40,192 to see the Giants, Jeff Kent hit an opposite field home run . . ." You try to look at the video before you go on air just for little things like that so you can say, "Look at the catch made by that fan after the home run."

You can tell when you're delivering it and watching it whether or not you hit it. It's almost like hitting a golf ball on the sweet spot; you know when you've hit it in performance, and that's what I live for.

Q: Are there any people at the network level that you admire or consider models for your work?

VG: I don't know if there's someone out there I would like to model or someone I'd like to be. I do have my favorites at the network level because they are so "non networky." Terry Bradshaw and John Madden come to mind because those are man's man kind of guys who will put things in laymen's terms, put things in a way you can understand.

I don't need someone telling me about the "two-three" zone or explaining the "pick and roll." I don't want to hear that! I want to hear Terry Bradshaw get worked up and wound up, and you can tell when he likes the subject because his eyes get kind of big and he starts gesturing with his hands and he gets so excited to talk about football and it's just great.

John Madden is the same way. I want to hear John Madden tell me, "He pulls, he knows his block, he knows his route, he gets his jersey all dirty and BOOM! he takes the guy out!" Any time you can get a guy at the network level and it just comes out of his pores, that's what does it for me. I don't like the ones who concentrate on how smart they are and how little you know; that's a pet peeve of mine.

Q: How do you handle distractions and unexpected problems and give the impression you're still in control?

VG: It's a comfort zone kind of thing that comes through experience. On a remote shoot, if there is sneezing or a heckler, you just keep on going. But when you first start out, you've got this tunnel vision going. You'll be projecting and then someone distracts you and then you see the talent get nervous and start stumbling and going down to their notepad. It just depends on how comfortable you are. We've all been there. Soledad O'Brien, who now works for NBC News, had her first live shot at Pat O'Shea's Tavern in San Francisco with some sports-related thing, and someone came up and pinched her.

You try to block out the distractions, but you know they are going to happen. Sometimes you have to say, "Hey, it's live TV, ladies and gentlemen," and keep going.

Q: If you were going to give someone one piece of advice concerning nonverbal communication and delivery, what would it be?

VG: I'd tell somebody, just before you go on and the floor manager yells "twenty seconds," take a couple of deep breaths, exhale, let it all out, and think of something that would let you know that this isn't brain surgery. You're giving out information the best way you know how in your own kind of style.

In time you're going to know what that style is. You're not going to know at first because your head is going to be filled with a mixed bag of other people you may have seen, ones that you admire and respect and model yourself after. In due time, you'll get a sense of who you really are or maybe if this is for you.

Maybe you would be more interested in doing something connected with television in general. You're going to find out in a hurry, is it for you? If it is, and you continue to be on camera, develop your own style.

Don't take yourself so seriously and don't try so hard. But when it comes to doing the job, take your job seriously; just don't take yourself so seriously. If you do that you will do better than you probably think.

Your show is never as bad as you think it is. There have been so many times when I've gotten up there and I feel like I'm dying up there. I'll review the tape and I say, "Hey, it wasn't that bad. There were a couple of things wrong but I can correct that." And the great thing about television sportscasting is you have two shows, so if you flub it on the five o'clock news at least you can make it up on the eleven.

You'll be able to tell from the feedback you get from people you don't even know are watching. Your friends are watching for the mistakes because they want to tease you about them, but go in knowing that you're going to make mistakes.

CHAPTER SIX

Working as a Team with Production Personnel

A number of books concerning video production and personnel have devoted pages to the video performer's relationship to the production process, but there are few pages concerning how the performer must interact with production personnel and how all can function as a team. Sometimes those working in front of the lens and those behind the camera find themselves in two different worlds. This can cause resentment and a less than satisfactory experience for all involved.

The Need for Teamwork

Performers must understand that a team concept is necessary in any production. Knowing how to interact with production personnel and understanding the capabilities and limitations of the video production facility can contribute to a better production and more positive interpersonal relationships.

It isn't necessary to learn every piece of equipment in the studio or control room, and you certainly do not need to become a "techie"; but you should have a basic understanding of what types of production values can be accomplished in a video facility along with the people working in the production process. This chapter deals with people and the interpersonal attitudes you must develop toward them in order to succeed as a video performer. Chapter 7 focuses on what you need to know about specific items of equipment.

The number of personnel involved in a video production can range from one or two general assistants to many specialists. A production facility can be a sophisticated, state-of-the-art studio and control room or a small space with a camcorder or two. In Chapter 8 we will see that field productions may have one person or as many as a dozen shooting an interview or other type of feature.

In either case, the goal should be the same: giving the best performance you can with the tools you have. Before discussing the team players and equipment in the production process, let's look at the five overarching principles that the video performer should keep in mind.

■ **Empathy**   Often the performer(s) and the production personnel are not on the same page. Some performers feel that it is up to the production people to make them look good and that they have little or no responsibility in the process. In other cases the performer does not understand the limitations of the production facility and has unrealistic demands and expectations of the personnel.

Performers need to understand the pressures and limitations of the human beings and machines involved in any production. Those who are new to video performance may simply not understand how complex the production process is; just getting an image onto the screen requires the expertise of many people.

This chapter introduces the various people involved in the process and explores the demands they face. Understanding and empathizing with them can make the production a much more rewarding experience for everyone involved.

■ **Preparation**   The three most important concepts in creating a smooth production process are, once again, *preparation, preparation, preparation* (yes, preparation has been mentioned earlier in this book, and it is a key ingredient of your success). Novice performers sometimes arrive unprepared on the production set or location. Lack of preparation is one of the most frustrating obstacles to the production process and can cause major clashes between talent and production personnel. Consider the following examples:

- A performer who is supposed to have memorized a script (or at least be very familiar with it) has not done so. He keeps stumbling through the material, necessitating numerous retakes.

- The director of a local dramatic production is invited as a guest on a local live talk show to plug the opening. The producer of the talk show has invited the director as the only guest and, given the talk show's format, has assumed that it will be a sit-down interview.

  The play's director thinks it would be a great idea to bring several cast members to the studio to perform a scene from the play. He decides to do this without consulting the producer of the talk show and shows up on the day of production with the actors ready to perform. The producer tells his guest that the actors can't perform because of the limitations of the studio set and the lack of proper lighting. The director does the interview solo as planned but is unhappy with the outcome, while the producer is unhappy about having disappointed the director.

- The spokesperson for a local art gallery is invited to appear on the interview segment of a local morning newscast. She brings numerous slides of a new exhibit at the gallery and asks if they can be shown. Because the production crew has had no advance warning about the slides, there is no time to prep or show them.

Knowing what to mention to producers and what visual elements you may bring to a production are important skills for a video performer. This chapter contains tips for good performance preparation and explains what you should know and ask before you get to the studio.

■ **The Show Must Go On**   Almost anything can happen during a video production; at times performers have to work under adverse conditions. In the case of a recorded production, the crew can do retakes to solve any problems that occur during shooting, but in live productions it is more difficult to correct problems without making them obvious to the viewer. In cases where the unexpected happens, it is important for you to remain calm and perform to the best of your abilities.

Anything can happen (or in some cases, not happen). For example, you may be doing a newscast or interview show and need to go to a video story or b-roll (background video while you are speaking). Due to mechanical or human error, the videotape doesn't roll and appear on the monitor.

It's up to you to continue gracefully with the program without the videotape segment and without drawing excess attention to the mistake. Maintain your composure and don't get angry with the crew or staff. Finger pointing does not correct the situation; they are all trying to do their best.

Following the production, or during a break, try to find out what went wrong and whether the situation can be remedied. Also ask if there is anything you can do to help. In most cases there will be little you can do as a performer if the problem is technical; however, if the problem is one that can be solved by giving more lead time before a videotape is rolled or better warning cues to the crew, you should know this and try to make the adjustment. The crew will appreciate your proactive approach to the situation.

RATINGS POINTER

You can probably recall seeing a number of mistakes on television over the years, some of which have made their way to shows devoted to bloopers. One of the classic cases of "video Murphy's law" happened many years ago during NBC's *Baseball Game of the Week*. A smooth production was thrown a major curve when during one game all of the cameras went dead except one stationed near the press box behind home plate. For several innings NBC director Harry Coyle had to follow the action with one camera and the announcers had to provide a more detailed description of the game (adopting a radio play-by-play call) because of the limited visual capabilities of using a single camera. It was a case of announcers and crew having to work together to create the best result from an unfortunate situation. ★ ★ ★ ★

Time Is Money   Whether you are involved with a multimillion-dollar prime-time network program or a small-scale instructional video, you should remember the cliche that time is money. Nowhere is this truer than in video production, where even modest instructional or corporate videos cost many thousands of dollars. You can help keep production costs down by being prepared and proactive in your performance. Knowing what you're supposed to say and do, and when, can improve the entire process.

Sometimes performers (especially novices) are so in awe of appearing on television that they do not act in a professional way, thereby damaging their credibility with crew and staff. Be professional when you come to the studio or site and your production personnel will appreciate you and your performance. If you don't know what to do, ask and get clarification. Developing a reputation as someone who is easy to work with increases the probability that other performance opportunities will come your way.

Synergy   Synergy can be defined as "group energy," or creating a better end product by being cohesive and goal oriented. If you keep the first four guiding principles—empathy, preparation, the show must go on, time is

Crew at Golden Gate Productions preps for one of their many productions.

money—in mind, you will probably create better rapport between yourself and the crew. The production process becomes a team effort when people work together in a creative and problem-solving mode, and when everyone looks for ways to make the production better and feels free to make suggestions. The final product becomes one of which all can be proud.

With these five principles in mind, let's look at the personnel on a production team, keeping in mind that the number of people or positions involved varies with the scale and scope of the production.

Crew Members and Staff Members

The personnel behind the camera fall into two groups, production crew and production staff, but at times these roles are combined. Generally speaking, producers, directors, and writers are considered to be production staff, along with a number of associates and supplementary personnel. The production crew comprises technical people involved primarily with equipment or the hands-on aspects of production: camera operators, floor or stage managers, technical directors, associate directors, audio engineers, lighting directors, and various technicians.

You may at times hear the terms "above the line" and "below the line." These are budgetary terms referring to the creative personnel and cost versus the production personnel and fixed cost of equipment and facilities. Staff members are thus usually considered "above the line" and crew members "below the line" for budget purposes.

The Studio and Crew Members

Most video production facilities comprise two areas: the studio and the control room. Good studios are large rooms with very high ceilings designed for the suspension of lighting equipment. Studios usually have smooth floors that allow cameras to move quickly and smoothly. In a larger studio at a local commercial television station it is not unusual to see the sets from several programs, especially if they are interview or talk shows, in the same studio.

Network buildings have a number of studios, each devoted to a particular show. For example, at the NBC studios in Burbank, California, *The Tonight Show* has its own studio, as do other regular productions.

If you visit a studio at a local station or a network, you may also notice that everything on the set is closer together than you would see in a similar real-life setting. As we have seen, video exaggerates distance, so sets need to be small and the furniture or props close together.

Some of the colors used on the set may not look the way they appear when seen on a particular program. Again, the video system reproduces color differently than our eyes do. Many studio sets are painted with colors as they are meant to appear onscreen.

On a smaller scale, what is used as a studio in an educational or corporate environment may be merely a room or space equipped with lights and other video equipment. The number of people involved in the production will depend on the context and the sophistication of the production. The crew members you may encounter in the studio production situation include the following:

Floor Manager   **Floor managers** are the director's voice in the studio. They relay instructions from the director to the talent with verbal commands before the production and with hand signals after it begins. The floor manager can hear the director's commands via a headset linking the control room with the studio. The director may come into the studio briefly prior to the show but then communicates with the studio via the floor manager the rest of the time.

Floor managers may assist with staging and the setup of scenery and production equipment. They may also help the audio operator and performer by clipping on microphones, seeing that the performer has a glass of water, and telling the performer where to sit or stand. Other responsibilities may include being in charge of props, teleprompters, and graphics.

Good floor managers seek to establish rapport with performers before the production by providing necessary information. The floor manager will also alert both performers and studio crew to the time remaining before the program begins. If there are any problems during the production, the floor manager will try to find an opportunity to explain them to the performers and studio crew.

It's tempting for many beginning performers to look at the floor manager standing next to the camera instead of looking directly into the lens, because it is easier to look at a friendly human being than an unresponsive camera lens. Remember, though, that even the slightest glance off camera is exaggerated and gives the performer the appearance of not looking at the viewer.

Once the program is on the air, the floor manager cannot give verbal commands to performers, because they would be heard on mic; therefore, **hand signals** or large printed cards are used to relay the information. Some of the most common hand signals are the following:

■ **Stand by.** It is almost time for the production to begin. Everyone should be in place ready to speak, act, or perform production duties. Hand is extended above head. At this stage the floor manager will also probably give verbal command of "stand by."

■ **Cue to start.** Performer begins talking or action. Index finger is pointed at the person who is going to speak or perform the action. Some floor managers will point at the live camera instead of the performer. Make sure the floor manager clarifies this for you.

■ **Time cues.** The number of minutes remaining in the show. Arm is upraised with number of fingers in the air to indicate how much time is left in the show.

■ **Half minute.** 30 seconds left in the show. Two index fingers or arms form a cross.

■ **Wrap it up (can also be 15 seconds left in show).** Program is about to end. Finish discussion or action. Arm is upraised with knuckles of fist pointed at the performer. Floor manager makes a motion like knocking on a door.

■ **Cut.** Stop talking or action. Hand or finger moves across the throat in a cutting motion.

■ **Speed up.** Talk faster or speed up your action. Index finger rotates in clockwise motion—the faster the motion, the more you need to speed up.

■ **Slow down.** Slow down because too much time is left in the program. You may have to fill the time remaining. Hands pull apart as if stretching a rubber band.

■ **On time or OK.** Everything is on time or going well.

1. Floor manager makes a circle with the thumb and forefinger.
2. Floor manager touches his or her nose with an index finger.

Check in advance which signal your floor manager is using.

■ **Roll VTR (videotape recorder).** The videotape recorder is rolling and a taped segment is coming up. Hand is held in front of face and makes a cranking motion with index finger (much like a film projector cranking).

■ **Come closer.** Performer needs to move closer to the camera or bring an object closer to the camera. Floor manager moves hands toward self.

■ **Back up.** Performer needs to move back from camera. Floor manager moves hands away from self in a pushing motion.

■ **Walk.** Time for performer to move to the next area or set. Index and middle fingers make a walking motion.

■ **More volume.** Speak louder. Hand is cupped over ear.

■ **Less volume.** Speak softer. Hands make a pushing down motion.

■ **Switching cameras.** You will look at another camera because the director will be shooting you from a different angle. Hand is shaken under the active camera lens when the change to another camera is about to happen, and motions to the other camera when the camera switch actually occurs.

Floor managers usually go over the hand signals they will be using with you before the production. Don't be afraid to ask for clarification concerning any commands you don't understand. It is also important to note that while the commands pictured in this book are used in many production situations, some studios may have their own variations of cues and commands. You should adapt to the signals used by the personnel in that setting.

It is important never to start speaking until the floor manager signals you to do so. Starting before a floor manager's cue can result in an **upcut,** meaning that your first few words go unheard.

■ **Production Assistants** **Production assistants** (sometimes called utilities) or P.A.s perform a wide variety of functions and are usually involved with large, complicated productions. You may see production assistants doing any of the following tasks:

- arranging sets, setting up displays, moving scenery and props
- assisting camera people with camera movement by moving camera cables and helping at times to move larger equipment

- assisting performers with wardrobe and makeup
- providing the performer with water
- being available to perform tasks at the command of the producer or director
- helping with prompting devices such as teleprompters and cue cards

Production assistants can be valuable in helping you with details before and during the production, so you should establish a good rapport with your P.A. You should realize that in some cases P.A. is an entry-level position employing many younger crew people interested in production. If you respect your P.A.s, they will work well with you and make your job easier.

Camera Operators   In small-scale productions you may work with a single camera operator; in bigger projects you may work with ten or more. No matter how large or small the production, the camera operator must provide proper framing of the talent and objects (composition) and smooth camera movement.

Camera operators receive their commands from the director, and their responsibility is to carry them out as quickly as possible. The movement guidelines mentioned in Chapter 5 help camera operators to get better shots while minimizing frustration. More details regarding specific performer-camera interactions are discussed in Chapter 7.

Handheld cameras are used in both remote and studio situations. In some studio situations you may see one or two handheld camera operators moving about the studio. These cameras allow the director to call for a wider variety of shots; however, they can be a distraction to the performer as the camera operators move swiftly about the studio. Ignore them and focus on the camera lens shooting you or the person you are talking to on the set.

Microphone Boom Operator   Microphone boom operators are less common in studios than they used to be. Many studios and production facilities now use smaller wireless mics on each performer, but you may occasionally still see a large overhead mic attached to a boom that moves just above the performer(s). It is the boom operator's responsibility to maneuver the boom in such a way that the mic is pointed toward the sound source or the person speaking. The boom operator must also keep the boom out of the top frame of the screen when pointing the mic in any direction. Controlled movement on the part of the performer can assist the boom operator with keeping the mic out of the frame and pointed at the right source.

■ **Lighting Director**   Large productions have a person assigned to studio lighting. He or she sets the position of the studio or remote lighting instruments and operates lighting equipment while the production is in progress. Performers can make the lighting director's job easier by wearing the proper types and colors of clothing for a production and by standing or sitting in the illuminated areas.

Other assorted personnel may be involved in the production process. No matter how many are involved, it is important for you to understand the basic job description of each person and to be aware that you can play an important role in building a team concept. You are the front person in the process, and others will pick up on your positive or negative energy. Good performers make the crew want to work with them.

The Control Room and Crew Members

The second area in the production process is the **control room.** This is the area off the studio that contains monitors, consoles, tape machines, and other equipment necessary to produce a program. This is where crew members watch what is going on in the studio, call the shots, and prepare various program elements.

Depending on the situation, you may see one or two or nearly a dozen people in and around the control room. Most performers spend little or no time in the control room, but having a working knowledge of its procedures and personnel may help you contribute to a smoother production.

In many studios the control room adjoins the studio; in others (such as large commercial stations or network studios) the control room may be down the hall from the studio so that the performer has little or no face-to-face contact with control room personnel. Control room personnel may communicate to the performer via an intercom system or through the floor manager. You may feel uncomfortable having such limited contact with the control room crew, but these means of secondary contact usually suffice to get you through the production with the necessary cues and information.

During remote or field productions a remote unit truck or van may serve as the control room, carrying all the necessary video, audio, and transmission equipment. In these cases, performers are even more removed from the production crew and must rely upon headset, intercom, or floor manager for communication with the remote truck. Concentration is important in maintaining communication with the remote crew.

Some of the control room crew you will work with include the following:

■ **Audio Engineer**   **Audio engineers** are in charge of all aspects of sound during the production. You will see the audio operator in front of a large **audio console** with numerous controls, faders, and so on. He or she is responsible for taking volume levels before the production (for example, checking how loud the performer is speaking), maintaining levels during the production, playing the audio for sources such as music and videotaped material, and listening for distracting noises. The audio engineer also blends or fades sources such as music volume while the talent is speaking over the music.

The audio engineer can enhance the quality of your voice during the production through a process known as **equalization.** It is important for you to work with the audio engineer before the production so that the equipment can be adjusted for proper vocal volume and quality. This pre-production time with the audio engineer can help to maximize your vocal quality and make you sound your best.

Audio is often called the most neglected aspect of video production. A good audio engineer makes sure that it is not.

RATINGS POINTER

One major annoyance for an audio engineer is a performer who doesn't know how to do a sound check or doesn't take the check seriously. When the engineer asks you to do a sound check, you should speak at the volume you will use during the production and say something in a steady, continuous manner. Read the first few lines of your script or the introduction to the production. This will give the audio engineer a more accurate sample of your voice than just saying, "testing, one, two, three . . ." and will reduce the length of the audio check. The audio engineer will appreciate your using this time-saving technique. ★ ★ ★ ★

■ **Technical Director**   The **technical director** (often called the TD or switcher) does the switching or transition from one camera to another or to various video sources such as video playback. You will see the TD sitting behind the switcher, a large console with rows of buttons, knobs, and levers (that's right, the switcher sits at the switcher).

The TD sits next to the director and follows the director's commands regarding which camera or video source to put on the air or record on tape.

In productions with numerous cameras or video sources, the job of the technical director can be as demanding as that of an air traffic controller.

Following the director's commands, the TD will select the appropriate video source from one of several control room monitors; make transitions from one source to another by cutting, dissolving, wiping, and so on; and activate various special effects. You can imagine the pressure a TD faces during a production like ABC's *Monday Night Football* lasting over three hours, with dozens of video sources to activate and hundreds of commands to follow.

Assistant Director   Also called the AD, the **assistant director** helps time the program and attend to other details that the director may assign. The AD can make or break a production because of the importance of timing segments and keeping total program time.

Most larger studios and television stations employ several additional technical personnel. You will probably have limited contact with them, but they are an important part of the production process:

Videotape Operator   This person is in charge of videotape recording and playback during a production. He or she makes sure the program is recorded and cues and "rolls in" tapes during production. For example, if you were interviewing someone about whitewater rafting and there was action videotape of the interviewee rafting on the river, the operator would roll the tape in at the appropriate moment.

If videotape is an element of your production, you may communicate with the videotape operator via the producer or director. In small-scale productions you may communicate directly with the operator.

Video Operator   Also called the video engineer or shader, the **video operator** is in charge of overall video quality and the picture's appearance on screen. He or she will adjust the camera controls based upon conditions in the studio such as lighting, talent's clothing and skin tone, and colors in the set. As with the lighting director, you can make the video operator's job easier by following the guidelines for clothing and colors to wear.

Chief Engineer   The top crew member in regard to the technical aspects of production, the **chief engineer** is in charge of all technical personnel and equipment, as well as the day-to-day operations of the production facility. You will probably have limited or no contact with the chief engineer.

The number of people involved in a production is determined by its overall scale and budget. You may see some or all of a large crew, or you may encounter only one or two people, depending on the production. Some local cable news services operate with a single person: A reporter covers a story with a field camera, does a stand-up in front of the camera, and also edits the tape. In any event, it is important to appreciate the skills and abilities of the people you are working with and the challenges they face.

Producers and Directors

Even casual observers of television and film have some idea of what producers and directors do. Their responsibilities differ according to the medium. Some say that film is a director's medium whereas television is a producer's medium, because of the amount of influence the respective positions carry in each situation. We will limit ourselves to the responsibilities of producer and director in video.

Producer   The producer is in charge of the entire production and is involved in making decisions concerning program concepts and content, scripting, sets and other visual elements in the studio, personnel, and basically any other technical or nontechnical program elements.

The producer may analyze the intended audience, develop the concept for a production, and double as a writer. Producers must know something about all aspects of the production process and be able to communicate effectively with technical and nontechnical personnel. You will probably have at least some contact with the producer.

Large productions may have an **associate producer,** who assists the producer with various tasks. In some cases you may have more contact with the associate than with the producer because he or she works directly with the talent. The associate producer may telephone and book the talent in advance of the production while also pre-interviewing or briefing the performer(s) before shooting.

Some programs, such as talk shows or newsmagazines, may be divided into segments and have **segment producers** who are in charge of each portion of the show. CBS's *60 Minutes* is an excellent example of this.

You've probably seen the title **executive producer** in credits at the end of a program. This person may have the responsibility of dealing with the business end of the production by working with stations, advertising agencies, writers, talent and talent agencies, and investors. In other cases the title executive producer may be given to someone as a "perk." For example, some stars of successful television series are given the title of executive producer but have little or no added responsibility.

No matter which producers you work with, it is important for you to have open communication and give them as much information as you can to assure a successful production. Here are some things to consider when working with a producer:

- *Try to find out as much as you can about the program.* Ask specific questions about the intended audience and the format of the show.

- *Find out why the producer is interested in including you as a part of this production.* This may be obvious, but sometimes the reason or focus for your involvement may be unclear.

- *Give the producer as much information about yourself as you can.* Also, try to make his or her job as easy as possible. You may want to e-mail or fax a short biography. If your name is difficult to pronounce, include the phonetic spelling.

If you develop a reputation of being easy to work with, you will probably be asked to appear in other productions or programs. Producers often share information with one another concerning talent and their abilities and attitudes. There is always a market for quality people with friendly, professional attitudes.

RATINGS POINTER

One of my "pet peeves" is watching Hollywood stars on television talk shows promoting their upcoming films. These stars usually have a clip of their movie to show at some point in the interview. The host of the show will ask the star, "So, what are we going to see here?" In many cases the stars have no idea which clip is being used and respond with "I don't know." This response provides no context for the viewer and makes the clip less effective in promoting the film. You may never be a Hollywood star, but you should always be knowledgeable about any visual material you use in the show and talk about its use with the producer. ★★★★

■ **Director**   Many people (even producers and directors) confuse the functions of producers and directors. The analogy of building a house might clarify the roles. It is the architect who develops the blueprint and design of the house, suggests the materials to be used, and secures all of the building materials needed. The contractor is the person who actually builds the house, trying to reproduce the original design concept as faithfully as possible.

When building a production, the producer is the architect and the director is the contractor. The director may need something of a hard hat to survive the production process. He or she is in charge of determining what the viewer will see and hear, and when.

Some programs, such as interview shows, can be relatively easy to direct, whereas sporting events require split-second decisions involving over a dozen cameras. The director's responsibilities start well before the production when he or she reviews and writes commands on the script. This marking of the script enables the director to call for camera shots, audio, and talent cues at specified points in the production.

Directors must decide on talent movement, known as blocking, and convey the information to the camera people and other technicians. It is important for you as a performer to listen carefully to the director's discussion of blocking prior to the show. Failure to do this may result in problems during the production such as being in an unlighted area or catching a camera out of position. You'll learn much more about how to work with a director during pre-production in Chapter 7.

Some video directors may work like film directors by teaching the performer how to deliver or emphasize certain portions of the script, or how to play a certain character. This is sometimes a "gray area," and both producer and director may be involved.

The director has the responsibility of communicating with the crew prior to showtime, arranging with camera operators where cameras are to be located and who is to get each shot. The director also consults with audio and lighting technicians during this pre-production period.

The director and producer also explain the program content and any changes that occur. The performer is often part of this pre-production session because changes will obviously affect what he or she says and does during the program. Failure to inform the performer of script changes can give him or her some embarrassing moments, such as introducing segments that are no longer in the script, or failing to introduce new segments.

Perhaps the most challenging aspect of directing comes during the actual performance, when the director must communicate with the crew via verbal commands relayed through headsets, via hand signals relayed by the floor manager, and during breaks.

Every performer should watch a director in order to develop greater empathy for the complexity of his or her task. You will see the director looking at numerous monitors in the control room and deciding which shot to select next, then prepping the camera operators. Time cues must be relayed to the floor manager and audio cues given to the audio operator. Hundreds of commands, sounding like a new language, are rapidly fired off. At the end of the program the director usually thanks the crew and all involved. Good performers reciprocate by thanking their directors and appreciating the challenging work they do.

RATINGS POINTER

If you have the opportunity to be part of a studio audience watching a network or local television show being taped, notice what happens during the commercial breaks. These serve as an opportunity for performer and crew to regroup, comment on things that are going well, and troubleshoot.

For example, during the taping of a talk show, the floor manager, producer, and talent usually meet around the talent's desk during each commercial break, discussing how the program is going and what will be coming up next. Breaks are a welcome part of the process, not only because commercials pay for the show but also because they serve as much-needed "breathers" for those involved. ★ ★ ★ ★

Rewind and Fade to Black

In order to perform at your best, you need to understand the basic responsibilities and challenges of the production crew. You should be proactive by communicating ahead of time with producers and directors regarding program content and presentation. Knowing how to participate in a video production involves learning the language used by production personnel, including verbal commands and gestures. Every studio has unique variations on terminology, but the terms discussed in this chapter provide a good foundation for communicating with crew and staff.

Often there is a gap in understanding between the performer and the technical crew, resulting in a less than satisfactory production. If crew and performers have empathy for each other, the probability of an excellent production is much higher.

Exercises

1 Watch a director at a local television station direct a program such as the local news (stations will often allow you to do this as part of a station tour). Watch the process before and during the program, noting the interpersonal communication style and command vocabulary.

2 Prepare an outline for a production promoting some aspect of your organization or educational institution. What visual elements could you include (videotape, still photos, charts, etc.)? What would you have to communicate to the producer or director prior to the production?

3 Watch the floor crew (cameras, floor manager, etc.) during a production. Who does what? How do they communicate with the control room? Do any problems arise? If so, how does the crew correct or deal with them?

4 Try to observe a performer and crew communicating with one another. How do they work together to assure a high-quality production?

INTERVIEW

Fran Andrews

Client Coordinator, Golden Gate Productions

Fran Andrews was introduced at the end of Chapter 2. This time she talks about how a performer can help in the production process by having some familiarity with the studio environment.

Question: What are some of the key things that performers need to do before coming to the studio?

Fran Andrews: For the new person coming into a studio environment, it's coming in the door and knowing what you are going to do and say. You have to be well rehearsed and know the topic you're going to be talking about. This is everything. Even if you haven't performed on television before, everything seems brand new, and there are things you don't know, you

will find that most crews are very forgiving of new people with little things they don't know if the performer comes in with two things: first, being thoroughly prepared with the material and two, not having a "holier than thou" attitude. If you come in as a regular, basic person, doing your job, thoroughly prepared, and flexible with anything that may come up, you'll have no problems working with most crews.

Flexibility is a key thing because every facility is different. Some facilities may want you to do a lighting check and they will have you come and sit in a chair to do the lighting, then send you to makeup. You may have no time to practice your script even if you were hoping to do so. You may not have a chance to get anything to eat. You may get water and no coffee. You can never tell about what may happen when you walk through the door. Flexibility, preparation, and a good attitude will help you succeed with your crew and in the studio environment.

Q: Do you find that people make assumptions about what you can do in your facility and don't give you advance notice concerning the kind of production elements they want?

FA: Of course. The only thing to do there from the point of view of the facility is to explain to the person why something can or can't be done. Again, the performer has to be flexible. It is easy to make assumptions concerning what someone else's job is and what can be done. Unless you are an expert in the technical side of production, you need to leave the technical aspects to the experts. If you walk in saying, "I'm not sure how to do it, but this is what I need to accomplish. Please help me figure out how to get it done," I think you will be very well received. Most crews will try to help you in every way possible.

Q: I assume it helps to let the crew know what you want a week or more before the production.

FA: Yes. Discussing every possible element before you walk in the door, getting all your questions answered whether they are directions, or if something can be put on the screen as a graphic. Is there going to be a makeup person? If not, is there going to be any makeup there for me to do my own? Anything that may seem small, you should still ask about it in advance.

Q: Is the performer at an advantage if they know the roles of the crew members?

FA: I think that anything you walk into, you'll always have an advantage if you know how things are done. On the other hand, you don't have to know everything about television in order to be an effective performer. There are the things you need to be aware of like not fidgeting, how to sit in your chair, keeping eye contact with the host or camera.

It is helpful to know in advance from your director whether he or she is going to do a tight shot, or full body and whether or not viewers are going to see your feet. Also, can you hide a cup of water? Is it OK to wear your tennis shoes as opposed to dress shoes? Those kind of questions you want to have answered in advance.

It is important to know roles and who is involved. You should know who is giving you your cues. It helps to know who is the boss and who will be making the ultimate decisions as to what goes onscreen. That being said, you don't only want to address that person and overlook anything else that others might have to say, but you do need to know who the final decision maker is.

You know that the floor manager is going to count you in and cue you, but you don't want to look at them straight on. You want to look with your peripheral vision or at the camera lens above his or her hand. It also helps to know if you're going to have to put on your own microphone or if the floor manager or audio technician will help you put it on. A basic thing to know is that if the tally light on top of the camera is on, then that's the camera that is on. You may not know that if you're new to video performance.

If you're going to use a teleprompter, practicing with the prompter and its

operator is a good thing because everyone speaks at a different rate and your
prompter operator will want to run
through the script, even 15 to 30 seconds,
with you to get a feel for how you speak
so that he or she can get your speed. Of
course you have to be careful not to move
your eyes as you read the prompter.
Sometimes we get performers who move
their eyes as they read the prompter and
this is distracting for viewers.

Q: It sounds as if most of your clients
come to the studio well prepared; however,
can you remember a time when there
was a stressful situation due to poor
performer-crew relationships?

FA: We've been very fortunate in that regard. Technical difficulties are always the
most stressful because you feel as if you
should be on target. Everyone has to try
and adapt to the situation because in
most cases it's no one's fault. The performer has to keep his or her energy level
up even though there may be several minutes before the problem is corrected.

The other thing that can happen is if a
guest doesn't show up for a live production and the host has to wing it to keep
the show going. This is a real challenge for
the host in regard to his or her impromptu
skills. Fortunately, that hasn't happened
often to us or the performer.

CHAPTER SEVEN

What Performers Need to Know about Equipment

Many people pursuing careers in television *want* to be in front of the camera lens, while some in other careers, such as politicians, educators, clergy, and businesspersons, find it *necessary* to be in front of the lens. Both groups of performers want to perfect the verbal and nonverbal aspects of their performances but have little concern for what goes on behind the camera and what equipment is used.

As we saw in Chapter 6, the ability to work with and understand the responsibilities of crew members can help performers to be better and more relaxed. Basic knowledge of production equipment is also helpful. Knowing the capabilities and limitations of equipment enables performers to present themselves more effectively onscreen and aids in a smoother production process.

A practical consideration for those seeking careers as broadcast performers is that many production houses and cable news services look for people who can wear a number of hats, including equipment operation. It is not uncommon for some local cable news services to have reporters shoot their own stories as well as appear in them. In these cases, the performer must know camera operation, video editing, and other production skills.

Your career aspirations and how you use television to communicate your messages will dictate what you need to know about equipment. This chapter provides information that almost any performer should know in regard to production equipment. The intent is not to intimidate you with a lot of technical terminology or jargon, but instead to give you the basics regarding the tools you'll be using when performing.

According to some educators and communication consultants, performers should be performers and not turned into "techies," but you don't need to be a "techie" to understand the functions of television equipment.

Note that the emphasis in this chapter is on basic equipment operation as it affects performance. This is not a production text, and if you want
to know more about the television production process, you should consult
one of the excellent production books listed in the Resources section at the
end of this book. Some people start out pursuing careers as performers but
find that they are happier behind the camera .

One further consideration is that because equipment changes rapidly,
even the most current production books will not mention all the latest technological changes and innovations. This chapter provides general information that should help your performance in the immediate future. The two
primary pieces of equipment used by performers are **microphones** and
cameras.

Microphones and Mic Techniques

Audio and video production books provide more detailed technical information about microphones. This section groups microphones by those most
commonly used and describes the characteristics of each mic.

Lavaliere Microphones   **Lavaliere microphones** (also called lavs or
clip-ons) are probably the most commonly used mics in television because of their small size and simple operation. You have seen a variety of
performers using these mics on newscasts and talk shows. The average
viewer forgets that the performer is wearing a mic because lavaliers are so
unobtrusive.

Lavaliere mics can be clipped to a blouse, shirt, tie, or lapel. If you
know that you will be using a lavaliere mic, you may want to take this into
consideration when choosing what to wear for your performance (sweaters
and shirts without collars make it a little difficult to clip on the mic, but you
can run the mic under your sweater or shirt and clip it on the collar so the
mic wire doesn't run in front of your clothing).

No matter what you are wearing, you can experiment with the best way
to conceal the microphone wire, such as hiding it behind a tie or running it
under a shirt or blouse. A floor manager or audio engineer can often assist
you in finding the best way to conceal the wire.

Make sure you clip the mic close enough to your chin (about six
inches) so that you achieve the best audio presence (presence is the degree
to which you sound **on mic**). Clipping the mic too low causes you to sound
as if you are in a large open area or a cave instead of talking directly to the
viewer. Be careful that the mic does not rub against or become covered by

clothing. As mentioned earlier, jewelry rubbing against the mic can cause sounds that resemble a small earthquake.

If you are hosting an interview program with one or two guests and they are on your left side, you may want to put the mic on your left lapel. This position will help audio quality, since you will be looking left most of the time.

By all means, remember to clip on your mic before the production. Even experienced performers sometimes forget to clip on their mics in a live situation and have to be reminded to do so while on camera. In other cases, guests during an interview show have actually been seen sitting on their mics at the beginning of a live production. This shouldn't happen if the audio engineer has taken a level and done his or her job, but for some reason it still does. If you're the host of an interview show make sure that your guest is wearing a mic before the program goes on the air, and that you and your guest(s) unclip your mics after the show so that you don't damage them or your clothing.

Nervous novices sometimes play with the mic cord, causing rubbing sounds to be heard on mic and highlighting their own anxiety. Use some of the suggestions for channeling nervousness mentioned earlier in the text, and watch out for novice guests who may be tempted to play with the mic wire.

Lavaliere mics are often battery powered, with the battery contained in a small housing down the mic cord. The audio engineer will take care of putting a battery in the housing, but if you're not getting sound during a sound check, it may be due to a bad battery or no battery at all.

Sometimes a lavaliere mic will cease working during a live production for any one of a number of reasons (this is rare but it does happen). If your mic stops working in a live situation, someone will signal you and hand you a new one. Technical problems do happen, so try not to worry about having to put on a new mic and do your best to make a smooth transition.

Lavaliere mics give you some flexibility if you have to move around a set or open area, because there is trailing wire or, in the case of a wireless mic, a small transmitter that provides even more freedom. Weather forecasters and other performers who need to stand at a map or demonstrate a product especially appreciate the freedom of movement these mics allow. Know the limitations of your wire or transmission range before the program starts.

Overall, lavaliere mics provide good sound quality for speech (not so for music) and many advantages for a variety of production situations. Their simplicity and compact size make them a favorite for performers and production personnel alike (on *The Tonight Show with Jay Leno* guests now come on the set and clip on their own mics after they sit down).

Floor manager will often help performers put on microphones.

Boom Microphones   **Boom microphones** are less in evidence today than in the past because of advances in wireless technology. They are still used in a variety of studio situations, however, such as a drama or slice of life, in which there must be no evidence of a microphone visible on the talent or set.

Boom microphones are mics attached to the end of a pipe or adjustable extension pole. Studio booms are often attached to dollies so that they can be moved around the studio, whereas booms used in the field (sometimes called "fish poles") are carried by hand. An advantage for performers is that the boom follows them as they move, giving them a little more freedom of movement than they have with other wired mics.

One drawback of the boom is that it requires an operator to point the mic in the direction of the person talking or other sound source. Another problem is that sometimes a performer sitting in a chair suddenly stands, causing the boom to be visible at the top of the screen. Booms can complicate lighting because they may cast shadows on sets and people. Despite these problems, booms do offer high-quality audio for situations in which it is unacceptable to see a microphone onscreen.

Handheld Microphones   Performers often use handheld mics during remote telecasts, interviews, and audience participation shows. These mics offer the advantage of being able to be used by others as well as the host. They also allow the performer to control a remote or studio audience situation by pointing the mic at a person to allow him or her to speak.

Handheld mics limit your range of movement and gestures. Performers need to check them before the show to see how far they can move. Beginning performers should practice gestures before using the mic and learn to gesture with one hand. Viewers recognize novice performers when they wave the mic in front of themselves as they gesture. Another common beginner's mistake is to interview someone but forget to point the mic in the direction of the interviewee during the person's response. In most cases it is not a good idea to hand the mic to the other person, though, because the performer needs to maintain control of the interview and how long the interviewee speaks.

Using a handheld mic outdoors may require the use of a wind screen to prevent wind noise and other unwanted sound from being heard on mic. One marketing advantage of a handheld mic is that it can bear a logo identifying the network, station, or cable service.

■ Desk Microphones   Still in use today for situations such as political speeches, panel and round table discussions—and almost anything broadcast on C-Span—desk mics provide flexibility because they can pick up more than one person's voice. However, people can sometimes sound off mic if they don't move the mic close enough to them, and distracting habits such as rustling paper or tapping fingers can cause unwanted sounds.

In many situations that formerly required desk mics lavaliere mics are now used instead. Desk mics are sometimes used for decorative purposes. On the David Letterman show, the lavaliere mic picks up the sound from Letterman, while the desk mic is merely a prop.

The desk microphone for David Letterman is decorative. The lavaliere mic is picking up his audio.

■ **Headset Microphones** Performers who do sports play-by-play announcing or announce large public events such as a parade may use a **headset microphone.** The small mic attached to a headset allows them to keep their hands free to hold notes or write during the program. The mic must be placed directly in front of the performer's mouth, and there should be a pop filter on the mic to control popping of plosives.

Lavaliere, boom, handheld, desk, and headset microphones are the types most commonly used in video production. You will encounter other microphone types if you do radio production or voiceover work, and audio production textbooks discuss these mics in detail. Audio production books also explain the internal structure of microphones and how they take sound waves and turn them into electronic impulses. Most performers don't need to know this information.

Microphone pickup patterns are one technical aspect of microphones that it's worthwhile for performers to know about, since they can assist performance.

Microphone Pickup Patterns

For best audio quality and presence, performers should have a general idea of the pickup area around the mic they are using. Microphones have the following **pickup patterns:**

- *Unidirectional.* Picks up sound from one side. These mics usually have what is called a **cardioid** (heart-shaped) pattern, with good pickup in front of the mic and some pickup on the sides.
- *Bidirectional.* Picks up sound from two sides (also called a figure eight pattern).
- *Omnidirectional.* Relatively good sound pickup from all sides of the mic.
- *Multidirectional.* Patterns alterable by adjusting a control.

Knowing the pickup pattern of the microphone you are using helps you achieve the best on-mic quality while helping to minimize unwanted sounds. Audio engineers can assist you in determining what mic pickup pattern you will be using.

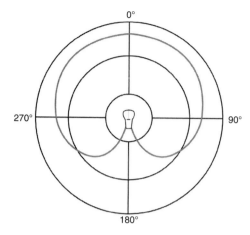

Unidirectional microphone pickup pattern.

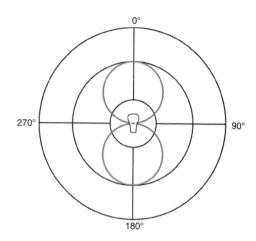

Bidirectional microphone pickup pattern.

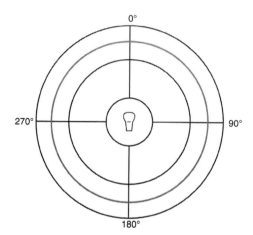

Omnidirectional microphone pickup pattern.

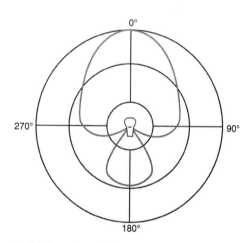

Multidirectional microphone pickup pattern.

Here are some final general considerations for proper microphone use:

- Know the range and pickup limitations of the microphone you're using, and make sure that you don't move out of the mic pickup pattern or range.

- Use your normal voice at the volume you will be using during the production when doing mic checks. As mentioned in Chapter 6, it is better to read part of your script or do the first few sentences of your introduction than to say "testing, one, two, three."

- When doing the check, stand or sit in the same place you will be performing to assure accuracy. Don't hit or scratch the top of the mic and ask, "Is this thing on?"

- Avoid distracting habits such as talking loudly, yelling across the studio, or clapping your hands near a mic after a level has been set. Your production people will thank you for this.

- Remember that mics are delicate pieces of equipment; you should handle them with care when attaching or detaching them. Audio operators can assist you with microphone care.

Cameras

Earlier chapters discussed camera operators, movement, and how to use the teleprompter placed on the camera. There are several other performance considerations concerning cameras. Television production books can provide you with technical information about how the camera sees your performance; what follows is basic information regarding your relationship to the camera.

■ **The Camera as Unsophisticated Eye**   The camera never blinks. This may be the one advantage the video camera has over the human eye. For the most part, the electronic eye is less sophisticated than our eyes, so knowing its limitations can help you tailor your performance for video.

Cameras are less sensitive to light than human eyes, so productions usually require intense lighting. In field productions, the sun can cause problems with video quality, making it necessary for the camera operator to keep the sun at his or her back, unless special filters are used.

Human eyes have the advantage of keeping most things in the field of view in focus and being able to move from side to side without blurring the images in front of them; video cameras do not have this capacity. The following are key guidelines for appearing on camera (some of these are also listed in Chapter 5):

■ **Stand still.**   It's been mentioned several times before that video exaggerates movement. Any rocking or swaying on camera makes you look as if you're on the deck of a boat. You want to be comfortable, but you must control the urge to move as you might in normal conversation. Remember, the tighter the shot, the more exaggerated your movement appears on camera and the more your camera operator has to adjust to keep you in the frame.

■ **Sit still.** As with standing, excessive movement and rocking while sitting can cause you to move out of the frame, while moving toward or away from the camera can cause you to go in and out of focus. Excessive movement makes you appear anxious or less in control, so work on slower natural movement when sitting, without appearing stiff.

■ **Hit your mark.** Performers like Jay Leno and David Letterman come on stage and stand in the same place each night to deliver their monologues. This is called **hitting the mark.** Directors and lighting technicians will determine blocking (where and when performers should move and the spots where they will stand). The director will mark where you should be and it is important that you hit the mark, for the following reasons:

1. *Lighting.* Lighting has been predetermined, and if you don't hit your mark you may be outside your lighted area (it is much easier to move people than to move lighting instruments).

2. *Camera composition.* Camera operators make the necessary adjustments for good camera composition based upon your predetermined mark. Don't force them to adjust because you are in the wrong place.

3. *Focus.* If you move too close to or too far away from the camera, you may be out of focus, causing more problems for the camera operators. Hitting your mark makes the production process smoother and less problematic. Try to do several run-throughs if time permits to help you hit your marks naturally without staring down at the floor to look for them.

■ **Telegraph your movement.** When moving from one area to another or standing up after being seated, you should nonverbally warn the production staff that you are going to move. Start any movement more slowly than you would in a live situation, pause a bit, then continue. This ensures that you will not move out of the frame or out of focus. Know when to move or stand so that your director, camera operators, or others are not caught off guard.

■ **Play to the camera.** During some interviews you will be asked to sit at an angle that seems unnatural for you, or your chair will be angled slightly toward the camera instead of facing the other person head-on. This "playing to the camera" provides a better-angled shot of you that avoids a profile. Viewers will be able to see more of your face, and the overall effect will look natural on screen.

Sometimes you must tilt an object forward to minimize glare.

■ **Play props to the camera.** There may be times in production when you have to hold objects (known in theater, film, and television as **props**) in various situations, ranging from a product in a commercial to an author's book during an interview program.

The key thing to keep in mind is that the viewer wants to see what you are holding, so you must play the object to the camera that has the best angle of shooting the prop (the director will let you know which camera this is). Too often a performer holds a prop with little regard for which camera is shooting it or whether the viewer can see it. If you are holding something with a reflective surface, such as a CD cover, a book with a dust jacket, or a product with a shiny package, you should tip it forward just a bit to minimize glare from the studio lights.

Pictures, books, charts, maps, and any other props that require a close-up should be held with a steady hand. Practice holding the prop in its placement before the program. If you have to point to areas on the prop, make sure you know where you're pointing and work for controlled movement of your finger and hand. The camera will have problems if you point or gesture too quickly.

RATINGS POINTER

There are a couple of tricks you can use when showing props in close-up. Many talk show hosts use a prop holder on desks when showing pictures, charts, or other visuals mounted on cardboard. There is usually a slot cut in the holder to hold the prop.

A mark on your desk shows where you should place the holder to give the camera the best shooting angle. If you have to hold a book or other object in front of your body, you can rest your elbows against your torso for added support. Work with a studio monitor before the show to check that you are holding the prop for the best camera angle. ★ ★ ★ ★

Demonstrations with props provide another set of challenges. When you're doing a demonstration such as a home improvement project or preparing a new food entree, you shouldn't feel compelled to talk every second, since viewers want to see what you're doing as well as hear your description. One of the advantages of a demonstration is that it is **primary movement** (movement in front of the camera lens) that is interesting to the viewer. Directors usually shoot much of a demonstration with close-ups to give the best perspective on what you are doing. Let the action do some of the talking.

When demonstrating an object, work with it in advance so that you will feel comfortable when doing the on-camera demonstration. This will give you a higher comfort level during the taping or live presentation.

▨ Robotic Cameras   Robotics have invaded the realm of camera operations. It has been possible to operate cameras without humans in the studio for a little over a decade. **Robotic cameras** move about the studio via

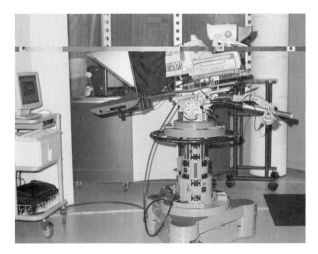

Robotic camera.

remote control, thus allowing one person in the control room to operate several at once. This technology makes it even more important to follow all the guidelines listed above regarding movement and hitting your marks.

Using Prompting Devices   Prompting devices such as cue cards and teleprompters are standard tools for many video performers. Most viewers who watch late night talk show hosts do their monologues have seen a production assistant holding cue cards near one of the cameras. Viewers also expect newscasters to talk directly to them via a teleprompter without looking at a script. Politicians also have special prompters so that they can deliver speeches while maintaining eye contact with the audience.

Prompting devices can aid performers who might forget their lines or who are operating under time constraints and cannot remember all the scripted information—for example, in a newscast. Sometimes performers who are very familiar with their material still feel the need for a prompting device as a security blanket. Performers must be able to read any prompting device without losing contact with the camera or giving the impression that they are not looking at the viewer.

Even if you have cue cards or a teleprompter, you should try to be as familiar with your material as possible so that the prompter acts only as a

Proper placement and holding of cue cards.

guide. This allows you to sound more natural, creating the impression that you are not looking at a device.

■ **Cue cards.** Cue cards have been aids to performers since the early days of television. They are usually used for short pieces of information. Cue cards may be used for commercials or for introductions to segments.

In most cases these cards are hand-lettered poster boards held by a floor manager or production assistant. Effective reading from cue cards is a team effort between the performer and the person holding the cue cards. Performers look amateurish if the cards are improperly located or held.

The person holding the cards should hold them as close to the camera lens as possible, remembering that any eye movement away from the lens gives the impression that the performer is not looking at the viewer. Floor managers or production assistants should never hold cue cards with their hands covering up part of the copy. Make the holder aware of any such problem before the production begins.

Skillful operators hold the cards so that they are reading along with the talent. They also move the cards up in such a way that the line the performer is reading is at the same height as the camera lens, so that the performer doesn't look above or below the lens.

In case the card holder forgets to change a cue card (which won't happen if the holder is reading along with you), you should have a general idea of what is on the next card so that you can ad-lib until the card is changed. You may be able to ask the director to stop tape, but in a live performance it is important to give the impression that everything is normal even if there is a problem with the cards. Performers can be proactive in preventing cue card mishaps by meeting with the holder in advance and by checking the order of the cards before the production begins.

You should learn to read cue cards with your peripheral vision, thereby looking more at the lens of the camera than at the card. With practice you will find this relatively easy to do.

■ **Teleprompters.** Teleprompters are used by performers at most television stations and in larger production houses and studios. The teleprompter uses a small monitor to display moving copy. The monitor screen is reflected onto glass placed directly over the camera lens so that the copy moves line by line in front of the lens. This allows maximum eye-to-lens contact. The copy's rate of movement can be adjusted to the performer's comfortable reading speed.

Usually, the script is typed into a word processor and then fed to the teleprompter. If the production requires multiple cameras, the same copy is fed to the teleprompters on each camera. This allows the talent to turn to or change cameras without breaking the reading flow. Another advantage of the teleprompter is that the camera holding the prompter may be placed close to the talent for easier reading. This placement, along with large fonts typed into the prompter, prevents many problems due to poor vision.

When watching a newscast you may have noticed the anchor holding a copy of the script in his or her hands, occasionally glancing down at it between stories. This breaks contact with the lens for a short period of time to provide a "breather" between the anchor and the viewer.

If the teleprompter malfunctions, the performer (as with cue cards) should be familiar enough with the script to ad-lib, or read from a hard copy of the script if doing a newscast. If you watch newscasts on a regular basis, you may have seen less experienced anchors show momentary panic when the teleprompter fails.

There are still times when a performer must use a script instead of a teleprompter. If you have to read from a script, you should avoid looking up at the camera at regular intervals; try instead to vary the pacing of your contact with the lens. This avoids the "yo-yo" effect of bobbing your head in a predictable way.

Portable teleprompters, called field prompters, are used for productions outside the studio; they operate in much the same way as the studio teleprompter. A mechanical teleprompter can be made by placing a roll of paper below the camera lens. The paper may be moved by a motor or by human hands. These portable devices provide the same advantages to the performer as the larger studio versions.

Here are some basic tips on how to read from teleprompters:

- Read at a steady pace. This will make it easier for the prompter operator to "feed" the copy at a reading rate that is comfortable for you.

- Try to read slightly ahead of the line appearing at lens level. This will help you to become familiar with what is coming up next and you'll avoid surprises.

- The reader should set the reading pace. Don't let the prompter operator set the pace, or it may be faster or slower than you would like.

- Remember to look down from time to time to give the viewer a break from eye contact. If the prompter breaks down try to keep from showing panic or looking like a "deer in the headlights." Know where you are in the copy so that you can refer to it if you need to.

RATINGS POINTER

Even the most influential people in the world can have bad experiences with prompting devices. During an address to Congress in 1993, then President Bill Clinton was unexpectedly faced with the text of a different speech on his teleprompter screens.

President Clinton was familiar enough with his text to improvise for the first few minutes of the speech until Vice President Al Gore was able to summon assistance. Eventually, the correct disk was found and loaded, and the president was able to read from the proper text.

While the teleprompter used by the president and other politicians in such situations is different from the prompters used by news anchors (the two clear pieces of glass you see to each side of the speaker are his/her prompters and the text is visible only from the sides) the principle of being familiar with your text in case of emergency applies to all performers. ★ ★ ★ ★

Using Peripheral Vision   As when reading from prompting devices, you should use your **peripheral vision** when looking at the floor manager or production assistants for signals and cues. You'll find that you won't need much of your potential peripheral vision, because good floor managers will stand as close to the camera as possible when giving you cues and time signals. Concentrate on the camera lens while receiving information from the floor manager.

Basic Camera Shots

Knowing basic camera shots can help you work more effectively with your camera operator in either studio or field situations. Three of the most common are close-up, medium, and over-the-shoulder shots.

Close-Ups   Most video production books define the standard **close-up (CU)** as a shot in which the top edge of the screen is slightly above the head (providing what is known as "headroom" so that the top of the screen doesn't touch the hairline), while the bottom edge of the screen hits just below the shoulders. Some directors and camera operators use the armpits as the target for the bottom of the screen. This technique provides a shot that focuses on the face of the performer and fills the frame.

The **extreme close-up (ECU)** frames the performer in such a way that the top edge of the screen cuts across the top of the head (usually just below the hairline) and the lower edge cuts slightly below the top part of the shoulders. The ECU is often used to emphasize facial features and intimacy or during compelling moments of an interview.

Head movement during close-ups may be distracting to the viewer (not to mention the production crew trying to shoot the performer), and the tighter the close-up, the more noticeable the problem. Excessive head movement can give the viewer the impression that the performer is on some kind of amusement park ride, making it difficult to watch for an extended period. Gestures must also be smaller and more controlled during close-ups. Refer to Chapter 5 on nonverbal communication for advice on performing within the confines of the close-up.

Medium Shots   In most cases the **medium shot** of a solo performer includes an area from just above the top of the head to below the waist. This is usually the shot you see of a weather forecaster during weather segments on your local newscast. The performer has a little more flexibility of movement and gestures in a medium shot, but should make sure that all movement is still within the shot.

Over-the-Shoulder and Other Shots   You've seen the **over-the-shoulder shot** many times during studio and field interviews: The camera looks over the shoulder of one person and shoots the other. In the foreground you can see the back of the head and shoulder of the person nearest the camera. As with the close-up, performers must avoid excessive movement when they know that the director will be using over the shoulder shots, because it is easy to move out of the frame.

Your director and camera operator may also use **long shots,** bust shots, knee shots, and two shots. The photographs on the facing page show examples of proper composition for all shots.

We've covered in detail cameras and microphones, the primary pieces of equipment in any television production. Secondary equipment includes videotape recorders and editing systems, character generators, and image storage systems. Again, for in-depth information concerning additional equipment, functions, and operations, consult a television production textbook. What follows here is a basic, user-friendly overview of the equipment performers may encounter and how this equipment may affect performance.

Close-up (CU).

Extreme close-up (ECU).

Over-the-shoulder shot (OSS).

Medium shot (MS).

Long shot (LS).

Bust shot.

Knee shot.

Two shot.

Videotape Recorders (VTRs)

Most people have used a consumer **videotape recorder (VTR),** also known as a videocassette recorder (VCR) at home or for instructional purposes to record programs for future playback or preservation. For this discussion we will refer to VTRs and VCRs under the heading of VTRs.

Many educational institutions and corporations also have video editing equipment so that taped segments can be pieced together or material eliminated from a tape. Corporate video facilities and archives are often comparable to those found at commercial and public television stations and cable services.

Production houses and television stations have sophisticated video recorders and editors, giving producers and talent more options in creating programs. Here are some basic concepts performers should know regarding recorders and editors. Much of your involvement with the following equipment will be determined by your specific function, where you work, and union restrictions.

■ **What is actually recorded onto videotape?** There are four tracks on videotape that record video, audio, and synchronization information. The **video track** records picture information and there are at least two **audio tracks** containing the sound. The **control track** records synchronization information of the video frames. If you've had any experience with editing film versus videotape, you know that one obvious difference between the two is that the audio is recorded and synchronized onto the videotape, whereas you must synchronize the sound with the picture before editing film.

■ **What are some VTRs I may be working with in the future?** As you might imagine, the technology is changing rapidly as VTRs improve in image quality and become more portable. Digital VTRs reproduce high-quality pictures through a process known as sampling: Essential parts of the signal are selected, digitized, then turned back into an improved analog signal.

Tracks on videotape.

Video

Audio
Sync
Cue

Digital VTRs produce high-quality original images and copies (**dubs**) and do not deteriorate in quality even after a number of taped **generations** (a generation is the number of dubs recorded away from the original). Think in terms of photocopying a document from a photocopy instead of the original and how it loses quality with each copy. This was a problem with analog VTRs, but not with digital ones.

■ **Do I need to know specific types and model numbers of VTRs?** Again, it depends on your goals and roles as a performer. Many performers don't need any specific knowledge of hardware; others need a working knowledge. The key concept here is to know what the video recorder and video editing system allow you to do in adding visual components to your production.

Video Editing Systems

Editing is the process of selecting portions of events shot on videotape or film and putting them into a sequence. Video editing systems allow you to arrange segments in any way you want for a final tape. For example, you can put together a sequence of highlights from a football game, cutting unwanted material, communicating meaning through the juxtaposition of images, and correcting mistakes.

Performers should realize that while video editing contributes to an aesthetically pleasing final product, it cannot correct all mistakes. For example, if the performer's coat is buttoned in one shot and not in another, the problem cannot be fixed during the editing process (post-production).

Be attentive to detail while videotaping a production, and remember that consistency is the key to avoiding mistakes that cannot be corrected by editing. You can also help your technical crew by alerting them if they need to retake a segment because of a minor mistake. It is easier to reshoot a segment than deal with mistakes in post-production.

Like video recorders, video editing systems come in various brands and model numbers. For our purposes, here is general information regarding **linear** and **nonlinear editing.**

■ **Linear Editing Systems**   Linear editing, the older type of editing process, usually involves using two VTRs and a piece of equipment called a **controller.** One VTR is the *source* that allows you to select your original shots, while the second VTR is the *record* machine that allows you to join them together. The controller, the brain of the operation, selects the beginning and ending points for edits, and tells both source and record machines when to start the editing process.

Nonlinear Editing   The newer type of editing system, nonlinear editing, uses computers instead of VTRs. Video and audio information is stored not on tape but on high-capacity hard drives. Consequently, you can call up any shot from a time code and go directly to that shot without searching through videotape to find it. Another advantage of this system is that you can display a variety of frames and create "bins" in much the same way that you use a light tray to arrange and view photographic slides.

While there are some disadvantages to nonlinear editing, such as the need to transfer the information from source videotapes to the computer's hard drive and learn the complexities of the system, nonlinear editing is the system of choice at most commercial and public television stations and production houses.

Electronic Still Store (ESS) System   An ESS system is like a digital slide projector that can take any video frame, store it, and access it in a split second. You can take shots of still pictures, slides, or a single video frame and store them in this system. The graphics box you see over the shoulder of a newscaster is an example of ESS use. ESS systems can help you add visual elements to a production from a variety of sources.

Character Generators   Most of the printed information you see on the television screen comes from a **character generator,** a machine similar to a word processor. Character generators allow you to add printed information such as names (identification of performers), credits, weather conditions, stock quotations, and many other types of information best conveyed in a print format. Work with production staff prior to your performance so that they can format and present your printed information in the best way possible for the viewer.

Switchers   Chapter 6 contained some information regarding video switchers. **Switchers** are located in the control room and feature many rows of buttons (**buses**), levers, and knobs. The switcher allows the director to cut between cameras and other video sources such as VTRs, as well as add special effects to the production. The switcher is operated by the technical director, who follows the commands of the director. You may never have to operate a switcher, but it is a good idea to know its most common functions so that you can speak the same language as the technical crew:

- **Cut or take**—an instant change from one image to another.
- **Dissolve**—A gradual transition from one image to another, with the images overlapping on the screen for a brief period of time determined by the director.
- **Fade**—Involves black (no image) usually fading up from black to an image or fading from an image to black. Be careful not to confuse dissolves with fades when speaking to production personnel.

Chroma-Key   As mentioned in the section on clothing in Chapter 3, **chroma-key** is not a specific piece of equipment but a function of the video switcher that cancels a color on the set such as green or blue and electronically replaces it with other image information (still picture, map, graphic, etc.).

One of the most common uses of chroma-key is for weathercasters when they display maps and other visuals. The weathercaster stands in front of a green or blue background in the studio, while maps and other information appear in the background. These visuals are not seen in the studio and the weathercaster must look at monitors to see what is onscreen (more about the use of chroma-key for weather in Chapter 8).

Chroma-key can enhance the visual aspects of your performance, but there is a temptation to use it as a visual gimmick. Think about what you want to communicate to viewers and whether chroma-key or some other visual technique best meets your needs.

Rewind and Fade to Black

The intent of this chapter has been to give you information about video equipment so that you can begin to consider how equipment can assist you with the visual aspects of your performance and communicating with your crew. Most of the chapter was devoted to the primary equipment of microphones and cameras, because performers are directly involved with these. Other items such as video recorders, editors, switchers, and character generators are secondary equipment.

Many video production professionals tell those entering the field that it is more important to think in creative terms regarding production visualization than to understand all the technical aspects of the equipment. Many production personnel say, "We can teach button pushing, but we can't teach creativity." Technology continues to change, but creativity and the ability to communicate ideas are always valued. Think in terms of message and what you want viewers to see while always being the "unselfish performer" described in Chapter 3.

In the movie *The Wizard of Oz,* the Wizard projects himself as larger than life with special effects, smoke, and sound effects, but when Dorothy and her friends pull back the curtain from the Wizard's control booth, he turns out to be a small person. Don't let technology turn you into a small performer; instead, use it to build, enhance, and clarify your message. Remember that you are the star, not your equipment.

Exercises

1 Check out the production facility you will be using as a performer. What equipment does the facility have and what are its capabilities? Keep a log of your findings and use this for future planning.

2 Choose a production you may work on in the near future and plan how you can communicate with production staff regarding equipment to add visual elements to it.

3 Visit the website of a video equipment manufacturer (such as Sony) or local video equipment dealer. Try to get an idea of new trends and advances in technology.

4 Think in terms of "low tech" for a production you are planning. How might you use items such as models or other basic visual aids to communicate your message while maintaining audience interest?

INTERVIEW

Craig Miller

Former Reporter for CNN, KDKA Pittsburgh, and KPIX San Francisco

Craig Miller now has a program called *Miller's Attic* on HGTV. He has worked as a news reporter in a number of major markets. Here, he talks about the importance of understanding what your equipment and engineers can do in shooting news, features, and interviews. He also urges students not to become frustrated if they are not learning on state-of-the-art equipment.

Question: How important is it for performers to know something about video equipment and those who operate it?

Craig Miller: Now in many stations in smaller markets they are making the same person do everything—shoot the pictures, write the story, edit the pictures. At larger stations, if you know what the constraints of the person in the editing booth are, it will inform the way you write the script. You can either make that person's job easy or very difficult. If you know what the constraints are of the camera operator, it will inform what you do in the field and what you do when you get back to write the story. I came to this way of thinking before stations started aggressively cross-training several years ago. Stations didn't do this to improve the empathy each person had for the other's task, to make a better, more seamless product; they were doing it so they could hire fewer people to do everything.

One of the cardinal rules is that you write to video. There were a lot of reporters who didn't do this and they would come back to the station and try to write the story as how they visualized it in their heads. They didn't pay any attention to what the photographer was doing in the field. They would write the story as if it were a newspaper or radio story as theater of the mind; then they would get into editing and panic because they didn't have any video to cover the story. I remember reporters running around the station and yelling, "Where do I get a picture of a 'blank.'" The solution to that is very simple; if you don't have it, you don't write it. If you write to what you have, it makes everyone's job easier.

Q: On the flip side, many people take field trips to television stations and see all the state-of-the-art equipment. They come back to campus and say, "We don't have that. We can't do quality productions." How important is it for students to learn on state-of-the-art equipment versus learning concepts and creativity?

CM: It's not important to learn on state-of-the-art equipment. It's more important to understand where to point the camera and concepts such as during a stand-up what to do and what not to do. The rest of it will come and be a result of how much money your station has to spend on equipment.

You should learn to do things with "bare bones" equipment, because if you can do it with that you can do things with better equipment. When people get their first jobs, they are not going to start in New York, they will probably start in places like Eureka, California, where they have old, bad equipment. They will be somewhat constrained because if they are a "one person band," there will be certain things they won't be able to do. Still, creativity is the key over button pushing.

Q: Do you think there are times when video technology is misused or used as a gimmick?

CM: In television news one of the biggest misuses is with the live shot. It has become a huge tail wagging the dog. You can turn on the news any night and see it. The live shot is often used as a production tool. There can be a drive-by shooting in Oakland that happened six hours ago and we go to the reporter live on the scene. There's a dark empty street in the background with some crime scene tape and there is no compelling reason to be there at the moment. But there is something about a live shot that fosters immediacy.

The live shot implies that just because something is live it is important. Nine times out of ten, it's not.

Our medical reporter in Pittsburgh was suspended from a newscast because of a disagreement about her being in a live shot. It was the dead of winter, and the woman had spent the day doing a story on the dangers of cold exposure. For the six o'clock news they have her go to the top of Mount Washington where there is this blizzard and she's standing up there without the appropriate clothing. She starts telling us some of the do's and don't's of winter preparation and in the middle of the report she just snaps and says, "For instance, don't do any of the things I'm doing right now like standing in the freezing cold, with open-toed shoes, and no hat, only because my news director insisted we do a live shot up here."

The other thing is that if you have to do a live shot at the end of a recorded story and you're stuck in traffic getting to the location, you can't do last-minute editing or find more graphics to help make the story more interesting. That's why I never did live shots unless they were absolutely necessary.

CHAPTER EIGHT

Interview Programs

All you have to do is pick up a *TV Guide* or scan the television listings in your local newspaper to see that interview and talk shows are a major component of programming throughout daytime television. Interview shows ranging from big-budget late night talk shows to local public affairs programs produced on a shoestring budget provide viewers with a variety of personalities and information. The types of interview and talk shows we see usually fall into specific time slots throughout the day.

Types of Interview Shows

■ **Early Morning**   Interviews seen early in the morning tend to be both informative and entertaining. Programs such as NBC's *Today* and ABC's *Good Morning America* have for years featured people in the news, such as politicians and government officials, as well as entertainment-oriented guests, such as movie stars, musicians, and authors. Early morning network shows provide a forum for public figures to discuss their political positions and an audience of potential customers for show business personalities promoting a movie or concert. It is not unusual to see an author promoting a new book on a number of interview or talk shows in quick succession as part of a tour.

Early morning shows.

	6 am	6:30	7:00	7:30	8:00	8:30	9:00	9:30	10:00	10:30	11:00	11:30
FOX **2**	Morning News		Good Morning on 2				Ricki Lake		People's Court		Ananda Lewis	
NBC **4**	News		Today						Sally		Judy	News
CBS **5**	News		Early Show				Martha Stewart		Price is Right		Young - Restless	
ABC **7**	Morning News		Good Morning America				Regis and Kelly		The View		News	Port Ch.
CNBC	Squawk Box		Market Watch				Power Lunch				Street Signs	
CNN	CNN This Morning						CNN Today		Burden	CNN Today		

These interviews often last three minutes or less, as producers attempt to provide viewers with fast-paced shows containing many segments. As a result, they may lack some of the depth of interviews seen later in the day, when one guest may be interviewed for a major portion of a program. Viewers may perceive morning interviews as longer than a few minutes because interviewers skillfully cover a wide variety of topics and look natural while maintaining a fast pace.

Some independent stations air localized versions of *Today* or *Good Morning America.* These programs contain interviews with guests visiting the station's city along with news, weather, and sports reports. Many local stations produce early morning newscasts that contain interview segments, as do local cable news programs. Generally speaking, the interviews we see early in the morning are informative in nature, even when the guests are celebrities.

Midmorning   As the morning progresses, talk shows become lighter, focusing more on entertainment and less on hard news. These programs are for the stay-at-home audience, providing hosts and guests who focus on entertainment and issues that are important for homemakers and retirees. NBC's final hour of *Today* covers some of the same topics as earlier on *Today* while featuring other segments about child care, cooking, and home projects.

Many talk shows seen throughout the day are syndicated programs. The Federal Communications Commission defines a syndicated program as "any program sold, licensed, distributed, or offered to television stations in more than one market within the United States for non network television broadcast exhibition but not including live presentation."

Later Morning and Midday   Many types of interview and talk shows are broadcast during late morning and around noon. Some, such as *The Jerry Springer Show, Ricki Lake,* and *Jenny Jones* present bizarre guests and situations along with audience participation. Some critics have called

Midmorning shows.

		6 am	6:30	7:00	7:30	8:00	8:30	9:00	9:30	10:00	10:30	11:00	11:30
FOX	2	Morning News		Good Morning on 2				Ricki Lake		People's Court		Ananda Lewis	
NBC	4	News		Today						Sally		Judy	News
CBS	5	News		Early Show				Martha Stewart		Price is Right		Young - Restless	
ABC	7	Morning News		Good Morning America				Regis and Kelly		The View		News	Port Ch.
CNBC		Squawk Box		Market Watch				Power Lunch				Street Signs	
CNN		CNN This Morning						CNN Today		Burden	CNN Today		

Late morning and midday shows.

	6 am	6:30	7:00	7:30	8:00	8:30	9:00	9:30	10:00	10:30	11:00	11:30
FOX 2	Morning News		Good Morning on 2				Ricki Lake		People's Court		Ananda Lewis	
NBC 4	News		Today						Sally		Judy	News
CBS 5	News		Early Show				Martha Stewart		Price is Right		Young - Restless	
ABC 7	Morning News		Good Morning America				Regis and Kelly		The View		News	Port Ch.
CNBC	Squawk Box		Market Watch				Power Lunch				Street Signs	
CNN	CNN This Morning						CNN Today		Burden	CNN Today		

	Noon	12:30	1:00	1:30	2:00	2:30	3:00	3:30	4:00	4:30	5:00	5:30
FOX 2	News	Hatchett	Mars/Venus		Woody	Transformers	Rangers	Digimon	Crossing	Crossing	Baseball	
NBC 4	Passions		J-Brown	J-Brown	Jenny Jones		Days of Our Lives		News	Judy	News	NBC News
CBS 5	News	Bold	As the World Turns		Guiding Light		Martha Stewart		Tell Truth	News	News	
ABC 7	All My Children		One Life to Live		General Hospital		Rosie O'Donnell		Oprah Winfrey		News	ABC News
CNBC	Street Signs		Market Wrap		Market Wrap		Business Center			News	Hardball	
CNN	Talkback Live		News Site		Inside Politics		Moneyline		News	Crossfire	Walt Blitzer	The Point

these programs "side show television"; but there is no denying that they draw large audiences. Syndicators and local stations airing these shows also make large profits, because they are relatively inexpensive to produce.

At the other end of the spectrum, informational interview segments appear on local stations' midday newscasts. You may see the same types of interviews at midday as you would on early morning newscasts.

■ **Afternoons** Syndicated programs such as *The Rosie O'Donnell Show* and *The Oprah Winfrey Show* feature entertaining and informative interview formats hosted by well-known personalities. These programs provide many local stations with good lead-ins to tabloid news shows such as *Hard Copy* and *Current Affair* or to their late afternoon and early evening local newscasts.

Cable services such as ESPN or CNN may have late afternoon interview shows sandwiched between newscasts or sports events.

Afternoon shows.

	Noon	12:30	1:00	1:30	2:00	2:30	3:00	3:30	4:00	4:30	5:00	5:30
FOX 2	News	Hatchett	Mars/Venus		Woody	Transformers	Rangers	Digimon	Crossing	Crossing	Baseball	
NBC 4	Passions		J-Brown	J-Brown	Jenny Jones		Days of Our Lives		News	Judy	News	NBC News
CBS 5	News	Bold	As the World Turns		Guiding Light		Martha Stewart		Tell Truth	News	News	
ABC 7	All My Children		One Life to Live		General Hospital		Rosie O'Donnell		Oprah Winfrey		News	ABC News
CNBC	Street Signs		Market Wrap		Market Wrap		Business Center			News	Hardball	
CNN	Talkback Live		News Site		Inside Politics		Moneyline		News	Crossfire	Walt Blitzer	The Point

Evening shows.

	6 pm	6:30	7:00	7:30	8:00	8:30	9:00	9:30	10:00	10:30	11:00	11:30
FOX 2	Baseball San Francisco at Houston				Guiness World Records		Night Visions		10 O'Clock News		Seinfeld	Seinfeld
NBC 4	News		Frazier	Entertainment tonight	Friends		Will and Grace		ER		News	Tonight
CBS 5	CBS Evening News	News	Evening Magazine	Hollywood Squares	48 Hours "Living with the Enemy"		Big Brother 2		Tell Truth	News	News	Late Show
ABC 7	News		Jeopardy	Wheel of Fortune	Whose Line is it Anyway?	Whose Line is it Anyway?	Who Wants to be a Millionaire		Primetime Thursday		News	Nightline

	6 pm	6:30	7:00	7:30	8:00	8:30	9:00	9:30	10:00	10:30	11:00	11:30
CNBC	Riviera Live		News with Brian Williams		Hardball		Riviera Live		News with Brian Williams		Business Center	
CNN	Larry King Live		CNN Tonight	Greenfield Large	Sports	Moneyline	Larry King Live		CNN Tonight	Greenfield Large	Sports	Moneyline

■ **Evenings** Local newscasts have interview segments produced in the studio or in the field. Videotaped news stories, known as packages, feature edited portions of interviews, known as soundbites (field interviews and soundbites are explored in detail in Chapter 9).

Reporters frequently do remote interviews with newsmakers, and it is not unusual for sports anchors to go on location before a big game to interview athletes or coaches. Interviews in one form or another are important components of network and local newscasts.

Interviews are also a staple of newsmagazine programs such as *60 Minutes, 20/20,* and *Dateline,* which continue to thrive on network television. Some television critics believe that in the near future networks will start airing prime-time network newscasts at 10 P.M. If this happens, interviews in one form or another will be included in these newscasts.

Cable services such as CNN and MSNBC offer numerous interview shows while local origination and public access cable offer programs that cater to specific audiences and tastes. Some local stations offer early evening interview shows discussing local issues or highlighting sports teams, although most of these programs have given way to less expensive and more profitable syndicated programs.

■ **Late Night** When we think of late night television we usually think of local news and entertaining talk shows such as *Tonight* and the *Late Show.* Late night talk shows have high production values, elaborate sets, and

Late night shows.

	Midnight	12:30	1:00	1:30	2:00	2:30	3:00	3:30	4:00	4:30	5:00	5:30
FOX 2	Mad	Change	Street	Street	Paid	Paid	Paid	Paid	Arrest	News	Morning News	
NBC 4	Tonight	Late Night		SCTV	Jenny Jones		Paid	Paid	Paid	Early	News	
CBS 5	Late Show		Late Late Show	News	Sexwars	CBS Up To The Minute				CBS News	News	
ABC 7	Politically	Lyania		News	ABC World News Now					ABC News	News	

	Midnight	12:30	1:00	1:30	2:00	2:30	3:00	3:30	4:00	4:30	5:00	5:30
CNBC	Paid	Paid	Paid	Paid	Today's Business				Squawk Box			
CNN	Larry King Live		World News	Newsroom	Moneyline		Money Morning		AT Daybreak			

music. Production costs for these shows are lowered slightly by the fact that celebrities appear for relatively little money, known as union scale, in order to promote their latest film, book, or CD. Emphasis is usually on entertainment as opposed to hard news.

Your late night local news sometimes contains interviews, especially if there is a late-breaking story and the principals involved are available for interviews. In most cases, late local news is a recap of the day's events plus significant stories that have developed since the early newscast.

An interview show that seems to go against the grain and is often seen late at night in many markets is PBS's *Charlie Rose*. Charlie Rose interviews a wide variety of guests, ranging from politicians to musicians, for an extended time. The production values for this show are simple; it is shot with robotic cameras on a small set with a low ceiling at Bloomberg Financial Services in New York. Rose and his guests sit at a simple wooden table, and the emphasis is on conversation rather than flashy sets and production values. Charlie Rose effectively models the extensive preparation an interviewer must undertake to ensure an interesting and natural-sounding interview.

■ Public Affairs and Public Access Programs

On weekends, especially Sunday mornings, we see a variety of public affairs programs. These programs may be locally produced, dealing with issues and public figures in that city, or they may be network programs such as *Meet the Press* or *This Week on ABC*. The emphasis is on information, with public officials using these programs to forward their agendas and interviewers attempting to get answers to difficult questions.

Interview programs on public access television appear at almost any time of day and any day of the week, with subjects ranging from local politicians to cultural figures. For many who move on to larger arenas or more significant positions, the public access interview marks their first appearance on television.

Internet streaming video may soon provide the same service as public access television, giving individuals a cybersoapbox for their views. Local

Sunday morning shows.

		6 am	6:30	7:00	7:30	8:00	8:30	9:00	9:30	10:00	10:30	11:00	11:30
FOX	2	Lifestyle	It Is Written	In Ministries	Hour of Power		49ers	Fox NFL Sunday		Football	Carolina Panthers at Minnesota		
NBC	4	Today		Meet the Press		News		Living	Garden	Wakeboarding		Golf	Williams
CBS	5	Mosaic	Bay Sunday	Sunday Morning			49ers	NFL Today		Football	Oakland at Kansas City		
ABC	7	Entertainers		News		This Week		Cycling	San Francisco Grand Prix				

	6 am	6:30	7:00	7:30	8:00	8:30	9:00	9:30	10:00	10:30	11:00	11:30
CNBC	Paid	Paid	Paid	Paid	Paid	Paid	Paid	Paid	Paid	Paid	Paid	Paid
CNN	Sunday Morning		NFL Preview		Evans	Sources	Late Edition				World Report	

commercial stations are now producing Internet streaming video interview shows to complement their on-air offerings.

We've surveyed the wide variety of interview and talk shows, hosts, and styles. In an age of shows that sometimes go "down market" or attempt to provoke controversy at almost any cost, it is important to remember that many of the most popular and longest running programs have well-informed, prepared hosts who know how to elicit information from guests while making the interview look easy and conversational. Again, you will need to decide how you want to be perceived in the long term as a video performer. Following are the central principles that good interviewers use during their programs and segments.

Preparing for the Interview: Research

Television interviews may look like natural, conversational encounters, and they should; however, casual viewers usually don't consider the amount of preparation needed to create questions and research guests' backgrounds before the program. As an interviewer, you must first gather as much information as you can about the person you are interviewing.

Although you will interview a variety of people, they will probably fall into two categories: *personality* and *informative.* Personality interviews are film stars, politicians, musicians, authors, and other celebrities. You show viewers that you are interested in these people by using a friendly tone with little or no confrontation.

Informative interviews are interviews with experts or authorities. These people may have lots of television experience or none at all, so there can be special challenges here. It's your job to draw out the facts from these subjects and clarify information when necessary.

Viewers have come to expect interviewers to have done their research on guests and issues. Several sources can aid you in your preparation:

Press Kits   If the person you are interviewing is well known or is scheduled by a booking agent, you may be provided with a **press kit.** Press kits often contain basic biographical information and past accomplishments. They can be a valuable shortcut in preparation and research as long as you use them wisely, remembering that the kit will try to present the guest in the best possible light. You should also study the press kit to discover interesting facts about the guest or accomplishments not known to the audience. Be aware that press kits sometimes contain wrong information about a guest, so you should know how to backtrack gracefully from a question asked in error.

■ **Data Banks and Library Resources** Television stations have their own data banks in which you can find information on most public figures. Data banks also exist for articles in periodicals or newspapers about potential interview subjects including the *New York Times Index* or *EBSCO Host.* Many of these data banks allow you to access the full text of articles.

■ **The Internet** Online sources make short work of research for many interviewers. Websites, online newspapers, and other periodicals provide current information on people and events, but there is a downside to online research. As you may already have discovered when researching your own projects, the information thus obtained may lack credibility and relevance; therefore, you must do some basic critical thinking and source evaluation.

For example, suppose you were going to interview Joan Ganz Cooney, the creator of the children's show *Sesame Street,* and wanted to do some basic background research. You discover that Joan Cooney is in The Women's Hall of Fame and the Television Hall of Fame, but you also find websites of white supremacist groups protesting against Ms. Cooney because of *Sesame Street*'s multiracial cast. Obviously, the Internet is a valuable and speedy research tool, but as is clear from this example, let the researcher beware.

Here are some points to consider when evaluating web pages:

■ **What is the source of the page?** Who wrote it and what are their credentials? Evaluate web pages for credibility as you would other conventional sources such as periodicals and books. Also look to see if there is an "About us" section that expresses the organization's mission or philosophy.

■ **Who published the page?** What type of domain is it from? Basically defined, a domain is the hierarchical scheme for indicating the categorical and geographical venue of a web page from the network. Common domains in the United States include edu (education), gov (government agency), net (network related), com (commercial), and org (nonprofit and research organizations). Outside the United States, domains indicate country, for example, ca (Canada), uk (United Kingdom), au (Australia), jp (Japan), fr (France), and so on.

Check to see if there is a tilde (~) in the URL (uniform resource locator, the unique address of any web document); this frequently indicates a personal page. See if the publisher takes credit for the content of the website and evaluate whether it will still be there tomorrow.

■ **Is the web page current, timely, or dated?** Individual pages may be updated at different times, or the entire website may contain old information. Examine when the page was last updated by looking at the bottom of the page.

■ **Is there bias?** Is the website selling, promoting, or ranting? Is it giving you links to other viewpoints? Does it seem balanced or one-sided? Is it annotated? Is it sponsored by an extremist organization? Examine what is *not* said as well as what is said.

■ **Is it unmodified or unedited if it is reproducing a published piece?** See if you can determine whether a published piece has been altered in any way, and if so, why.

■ **Ask yourself if you should consult other conventional sources to substantiate your online source.** Recently, both print and electronic journalists have made major factual errors by consulting online sources. There were several instances during the Clinton–Lewinsky affair that journalists made serious fact errors due to consultation of online sources. Make sure you've done your homework by consulting as many sources as you can given time and other limitations.

The Item or Event Your Guest Is Involved With

Guests often appear on interview programs to promote a book, concert, special event, and so on. If the guest has written a book, you should try to read it along with its reviews. Try to be familiar with the author's other books too, so that you have some basis for comparison. Sometimes you are unable to read the entire book due to time limitations, but you should at least attempt to read representative or significant passages. Don't pretend in an interview that you've read the entire book if you haven't.

If your guest is involved with a special event, you should do some basic research regarding the event and its history. Is this the first time the guest has been involved with this event, or is there an ongoing relationship? If the guest is promoting a concert or CD, make sure you are familiar with his or her music.

You may some day interview film stars promoting films. In many cases the film distributor will send a press kit and a videocassette of the film to aid you in preparation for the interview. There may be a film clip that is rolled in to the actual interview as well.

Some interviewers claim to do hours of research while others, such as Larry King, claim to do little or none before an interview. As you progress as an interviewer, you will discover how much research you have to do to conduct a quality interview. One thing is certain; audiences can tell if an interviewer is well prepared or simply getting by on style over substance.

Upon completion of your research, you can begin to focus on the interview topic(s). Your choice of topic will often make or break an interview.

Choosing a Topic

The basic question you must ask is, "Is this topic interesting?" or, "Can I make this topic interesting?" Some guests can take even the most mundane topics and make them fascinating, whereas other guests can make compelling topics boring. You can't always control the dynamism of the guest, but you can control the quality of the topic(s).

One way to test topic interest level is through the "two Qs" of **qualitative** and **quantitative significance.** Qualitative significance is usually the best, the most, or the first of something. If you are interviewing a medical researcher who has developed a vaccine that might prevent certain types of cancers, this invention has qualitative significance. Quantitative significance has to do with specific numbers or statistics, such as how much money is spent on certain types of entertainment or how many people are doing a certain activity. For example, if you are interviewing a consumer affairs advocate who makes the claim that 7 percent of items scanned at the checkstand at a store have scanning errors and that these mistakes cost consumers $2 billion a year, you are highlighting quantitative significance.

Another consideration is universality. Certain topics, such as money and health, seem to appeal to almost everyone. People want to know more about topics that affect their checkbooks and bodies. A way to test topic universality is through demographic and psychographic analysis. Demographic analysis considers audience characteristics, including age, income, geographic region, racial or ethnic background, and education. Some interview and talk shows appeal to a broad demographic; others appeal to a more specific audience. Psychographic analysis, often used to determine "hot button" issues for the audience, deals with attitudes, likes, dislikes, and pet peeves.

Timeliness and time of day will also assist you in topic selection. If the audience has already heard about a particular topic over a long period of time, you will have to find a fresh angle to make that topic interesting. For example, everyone knows that you can save money by shopping with coupons, but the average person may not know about Internet or e-coupons.

Time of day also determines topic choice, because some topics may be too heavy or comprehensive for early morning or late night audiences. Many critics have said that part of the success of *The Tonight Show* is that it stays away from heavy or controversial topics, opting instead for entertainment before viewers go to bed. If the program is videotaped, you must take into consideration what time viewers will be watching it. You may be taping a public affairs show at 10 A.M. on a Friday that will air the following Sunday at 6 A.M., so make sure your topic is appropriate for the air time.

Have a clear purpose and focused topic(s) for your interview. Write out a purpose statement of 25 words or less that sums up why you are doing this interview and what do you want the audience to get out of it. In many cases you'll find that the purpose will help you to focus your topic choice. The program length determines how many topics you can cover in depth; for example, *Charlie Rose* can cover more topics in one interview because the segment time with each guest is longer than interview segments on programs like *Today.*

If you are a student doing practice interviews, you should try to challenge yourself by finding the most interesting guests you can, while also developing interesting topics. Doing practice interviews with a friend or someone you know doesn't help you develop your skill as an interviewer, nor does it provide much audience interest. If you are appearing in a corporate interview program, always look for the most knowledgeable and dynamic experts you can find to ensure a quality production.

Once you have a good grasp of interview topic(s), move on to developing specific interview questions. By starting with an interview purpose and topics, you'll find it much easier to develop questions than if you had no foundation for the interview.

Preparing Questions

Before you prepare specific questions for an interview, you should put yourself in the place of audience members; what questions would they ask if they had the opportunity to interview your guest? This device will give you an attitudinal foundation for developing questions. However, it also helps to know the best types of questions to ask and which types of questions you should avoid.

■ **Open-Ended Questions**   General and less structured questions allow the guest some latitude in his or her response. Open-ended questions are often used to start out an interview, since they allow the guest to warm up to the interview situation. For example, you might ask, "What did you like about playing your character?" or, "What were the things you liked about Russia?"

Open-ended questions are most often used in entertainment-oriented interviews. News interviewers tend to use open-ended questions less, because they are not specific and take considerable time to answer. An interviewee may also end up answering *a* question but not *the* question.

Closed-Ended Questions Closed-ended questions are specific, as the interviewer attempts to find out various facts. Questions such as, "How much money do you expect this will cost taxpayers?" or, "How many people were involved with this crime?" seek quantitative information. Interviewers must be careful not to rely only on closed-ended questions, however, because they may create a static situation. With these questions it is also easy for interviewees to answer yes or no or fall into other predictable patterns.

Hypothetical Questions The beauty of hypothetical questions is that they can be used in a variety of interviews. In an informative interview you may be able to predict policy by asking a hypothetical question. For example, by asking "What would you do if the teachers in your district went on strike?" you can give viewers some insights as to what a public official might do if a certain action took place. Hypothetical questions can also be used in entertainment-oriented interviews, for example, "If you had a chance to play any character, who would it be?"

Leading Questions These tend to limit responses and force the interviewee into a corner. A question such as, "Most people think that Eric Jones should retire; do you?" shows a bias on the part of the interviewer. Leading questions can give the impression that you are being unfair to the guest, so limit your use of them.

Transitional Questions These questions are good for getting from one interview segment to another. For example, "Since we're talking about summer activities, what about your interest in jet skiing?" or, "After you finish painting the trim, what next?" Transitional questions show that you are listening to the guest while moving things along. The faster-paced the interview, the more likely you are to use transitional questions.

Interviewer Responses As you've probably guessed, these are not really questions but reactions to what your guest has said. "That's crazy!" or "Very interesting" are typical responses one hears from interviewers, although good interviewers use these sparingly because they can sound silly if overused. Remember that viewers want to hear your guest.

Many beginning interviewers want to know if there are so-called "best" questions to ask. Interview programs can be as fluid as a piece of jazz music, in which the best questions are determined by the guest's response and how the interviewer is able to react to and build on it. Here are some tips on asking good questions:

■ **If you don't ask you won't get.** Within reason, you have to ask the difficult question or the question that everyone at home would ask if they had the chance. You never know when the guest may be in the mood to reveal information or feel it is the appropriate moment to make a confession. Some will argue with the ethics of this approach; however, much is determined by the style of the interviewer. For example, NBC sports reporter Jim Gray was much criticized for asking former baseball player Pete Rose if there was anything that he wanted to confess to the public regarding his alleged betting on baseball games. The criticism came not so much because Gray asked the question, but because he persisted in that line of questioning. When asking difficult questions, you must be sensitive and pay attention to timing so that the audience perceives you as a fair interviewer.

■ **Ask yourself, "What does the audience know?"** In many cases, some of the best questions you can develop come from determining what the audience knows and what gaps need filling. Good interviewers don't assume that the audience knows what they themselves know. Simple, direct questions that clarify are some of the best you can ask.

■ **Ask questions to which you know the answer.** This is probably one of the best-known strategies of good interviewers. For example, if you are interviewing your city's mayor and have heard from reliable sources that the city is about to spend money on a new downtown mall, you can ask the mayor a question regarding what new projects are on the horizon for the city. You may have to persist and ask a series of questions in order to arrive at the specifics of the mall project.

■ **Favor "how" and "why" questions.** These questions deal with process, such as getting from point A to point B, while also offering insight into the interviewee's feelings toward certain issues. "How" and "why" questions can provide some of the most revealing answers during an interview.

■ **Present yourself as the "reasonable person" while asking questions.** This technique was perfected by Phil Donahue years ago when he would preface his questions with the plea, "Help me out here." In an era of talk shows with tenacious interviewers, this can still be a useful way to elicit information from a guest while also increasing your popularity with viewers. This approach also demonstrates that you are willing to give a controversial guest a chance, even if you don't agree with his or her views.

■ **Ask yourself, "What is the interviewee's point of view?"** It helps to know where your guest stands on a particular topic. If you're asking a political official a question about funding for education, it probably helps to know if the official has ties to public education, children attending public schools, or was once a school board member. Work on determining the audience's attitude toward the question and topics you are introducing.

■ **Define and clarify terms and jargon.** In the "dot.com" era new terms and jargon are constantly being introduced into our lexicon. Don't assume that just because you understand every word the guest is saying, the audience will too. Simplify and define technical terms and acronyms. Be specific about events and places you are referring to, and don't be afraid to repeat them several times throughout the interview.

■ **Be fair to your guest.** Don't ask questions that your guest can't answer. Putting your guest on the spot just to make you look good can backfire as your audience begins to side with the guest. Determine what information your guest has and what types of questions he or she can answer. Getting your guest to do too much speculating adds little value to a quality interview.

You should be prepared to ask spontaneous follow-up questions during most interviews. These are discussed in the During the Interview section of this chapter. Novice interviewers sometimes wonder what constitutes a bad question to ask. In general, you should avoid the following kinds of questions:

■ **Questions that lead to "yes" and "no" answers.** One of the most basic mistakes made by novice interviewers is asking questions that can be answered with a simple *yes* or *no*. Not only do these questions limit the amount of information you receive from the guest; they also contribute to an interview that looks visually jarring because the director has to "ping pong" back and forth between the host and guest.

"Yes" and "no" are useful responses if you ask a follow-up question for more explanation, but a series of these answers can be deadly. Make sure you vary your types of questions so that you don't fall into this trap.

■ **"How do you feel?" questions.** We've all heard interviewers and reporters ask, "How do you feel?" in situations ranging from triumph to tragedy. You can elicit the real feelings of an individual much better by asking more specific questions. For example, if you are interviewing a politician who has just lost a close election, you might ask, "At what point did you think you might lose this election?" On the other hand, during a moment of triumph you might ask a player who has scored a game-winning touchdown, "What was going through your head when you knew you were in the end zone for the score?"

When asking questions of people who have experienced a tragedy, it is especially important to show sensitivity. Experienced interviewers can obtain information from the guest while also demonstrating sympathy for what they may be feeling.

■ **Apologetic questions.** You may want to consider not asking a question if you have to preface it with an apology. Questions that begin, "I know this might sound silly to you . . . " can give the guest a reason to think that the question doesn't deserve an answer. One exception to this is a tough question that viewers feel must be asked of the guest. The "You know I have to ask this question . . . " approach often comes at the beginning or end of an interview if the guest has been associated with a controversial issue or topic.

■ **Unfocused questions.** Questions that have no focus or objective either lead to long, rambling answers or produce no answers at all. Asking, "So what has happened to you over the last year that you would like to talk about?" invites a long, unfocused answer or many seconds of silence as the guest tries to remember the events of the past year. Some unfocused questions aren't questions at all. For example, "Wow, you really finished her off in that match!" puts the guest in an awkward position. Questions should give the guest some idea of what information you want to receive.

■ **Questions with multiple parts.** Ask questions with no more than two parts. Questions with multiple parts confuse the guest and viewers about the sequence of responses. Asking a film star, "So did you enjoy working with your costar, being directed by Jill Jones, or shooting the movie in Canada the most?" invites a diffuse response. Keep your questions simple and to the point.

One final suggestion is to keep questions to less than three sentences so that the guest can remember the entire question. This is especially helpful when guests are inexperienced and relatively anxious.

After you have created a series of questions, organize them into one of several sequences. Some interviewers like to anticipate the sequence of questions they will use before creating their questions. Others like to work on specific questions first and then develop a sequence. After several interview experiences, you will find which method works best for you.

Sequence of Questions

Interviewers usually have a blueprint, or game plan, of how they will ask questions during the interview. Three of the most commonly used sequences are the **funnel,** the **inverted funnel,** and the **tunnel.** The funnel begins with general questions, then proceeds to more specific issues. You can often move from open- to closed-ended questions in this sequence. For example, you can ask the general question, "Why is the city experiencing a budget deficit?" and go on to, "Are there departments that are overspending?" "Does there need to be a tax increase?" and so on.

The inverted funnel, in contrast, starts with a specific question, moving to more general questions as the interview progresses. For example: "Did you vote against the proposed homeless shelter? Have you voted against other facilities for the homeless? Which ones? What is your philosophy on city government spending for the homeless?" This type of sequence allows you to discover philosophy and feelings about topics. The inverted funnel also presents the information in a manageable manner for viewers who may want to know a guest's opinions on specific issues.

The tunnel sequence combines a series of questions about the same topic. These can be all open ended: "How did you survive the accident? What did you see before impact? What were you thinking before it happened?" Or they may be closed ended, "How many cars were in front of you before the accident? Did you see the car come from the side? Did you see if anyone was hurt?"

After developing the questions and sequence(s), you can write your introduction and conclusion.

Introductions and Conclusions

The first and last impressions are sometimes the only ones viewers remember. You have only a few seconds to capture viewer attention as to why this interview is significant, and you want to end the segment on a positive note. Too often, intros and conclusions are written as afterthoughts rather than attention getters and means of closure.

Write out or outline your intro in advance, remembering that this is your chance to persuade the audience that this segment is worthy of their attention. Sometimes you can read the intro from a teleprompter or from a script, but if you read word for word, you must do so in a conversational manner. Many interviewers work better with an ad-lib style, using limited notes with the most important information about the guest and topic.

Intros should include the following information:

- Some attention-getter or "hook" concerning this guest or the topic's importance. Use what you have read earlier about audience analysis as a guide for your attention-getter.
- Name, title, and other basic biographical information concerning your guest. Think in terms of "here and now" as to what the guest is doing; don't dwell on the obvious or what the audience already knows about the guest.
- You can give a hint as to where the interview is going and why the guest is being interviewed.

Good conclusions provide a summary of what has taken place in the interview, along with a reminder of the guest's name, basic information, and why he or she was interviewed. This may be fully scripted, although you may often have to tailor the conclusion to match information revealed in the interview or time limitations. You could have 30 or five seconds to conclude at the end of the show, so you must be able to adapt.

Once all your preparation, from research to writing the introduction and conclusion, is completed, you can now focus on your guest and his or her needs.

The Guest

You may have opportunities to work with experienced guests who do multiple television interviews in the same day, as well as those appearing on television for the first time. In either case, you can make the experience more positive by following this checklist before the guest walks into the studio:

- Does the guest have directions or transportation to the studio? A prepared map helps, and you can now get customized maps online from services such as Yahoo!
- What time should the guest get to the studio?

- Do you have a way to get in touch with the guest in case of emergency? Can he or she get in touch with you if necessary?

- Does your set demand special physical preparation for this guest? Will he or she have to sit on a low stool? Will loose-fitting clothes work better? Are there certain colors of clothing that will blend with the set? Does the guest know to avoid certain patterns and colors of clothing?

- Does the guest need to know about makeup? Will he or she need to arrive at the studio early for makeup?

- Does the guest need to know that there are other guests on the program and who they will be?

- Should the guest know how much time you will be spending on the interview?

- Will there be a studio audience? Will the guest be expected to answer questions or participate in some other way with the studio audience? Could there be telephone call-ins?

- Does the guest know the specifications for any props or graphics to be included on the show? Are there other considerations, such as studio lighting or camera movement, that could affect production elements?

- Is there a deadline that must be met with your art department or other production personnel if the guest wants to bring in visuals or videotape?

- Does the guest know it is illegal to say certain things on the air?

RATINGS POINTER

Consulting firms such as Frank Magid and Associates work with a variety of performers, including those new to television. However, in an era of reality-based shows when an average person may become a celebrity overnight, virtually anyone may become an interview subject. Never assume that your guest knows even the most basic aspects of television performance. Err in the direction of giving too much rather than not enough information. ★ ★ ★ ★

The question often arises whether or not you should send questions to the guest in advance of the interview. Most experienced interviewers advise against doing this, because if the guest rehearses his or her responses, it takes away from the spontaneity of the interview. You must make a value judgment when a guest refuses to appear on your program without an advance list of questions. If it's an important guest and you really want the interview, you may end up breaking this rule.

Provide the guest with a basic idea of the focus and general areas to be covered in the interview. Also, if there's some special area or content you want the guest to cover, such as "the strangest or funniest thing that has happened to him or her," you may want to give advance warning.

Once your guest arrives at the studio, provide an orientation to the studio, control room, and personnel if available. Make sure you take care of basic needs such as getting the guest something to drink and any makeup or other pre-production preparation.

Some studios have **green rooms** where guests may wait, complete with snacks, beverages, and a television monitor, so that they can see what is happening on the program before they go on. Other studios have nothing more than a couple of chairs in a corner. In either case you should do everything you can before the interview to ensure the comfort of your guest.

During the time before the interview you should try to judge your guest's level of comfort and experience. As noted earlier, some guests may do several interviews in the same day (it is not unusual to see an author on a book tour interviewed on two different morning shows, a noon news show, and also a couple of radio programs). Other guests may have little or no experience in front of the cameras. You must determine what needs to be explained and how much coaching is necessary.

Be prepared to deal with hostile guests. Sometimes you will be aware of probable hostility in advance because of previous contact or controversial events in the news associated with this guest. Other times a normally congenial guest is simply having a bad day due to problems with travel, illness, or other factors. If you know that you'll be dealing with a hostile guest, you won't overreact or be thrown off guard if things don't go smoothly.

When talking to your guest before the program, review the general areas you'll be covering in the interview. Try to stay away from specific questions you will ask so that you don't burn out some of the best topics before you ever get on air. The conversation before the interview can establish a positive foundation, so try to look for experiences you might have in common with the guest, as you would in normal conversation.

As discussed in Chapter 7, once on the set you should make sure your guest is properly miced and help him or her through the audio check. You may have to do some basic coaching concerning where to look, how to sit in the chair, and so on. Some guests are tempted to look directly into the camera lens instead of at you. Tell them to treat the interview as they would a normal conversation, maintaining eye contact with you unless they want to refer some information to viewers such as an address or telephone number.

It may seem that you've done a tremendous amount of preparatory work before the interview, and you have—from researching the guest to making the guest feel and look good. This attention to detail increases the probability of success.

"You're On!"—During the Interview

After all your preparation, the tally light finally goes on and the interview starts. You've written an introduction that includes the topic, significance of the guest, his or her credentials, and why the audience should care about this interview. Give the audience the basics concerning the guest without giving too much information. You can also add more biographical information about the guest throughout the interview.

There is no hard-and-fast rule about how long an introduction should be, but use 15 seconds as a guideline. The length of the introduction is usually dictated by how much the audience knows about the guest and the length of the interview.

Make sure you are familiar with your introduction so that you can deliver it smoothly, remembering that by performing the first few seconds of presentation, you build your confidence level for the remainder of the program. Smooth delivery of the intro also sets the tone for the remainder of the interview, as viewers make judgments concerning whether or not this topic is worthy of their attention.

Once you're into the question-and-answer portion of the interview, you should follow a few simple rules:

Listen   Active listening is a major element of being a good interviewer. Inexperienced interviewers will often look at their notes, ask a question, then prepare to ask the next question without listening to the guest's response. Listening will help you ask more interesting follow-up questions that do not appear on your script. You can also encourage the guest with amplifications such as, "Can you tell me more about that? I've always been interested in how that was developed."

Listening also keeps you from asking a question that may have been answered in a previous response or failing to switch to a new line of questioning if the need arises. Good interviewers adjust and "go with the flow" in order to get the best information from their guests.

Use your listening speed to your advantage. You are able to listen and process information three to four times faster than someone can speak, so you can listen to the guest's reply while anticipating your next question.

RATINGS POINTER

A student interviewing a college basketball coach asked the question, "Do you think you will be able to recruit a power forward this year?" The coach responded by saying that he would be doing no further recruiting because he had just been fired by the athletic director. The student didn't listen to the answer and continued with "What are the team's greatest needs for next season?" Listening not only elicits good information, it saves you from potential embarrassment. ★ ★ ★ ★

Look Interested A guest who is an inexperienced interviewee may find it difficult to appear relaxed and comfortable. As mentioned before, television diminishes your onscreen energy level, and on the air, control and comfort sometimes look like boredom.

You will probably have to work a little harder than you would in normal conversation to express energy and interest through your facial expressions, gestures, and body posture. As discussed in Chapter 5, you will want to lean in somewhat to the guest and the camera when addressing viewers. Be careful that the lean doesn't become a comfortable slump. Television lighting can exaggerate your lean to the point that it looks as if you have back problems. On the other hand, you don't want to appear sloppy by sitting too far back in your chair. This can be a problem, especially if you are sitting on a couch. As mentioned earlier, these postures make you look heavier on television.

Where Do I Look? Most of the time you are looking at your guest as you would in normal conversation. You want to give the impression of conversing with your guest as the viewer looks in on your interaction. Direct eye contact, which gives guests the feedback and support they need, is another way of making guests feel comfortable. Look at the camera when you are supplying information directly to viewers, such as during the introduction, conclusion, and transitions. Make sure you know in advance which camera is shooting you so that you don't have to search for the camera that is hot.

Movement As mentioned in Chapter 5, controlled movement is fine. Your guest will probably mirror what you do, so it's important that you establish the lead in nonverbal communication. If a guest seems too animated in his or her movements, you may want to provide a gentle reminder during a commercial break to tone things down a bit.

Some hosts habitually touch or pat a guest. At times this can be reassuring, but it can also look like a power play and give the impression that you are trying to cut the guest off. Consider who your guest is and whether or not any physical contact is appropriate.

■ **Repeat the Guest's Name and Credentials**   Factors such as the interview length and the fame or notoriety of the guest determine how often you should repeat his or her name and credentials. One advantage in television is that this information is reinforced through use of **supers** or **keys;** for example, you see the printed information "Sen. Edward Kennedy, D-Massachusetts" at the bottom of the screen when the senator appears on a news or interview show.

It is still a good idea to reinforce this information verbally during longer interviews and before commercial breaks. You may need to give a more complete explanation of the person's title or credentials than is possible at the bottom of the screen.

■ **Maintain Control**   Don't let the guest get off track from the question. Be assertive and try to get the guest back on topic. Interviews are different from day-to-day conversation in that it is OK to interrupt. You can get guests back on the topic or switch to a more interesting topic by interrupting. This takes practice because you don't want to appear rude, but you can learn how to do it gracefully by watching hosts of interview shows as they skillfully interrupt guests in a firm but polite manner.

You will encounter guests who want to assert their positions on issues or make speeches. Try to be aware of this possibility before the interview begins so that you can redirect the guest if necessary.

Maintaining control also means that you look interested in the guest while appearing calm and in command of the situation. Sometimes this is difficult due to the high-pressured environment of the television studio, and even more so in live remote situations with people and distractions. There may be times when you have to say, "That's live television, folks!" and continue as best you can.

■ **Keep Clarifying**   Earlier in this chapter it was mentioned that you and the guest should not fall into using technical jargon or buzz words. If anything, you should go to the opposite extreme. In the film *Philadelphia* actor Denzel Washington's character repeatedly requests, "Explain it to me like I'm a four year old." Paraphrase what your guest is saying into language you think your audience will understand. Don't be afraid to admit if you're confused or don't understand what your guest is saying. Chances are your audience is also having problems with the information and appreciates your attempts to clarify what is being said.

■ Consider Your Audience You want to show concern for and interest in your guest, but ultimately you are doing the interview for viewers. Relate information to the home audience: Why should they care? This may be a difficult task, because some guests have trouble getting beyond their own specialized interests. It is your job to be an advocate for the audience by asking questions viewers would like answered, sometimes coaxing the guest to get beyond conceptual, theoretical information to more practical applications. If an oil company executive is talking about the high cost of refining oil you may ask, "Well, how does that translate to how much I can expect to pay for a gallon of gas this summer vacation season?" Your guest now has to talk in more practical terms instead of generalities.

■ Keep This a Conversation Television interviews are different from print interviews or press conferences in that they are in essence conversations between people. Avoid asking a series of questions without genuinely interacting with your guest. Feel free to add information, ask for clarification, or show your honest reaction to what your guest is saying. If you've prepared before the interview, you should be able to add intelligent comments to your guest's comments.

Viewers should feel as if they are eavesdropping on a dilaogue instead of watching a press conference. The best interviewers give the impression that the interview is a natural conversation, not a staged event.

■ Keep the Focus on the Guest Some interview and talk shows, such as *The Rosie O'Donnell Show, Tonight,* and the *Late Show,* feature well-known hosts who rival their guests in notoriety. Even in these situations, the hosts try to put the focus on the guests. As talented as these hosts are, if they didn't have guests, they wouldn't have shows. Don't forget that your guest is the person viewers want to see and hear. In many cases he or she will be an expert in some area, so don't try to match his or her expertise. Work on getting the best information and anticipating what the audience would ask if they were in your position. Remember that the audience may resent a host who is rude or seems to dominate an interview.

■ **Be Tough, Not Rude** Some interviewers have made a living from giving guests what are called "softball," easy-to-answer questions, whereas other hosts seem to thrive on asking "hardball" questions. Most good interviews contain a balance, with the purpose of the interview often dictating the type of questions.

There's nothing wrong with asking difficult questions, especially if you've done your homework and know the audience would like to know the answers. Don't be afraid to keep the guest focused and on the question. Listen to the guest's response and make sure he or she is answering what you've asked; if not, you need to pursue the answer to "the" question.

■ **Don't Be in Awe of the Guest** You will probably have the opportunity to interview famous and powerful guests. It is easy to fall into the trap of putting yourself in a "one down" position from your guest (especially early in your career) and putting yourself in an inferior position.

The guest is there for a reason: to sell a book, promote an event, or forward his or her agenda. Your program or segment provides an opportunity to do this. Be gracious to your guest, follow the advice given earlier in this chapter regarding host-guest relationships, and be professional in how you treat the guest.

■ **Give Only Nonverbal Reinforcement** One of the most common mistakes of novice interviewers is interjecting comments like "Uh huh," "OK," "I see," and others when listening to guests. This response is natural in day-to-day conversation, especially when we are interested in the person we are talking to and want to appear polite. But on television it is extremely annoying, especially when we are watching a close-up of the guest and we hear a voice from off camera saying, "Uh huh," "Uh huh." It is also difficult to edit such interviews for soundbites if the soundtrack contains extraneous comments by the interviewer.

Work on giving your guests nonverbal feedback by looking interested and maintaining eye contact with them. Consider the context of the interview to gauge whether or not nodding your head is appropriate feedback. Viewers could interpret this as agreement or disagreement with a guest regarding a political or controversial issue. Nonverbal reactions are important, because your director may want to cut away from the guest for a reaction shot of you. Reaction shots add visual interest to any interview program.

■ **Use Notes**   Most interviewers use notes and keep them in view of the camera. Notecards or a clipboard are the preferred ways of using notes. We see the best interviewers and reporters in television with notecards or clipboard in hand. Don't hold your notes in such a way that they become a barrier between you and the audience. On the other hand, don't try to give the impression you're not using notes by trying to hide them. If you use notecards, don't let your nervousness show by playing with or bending them during the interview.

Some beginners try to hide their notes in their laps, but then the camera catches them as they look down, causing the audience to wonder why they are looking at their laps. Other hosts try to hide notes by putting them next to their chairs. Again, the audience wonders what they are staring at on the floor. Be familiar with your notes but don't be afraid to check them when necessary.

■ **Make Good Transitions**   A smooth transition or "signposting" between areas lets your guest and audience know where you are going with the interview. Effective transitions blend what has just been covered with what is coming up next. Transitions also provide some warning to guests if you're moving into a more difficult or controversial line of questioning. Asking a guest a question about his or her family before abruptly jumping to a question about some scandal from the past isn't smooth or fair. Work on setting up areas of questions with logical transitions.

■ **Ask Follow-Up Questions**   Question types and preparation were discussed earlier in this chapter. During the interview there are times when hosts must clarify or expand upon the responses given by guests. Follow-up questions help to do this. When a guest answers a question, it is up to you to judge whether or not the response was clear or whether important information was omitted. Here are some basic follow-up questions:

■ **Forced choice.** Here you ask a guest to choose between two alternatives; for example, when interviewing your state's governor you ask, "Given this year's budget surplus it's been said that you might spend a considerable amount on either health care or public education. Which of these do you think will receive more money?"

■ **Paraphrase.** This is restating the guest's response in your own words for purposes of clarification. Paraphrasing allows you to check your understanding of the response while also demonstrating fairness to the guest.

■ **Ask for examples.** One of the most basic follow-up questions is, "Give me an example." If the guest is a police officer who says that road rage seems to be increasing on our local highways, you may ask, "Could give me some examples of what you would consider to be road rage?" or, "Can you describe a time you saw a recent act of road rage?" Examples clarify and add interest to interviews.

■ **Ask "how" and "why" questions.** Getting beyond basic answers and finding out how or why something happened gives more depth to the initial response. It also shows viewers that you are trying to get to the bottom of a question or issue.

■ **Capture the guest's feelings.** Sometimes you have to remind guests of their emotions during a past event. Asking questions such as, "Weren't you upset?" or, "Did you hate having to do that?" can help guests recall how they felt at a particular time, making the memory seem current for guest and viewer. This type of question can also lead to good stories from a guest.

■ **Fill in the blanks.** When guests, unintentionally or intentionally, omit information from a response, an obvious follow-up question is to zero in on the omission: "You didn't mention the cost of your plan to taxpayers."

■ **"Show me yours, and I'll show you mine."** Interviewers will sometimes compare past experiences or examples with a guest to get more information or depth from a response. This approach helps you to identify with the guest. Be careful not to overuse this technique, though, because the focus should remain on the interviewee.

■ **"Help me out here."** This is where you defer to the guest's expertise in order to clarify or get further information. When asking a baseball pitcher about concentrating on the batter, you might ask "I've never pitched in the big leagues, but I imagine it would be difficult to focus on the batter with 40,000 fans yelling in the ballpark."

■ **React to your guest.** A reaction before a follow-up question can often add impact. "I can't believe they plan on doing that! So you think their plan will work?" can elicit a more interesting and honest response from the guest, as well as make you seem more involved in the interview.

■ **Pause after a response.** Even experienced interviewers sometimes think that they have to fill every second with questions or conversation, whereas a slight pause after a guest's response may be one of your best assets. Guests will often expand upon their answers simply because you haven't jumped in with another question.

Visually, you give the director opportunities for good reaction shots when you use occasional pauses. Pauses, as noted earlier, also create anticipation and a sense of power; just be careful that you don't overuse them.

These are just a few types of follow-up questions you may use. As you gain more experience, you will develop your own questions and techniques.

Dealing with Problems
In most cases, television interviews go smoothly without major problems, especially if the interviewer is well prepared. But there are times, especially in live television, when problems do arise. Another aspect of being an experienced interviewer is dealing with unanticipated problems during the interview.

■ **A boring guest/interview.** In theory this shouldn't happen if you've done adequate preparation, but due to the guest's nervousness or poor pre-screening, the guest and interview may turn out to be boring. The responsibility for an interesting interview, however, lies with the host, and the audience will blame you, not the guest, if things get boring (in fact, viewers will probably vote with their remote controls by switching to another channel). You can coach your guest into a good, or at least acceptable performance, by doing some of the following:

- If the guest speaks slowly, try picking up your own pace.
- If he or she speaks too quietly, increase your volume.
- If the guest is lounging too far back in the chair, try leaning into him or her.

Your guest will often mirror what you do with verbals and nonverbals. If the interview is longer, with several segments and commercial breaks, make the guest aware of what he or she is doing (or not doing) during one of these breaks to correct the problem.

■ **The interview gets hostile.** Assuming that you're not doing a deliberately confrontational show, interviews can nevertheless contain some controversy and an honest exchange of ideas. Some guests respond negatively to tough questions. Unless you have a reputation as a tenacious, aggressive interviewer, it is probably best to keep from matching the guest's hostility level. Remain in control and remember the issues and information you want viewers to know. It's also a good idea to try to keep issues and personalities separate. A little controversy can increase audience interest in your program, so try to maintain your composure if your guest gets intense. Most viewers are fair-minded and will recognize when a guest is being unreasonable.

■ **You know the guest.** You may be wondering why this is a problem, but people you know can actually be more difficult to interview than people you don't. It's easy to fall into "in" jokes or stories that are fun for the two of you but less interesting for your audience. Keep the viewers in mind: Is some of your history with the guest really entertaining, or not?

■ **You run out of things to ask.** Again, this shouldn't happen if you've prepared well and developed an adequate number of questions. Listen to what is being said so that you can ask good follow-up questions and take the interview in any direction. Usually, the challenge is trying to stay within the program's time limits rather than trying to fill time.

■ **The guest tries to dominate the interview.** An interview is not a regular conversation in that you may interrupt your guest. Keep your questions coming, and take advantage of any opening and slight pause by the guest to regain control.

■ **Phone calls.** Some interview programs feature phone calls from viewers. There is a temptation for you to lose eye contact with the camera when you are listening to callers over the studio speakers. Keep your contact with the camera when you listen to callers. If you get a prank call, don't bring attention to it and try to make a smooth transition to the next caller.

■ **Conclusions** When asking your final question, you can give the guest some indication that you are running out of time so that the response should be short. Ask direct or closed-ended questions so that you don't put the guest in the position of having to answer an involved question in 30 seconds or less. If you have time to do so, summarize some of the more important points viewers have heard. Make sure you thank your guest and remind the audience of his or her name and credentials.

Directors will often use a set shot at the end of the program showing the host and guest talking to each other while the credits roll. The mics are cut so that you can talk conversationally. Alert your guest that this is happening so that it doesn't catch him or her off guard.

After the Interview

Following the interview you should try to get a tape of the show for review purposes. Watch and take notes on what you did during the interview. Was your purpose clear? Did you ask clear, concise questions? Did you take the interview in a different direction when you needed to do so? Did the guest seem comfortable with you and did you look interested in the guest?

When you watch the tape, compare it to other interviews you've done, especially those with similar types of guests. How does this interview compare with others; are you making progress as an interviewer? Get constructive feedback from instructors, students, and colleagues and keep a file of notes listing your strengths and the areas you need to improve in each interview.

If possible, edit portions of interviews you do and compile an interview highlight tape. This can be an impressive portion of a resume tape you create at a later time. There is always a need for those with good interview skills as hosts or reporters.

Interviews as Oral History

Many colleges, universities, and corporations invite guest speakers, consultants, or trainers for presentations or special programs. These guests come, do their presentations, and then move on to their next engagements. There is a missed opportunity here because many of these guest presenters are willing to be interviewed and videotaped sometime during their stay.

Celebrities ranging from politicians to actors may visit your campus or organization on one occasion, but a videotaped interview or oral history segment can be preserved for years. For example, suppose the Rev. Jesse Jackson comes to your campus as a guest speaker and you find that he is willing to be interviewed in your campus television studio. Imagine the range of topics that could be discussed and how this interview could be used in classes ranging from political science to history to ethnic studies.

In the corporate world, a visiting communications consultant may provide supplementary insights in the more relaxed forum of a videotaped interview, which could be used in the future as a refresher course in principles taught by the consultant.

Not all guests will have the time or inclination to be videotaped, and there may be copyright restrictions on some of the material they use; however, many guests enjoy the opportunity to share their insights via the oral history interview. Preparation and knowledge of interview skills can help you obtain a high-quality interview.

Many people conducting oral history interviews do not know the basic interview principles discussed in this chapter. As a result, questions are often created at the last minute and the guest is allowed to ramble through a series of stories with little direction from the interviewer. Oral history interviews should follow most of the suggestions given in this chapter for interviews, with a few exceptions:

First, the time for an oral history interview is usually less restricted than the time for a television interview, so you can allow the guest longer, uninterrupted responses and stories. Still, you should make sure that the interview has a sense of purpose and direction so that it doesn't become a session in which the tape rolls and the guest says whatever comes to mind. Preparation and research are necessary elements of good oral history interviews.

Just as in other interviews, you must be able to change direction or deviate from scripted questions when collecting oral history; in fact, flexibility is even more important here. A guest may share an interesting insight or story that you've never heard before or did not anticipate based upon your line of questioning. Your ability to follow this up during the session can add to the interest level and quality of information given by the guest.

Establishing a rapport with your guest is important in any interview. In oral histories it is even more important because much of the information will be personal in nature. The overall tone of the experience should be that of an extended conversation. In many cases, the guest forgets that he or she is in a studio and relaxes as the interview progresses.

Oral histories provide information that we may not obtain in other, more public forums. The information is accessible for years to come, long after the guest has left the premises. Those who did not have the opportunity to hear the guest may now review the videotape at their convenience. Many libraries and museums have discovered the value of oral histories. The Museum of Television and Radio in New York and Los Angeles and the Museum of Broadcast Communications in Chicago have extensive collections where people may view tapes of influential broadcasters and industry pioneers.

If your school or organization doesn't have an oral history collection, consider starting one. It could be a valuable future resource.

Rewind and Fade to Black

Interview and talk shows will continue to be a popular genre of programs in the foreseeable future. These shows are becoming more interactive as video and internet technologies continue to merge. Not only is the studio audience an element of some of these shows; now people at home can interact with host and guests.

The tone of some of these shows may continue down the road of conflict and controversy. There is no denying that such programs have found an audience and produce profits because they are relatively inexpensive to produce. The basic principles of interviewing discussed in this chapter can be used in program types ranging from news and public affairs to entertainment.

Only you can determine your style as an interviewer and the type of program you host. With practice, you'll discover strengths that contribute to your style and how you relate to guests. The best interviewers in the business are those who connect not only with the guest in the studio, but also with viewers at home. In the movie *Broadcast News*, Albert Brooks's character says that reporters find their guests' lives to be so interesting because their own lives are so boring. Hopefully, you will find your guests' lives to be interesting because of the issues and information they provide, the research you've done, and a desire to share this with viewers.

Exercises

1 Watch and compare interview segments on early morning programs such as *Today* and *Good Morning America*. Take notes and answer the following questions:

a. How long are the segments and how many questions are asked?

b. What types of questions are asked (open-ended, closed-ended,etc.)?

c. Are there stylistic differences between the interviewers on these programs?

2 Observe an interview program with longer interview segments, such as *Charlie Rose* or *Larry King Live*. Note how many topics are discussed and how the host adapts to the responses of the guest.

3 Choose a person of interest to a wide demographic for a five- to ten-minute interview. Prepare for the interview by doing the necessary research and question writing. After taping the interview, ask yourself if this is the kind of interview you see on local or national television. Isolate your strengths and areas for improvement along with the interest level of the guest.

4 See if you can observe an interview show at a local television station. Watch what goes on before and after as well as during the interview. How does the host relate to the guest? Does the host prepare or coach the guest before the interview? What happens during breaks?

5 Compare notes with other students, colleagues, friends, and instructors after watching several host/interviewers. Do you find common likes and dislikes?

6 Discuss in class or with friends why shows such as *Jerry Springer* and *Jenny Jones* seem to be popular. Do you think these shows will last? Give specific reasons for your answers.

INTERVIEW

Lori Hillman

Former *CBS Evening News* Producer

Field interviews, as you will see in upcoming chapters, have their own set of challenges for performers. Here Lori Hillman talks about the importance of **soundbites,** the video quotations in which we hear the person being interviewed, in news and feature story structure. Lori was a producer of *The CBS Evening News with Dan Rather* and has worked on numerous segments with Bill Moyers.

Question: What can beginning interviewers do to make their stories better and easier to edit?

Lori Hillman: Usually people ask the right questions and they have their little lists, but in many cases the beginning interviewer is thinking about the question more than the answer. He or she is not listening for soundbites. If you come back and you've asked all the right questions but you don't have the answer to put on television, you don't have the interview. This happens with inexperience and you figure it out as you go along, but you have to listen for soundbites.

You may have to ask the question ten times because all that really matters is what you have when you go back to the station. It doesn't matter that you're asking lots of questions in the field and sounding really smart: You can't assume the camera person is shooting all the pictures you will want. You have to be really involved with what's being shot, what's being said on tape, and what you can use. If you come back to your office and you don't have what it takes to put a story together, you don't have story. You may have all the information in your head, but unfortunately in television that's not good enough.

Q: So as simple as it may seem, it sounds like you have to be a good listener.

LH: You have to hear your soundbites. It's tricky, because you are thinking about your next question. You want to come across as being a professional, intelligent, journalist, so you have your own perform-ance issues during an interview. You're making an impression on someone else and some interviews involve very presti-gious people who know a whole lot more about the subject than you do. You are trying to have a conversation with the per-son, because that is how you get your best soundbites but you're also trying to un-derstand a very complicated issue while eliciting a soundbite.

Not much of an interview works on tel-evision. You come back and you think you heard the bite, but there are long pauses and people stumbling, that's just how people talk. Many people are not as elo-quent as we would like them to be when we turn the camera on. Other people are so articulate when you turn the camera on them that we call them a "walking soundbite."

It happens where you have so much that is good and you can only choose one or two bites. But usually you're sitting there and you're saying "Oh, just say . . . keep going . . . " and you want people to end "down" instead of ending "up" with their pitch because that sounds awkward.

Q: Is there a problem with people like politicians who are used to speaking in soundbites sounding natural?

LH: Yes, that's true, although personally I would rather have to deal with that than not have something in a 10- to 15-second form that I can use on television. I would rather deal with someone sounding too slick than not slick enough, depending on the story. If you're doing a homeless story, you're not looking for slick soundbites, you're looking for what's real. But for a spokesperson kind of soundbite, you want someone who can speak in complete sen-tences with some content.

RATINGS POINTER

HGTV host and former KDKA and KPIX reporter Craig Miller agrees with Lori Hillman concerning the importance of listening for sound-bites during interviews. He uses the bites to construct the story. Miller says that when he gets back to the station he listens to all the inter-views and puts together what he calls a "bite sheet"—a list of the best statements from all the interviews. Then he puts the bites in order on a sheet of paper and uses that as the outline for editing the story. Next he writes the narrative that connects the soundbites together. Miller believes that soundbites are the "lifeblood" of the story. ★ ★ ★ ★

CHAPTER NINE

Being Interviewed on Television

There's an old media joke that goes, "You know it's going to be a bad day when you come into your office and see Mike Wallace and a *60 Minutes* crew sitting in the waiting room." You may never be on *60 Minutes*, but as we have seen, many professionals appear on television at some point in their careers. Consider, too, that interviewers and newscasters such as Tom Brokaw and Larry King often appear as guests on programs other than their own.

This chapter covers what you need to know when you're sitting in "the other chair" as a guest on an interview or talk program, including information on preparation, appearance, how to answer questions, and appropriate behavior following the program. If you've read the preceding chapters, you have a head start on being a credible guest. This chapter will extend and build upon that information and give you some strategies for responding to questions.

Knowing how to appear as a credible guest not only helps you in this role; it also helps you to be a better interviewer and host because you know how the guest may act and answer questions. Employment interviews via teleconferencing will be discussed later in this chapter.

Some people feel threatened by the prospect of appearing on television; however, the video interview provides some major benefits to the individual and organization he or she represents, for example:

- You can reach more people with free publicity about your organization. Television is the most influential medium for reaching large numbers of people. Even an early Sunday morning public affairs program reaches thousands of viewers.
- The credibility of your organization is enhanced by a television appearance. Viewers perceive that this organization must be important because it appears on television. The medium provides a halo effect.

- You can set the record straight by correcting wrong information or misperceptions about you and your organization; and you can strike first by getting your position to the public before the competition presents its information.

- If you don't get your message out, it may not get out at all. There's also the possibility that if it does get out, it will be inaccurate. This is your opportunity to present your message unfiltered by gatekeepers.

- You can build relationships with interviewers, increasing the possibility of future appearances on their programs. Hosts are always looking for interesting, confident, and credible guests for repeat appearances.

For these and other reasons the television interview can be a powerful way to communicate information to a large audience.

Types of Interviews

Three of the most common interview situations are the following:

■ **Hosted Programs**   The majority of interview programs you may encounter are hosted programs. As discussed at length in Chapter 8, they range from early morning information and news programs to late night entertainment talk shows, usually with a single host (although programs like *The View* may have multiple hosts). In most cases you will have time to prepare for these programs by analyzing the show, host, audience, and other elements. Host types range from friendly to confrontational. Later in this chapter you will learn what you need to do to prepare for various hosts.

RATINGS POINTER

On a multiple-host interview show, guests sometimes become confused regarding eye contact when responding to questions. Do you look at the person who asked the question? Do you look at both or all the hosts? Or do you look between the hosts, as some guests seem to do?

You can start by looking at the person who asked the question, then make contact with the other host(s), and finish your response by looking again at the questioner. This makes the response seem like natural conversation. The other benefit of this technique is that if a host asks a tough or hostile question, you don't get into a closed loop with him or her. ★ ★ ★ ★

■ **Mediated Interviews**   ABC's *Nightline* provides examples of a **mediated interview:** The host conducts the interview with multiple guests in different locations. This presents special challenges because the people involved see each other over monitors instead of face to face. Employment interviews and some forms of distance learning are other examples of mediated interviews. Consultants may be asked questions by viewers in multiple locations; instructors teach students at multiple sites or even in their homes.

RATINGS POINTER

Experienced guests on mediated interview programs know that they must maintain contact with the camera lens during the entire interview for two reasons: (1) The lens is the eyes of the interviewer and the viewers and (2) mediated interviews often use a split screen format. Many times viewers see two or more of the interviewees on the screen. Make the assumption that you may appear onscreen at any time and maintain good eye-to-lens contact. ★ ★ ★ ★

Mediated, split-screen interviews such as ABC's Nightline require interviewees to look at the camera at all times.

■ **Press Conferences**   Press conferences provide different challenges because numerous people ask questions in quick succession on a variety of topics. The venue may be in a studio or on location. Respondents have to think on their feet, often under great pressure. The president's press secretary and a company spokesperson addressing the press during a crisis are two examples of individuals who respond to questions under fire.

Here again, begin and end your eye contact with the questioner, but include eye contact with others during the body of your response. When the questioning gets tough or heated, this technique is especially valuable in helping you not appear confrontational vis-à-vis the questioner. Another challenge during press conferences is maintaining concentration despite distractions.

Once the interview type has been determined, you can begin your preparation process.

Preparing to Be Interviewed

Chapter 8 explained that all interviewers must research and prepare information about guests before the interview. Conversely, guests, too, must prepare to be interviewed. Many inexperienced guests neglect to do this, assuming that they will simply answer whatever the host asks. Guests should consider the following points before interviews:

■ **Determine the Purpose of the Interview**   The host, or perhaps the producer in charge of developing interesting show ideas, will have had a specific reason for asking you to appear on the program. In either case, find out why you are being invited and what the program's purpose is.

Interview programs are more than two people aimlessly talking. Those involved with the program believe you have something to say and are giving you an opportunity to share your knowledge. Sometimes you may be unqualified to speak on the requested topic or for the suggested purpose. Be honest with the contact person if you can't speak knowledgeably about the topic, and if possible, recommend other, better-qualified guests. Suggest other areas you may be able to address on future programs, and tell the contact person that you would enjoy appearing on the program to discuss one of these topics.

■ **Develop Your Agenda**   Your agenda may not match the host's reasons for inviting you on the program. A politician's motive for appearing on a program is the desire to be elected to public office, whereas the host's interest is remaining objective while finding out the candidate's positions on various issues. Use the program as an opportunity to communicate *your* message. Don't assume that you and the host will be on the same page or that the host will ask you questions that forward your agenda. Be proactive and take control of getting out the information you want viewers to hear.

■ **Ask, "Why Me?"**   Closely linked to finding out the purpose of the interview is determining why *you* have been asked to appear on this program. In some cases this is obvious. In other cases it may be less so because of the availability of other experts. Determine the expectations the producer and/ or host have of you concerning what will be learned during the interview.

■ **Who Is the Host?**   Find out who is conducting the interview. Do you know the person, in person or by reputation? Is the host a newscaster, reporter, or public affairs person at a local station? What is his or her style of interviewing? Is the interviewer fair-minded and objective or known to have an "agenda"? If there is more than one interviewer, do their views and styles contrast? Is the person a veteran interviewer or relatively new on the scene? Can you find out any of the interviewer's interests so that you can develop examples that play to those interests? Does the interviewer use humor or take a no-nonsense approach? Also, does the interviewer have a constituency or does he or she appeal to a particular demographic? If so, how will you tailor your message to appeal to this group? Answering these questions will provide you with the foundation you need before appearing on the program.

If time permits, you should watch the interviewer in action before your appearance. Tape the show and study it, taking notes as you watch. You may not be able to do this; for example, you may be called late in the afternoon for an interview that will appear on that evening's local news. But you can still ask friends and associates what they know about your interviewer.

If it appears that you may be interviewed on a regular basis, you should watch a variety of programs and interviewers so that you can be familiar with them if they call. Most experienced politicians and other public figures know interviewers by their names and styles.

Finally, try to determine the interviewer's level of expertise. Will you have to do additional research on your topic because of the interviewer's knowledge in that area?

■ **Length of Interview**   A practical consideration is finding out how long the program or interview segment will be. This helps you determine the length of your responses and what you can cover within the time limit. In short interviews you have to prioritize what to say so that you adhere to your agenda, communicating the most important points to the audience. It is easy to let the time pass without mentioning the key points you want to make. Write these out before the interview and make sure you cover them.

Think in terms of economical word choice; can you say in 15 seconds what some people take 30 seconds to say? If so, this will make you provide more quotable material for soundbites (more about this later). You may find that three-minute interviews are harder than half-hour interviews because questions and topic areas come so fast. Also, you'll find that your perception of time speeds up during most interviews. Many guests ask "Is that it?" following their segments because of the nervous energy they used up during the program.

■ **Demographics**   The importance of demographic research has been discussed throughout this book. Learn as much as you can about the audience's average age, gender, educational background, political issues, and opinions concerning your topic(s). Find out if there are certain "hot button" issues for the audience and if you need to prepare counterarguments for them.

Try to create a complete demographic profile for the viewing area of the program. This is difficult, especially if you appear on a network program with national and even international coverage, but you can still get an idea of the types of viewers the program attracts. Find out if the program attracts more females or males, if it skews younger or older, and any other general demographic information that is available.

Take into consideration that even when you appear on a local program, cable coverage may mean that the program is viewed in other areas. For example, there are cable systems throughout northern California that carry both San Francisco and Sacramento stations. Superstation WGN in Chicago is carried on cable systems throughout the nation. In these cases you have to determine who is your primary audience, that is, the people you most want to reach with your message. If you're appearing on a public affairs program in Chicago and your goal is to influence local voters on a referendum, you should obviously focus on the local viewers. In fact, viewers from other areas who are channel surfing and happen to hit your program will probably switch channels in a few seconds unless they happen to be from Chicago.

The more demographic research you are able to do the greater your probability of success. Remember that your host will have done a significant amount of demographics homework.

RATINGS POINTER

Years ago, when there were three to six local stations in a market, it was relatively easy to do a demographic profile of the audience. Superstations and cable have made demographic analysis both easier and more difficult.

You may have heard the term "superstations" and not really understood what they are. Superstations are local on-air stations, such as WTBS Channel 17 in Atlanta and WGN Channel 9 in Chicago, that uplink for satellite distribution to cable systems throughout the country. If you've watched these stations, you know that they specialize in movies and sports but also carry local public affairs and news (especially WGN). Even low-budget Sunday morning public affairs programs on these stations can be viewed by a national audience.

Cable provides channels and programs for more specific audiences, often called "narrowcasting." For example, the slogan and branding strategy for **Lifetime** cable service is "Television for women"; **Oxygen** started in 2000 as another cable service for women, providing numerous interview and other talk shows.

Although superstations and cable services present some challenges in demographic analysis, they also provide potentially larger audiences for your message. ★ ★ ★ ★

Visual Support   A number of successful interview programs with intelligent hosts and interesting guests have proved that watching people talking to one another can be compelling. Still, we know that television is a visual medium, so you should try to add visual interest when possible. Photos, objects, and videotape can increase interest and clarify your information. Producers usually appreciate any visual support you can provide as long as you give them advance notice that you want to include visuals in the program. As noted earlier, showing up unannounced with visuals can provide problems for the technical staff because they then have no time to prepare the visuals or don't have the equipment to show them. The following are actual examples of occasions when guests wanted to use visuals but couldn't do so for technical reasons:

- A stamp collector brought part of his collection to the studio, but the stamps were too small to be shot by the camera during the interview. There was not enough preparation time to shoot the stamps in advance and put them in an electronic still storage (ESS) system.

- On numerous occasions authors and musicians brought a copy of a book or CD to the studio intending to show viewers the cover. If they had sent the object to the studio sooner it could have been shot and loaded into the ESS for a better close-up.

- Politicians came to the studio with charts and visual aids that did not meet the specifications of good television visuals (too small, too detailed, vertically based, on white background, etc.).

- A fashion designer brought many dresses to the studio and wanted all of them displayed during the interview. She had no practical way to hang or display them, and there were limitations on the set due to lighting.

- Guests wanted to use Powerpoint presentations during a segment, not knowing that the graphics do not reproduce well over the video system.

- Interviewees brought videotape that couldn't be used because of poor quality or format problems.

All of these problems would have been easy to solve had the host or producer of the program been contacted in advance. Your contact can give you information about what you can use and how the visuals can be adapted for television. If you want to use videotape as b-roll during a segment, ask about the playback possibilities and whether you should send the tape to the producer in advance to be dubbed or "bumped up" to another format that will improve its quality.

Space and movement can also be problems. Sometimes guests want to demonstrate movement such as dance or exercise, but space and camera mobility restrict them from doing so. Discuss what you would like to demonstrate with the host or producer before the show so that the crew can adjust for lighting and camera movement.

A basic rule regarding visual or other support, therefore, is that if there is anything you want to do besides sit in a chair and talk with the host, you should discuss it with the host or producer before the interview. That way, there will be no surprises for those involved with the production.

Keep in mind that many public affairs programs, especially those seen early on weekend mornings, are done on a sustaining basis; in other words, they receive no support from commercial sponsors and the programs make no money for the station. Rather they are produced as a public service for the community and enhance the image of the station, especially when its license comes up for renewal with the **Federal Communications Commission (FCC).**

Since these programs are not money makers for the station, executives sometimes take an assembly-line approach to producing them. Public affairs programs are often produced as quickly as possible with little preparation time or opportunities for breaks so that the studio is available for other productions. The hosts of these programs are often news anchors or reporters who are sandwiching interview taping between their other responsibilities. For these reasons, make everyone's job as easy as possible and keep up with the pace of the production process.

■ The Interview's Setting

Find out where the interview will take place. Will it be in the studio or on location? What kind of furniture and set pieces are there, and what is the background color of the set? Is it taped or live? Are other guests invited to the interview, and if so, should you know anything about them? Also, where do you need to be and when should you be there? These practical questions will help you adapt to the interview setting.

Knowing the physical setting of the interview is important so that you can look your best either in the studio or on location. As discussed in Chapter 3, you should choose clothing and makeup depending upon the background colors of the set and lighting. You can take a couple of sets of clothes to the studio if you have doubts about colors, patterns, and so on, but following the guidelines given in Chapter 3 concerning clothing should eliminate most problems.

If the interview is shot on location, for example in your office, you may want to do some basic cleaning and straightening before the crew comes for the shoot. How many times have you seen an interviewee's office and desk that looked as if they had been hit by a storm? Consider the metamessage an unkempt office sends to viewers regarding your organizational skills.

Another consideration is whether the program is taped or live. Obviously, a live program means that you will be seen at the time of your interview, allowing you to deal with issues and events up to the minute. A taped interview means that you will have to consider the viewing date and time. As mentioned previously, you may need to adjust your delivery style for the airtime—what works for a midday talk show may be too energetic for an early Sunday morning public affairs program.

You may be shooting a seasonal program, for example one with a Christmas theme, weeks in advance of the airdate. Adjust your thinking and mood to be consistent with the airtime of the program.

If other guests are involved, you should research their positions on the program's topics. Programs often book guests with opposing viewpoints, providing a variety of opinions and potential conflict. Basic research can assist you in determining counterarguments to the other guests' positions. Of course if there are multiple guests you must share the interview time, leaving you less time to get your message to viewers, so remember to think in terms of prioritizing the most important points and keeping them brief.

Finally, make sure of the time and location of the interview. The checklist for the interviewer given in Chapter 8 included a reminder that he or she should give you basic information concerning where and when the interview will take place.

Watch the Program before You Appear Whenever possible, watch an edition of the program before the taping or air date. You will become familiar not only with the host's style but also with the overall tone, and this knowledge will help you understand what approach to use and how to adapt your message.

If the show is entertainment oriented, lighten your approach a bit from how you would behave during a public affairs program. You'll also develop a higher comfort level by being familiar with the format.

Read your local newspaper before appearing on the program, because the host may ask you questions based on recent events applying to the topic. Reading the newspaper is especially important if your interview takes place in another city; get up to speed on important local issues. Also, if this is an out-of-town interview and time permits, see if the producer will send you a videotape of a past program so that you can familiarize yourself with the show's format and style.

Suggest Your Introduction This advice comes under the category of controlling what you can control. Once the interview starts, you have little control over the interviewer. An author recently told the story of how a producer did a pre-interview with him before the program and asked intelligent, detailed questions. The producer had read the author's book and underlined excerpts from it. Despite the fact that the producer had given the show's host information from this pre-interview, however, the host chose a different line of questioning. This surprised the author, who was expecting the same kinds of questions asked by the producer. The host's questions were less sophisticated and detailed than the producer's, necessitating a major shift in thinking for the guest.

You can help determine the direction of the interview if you prepare a one-page information sheet with your biography and topic in question. At the top of the sheet you should list your name, along with a phonetic spelling if it is difficult to pronounce. For example, the name "Dreibelbis" would appear as "Dra-BELL-biz" so that the host would have an easier time pronouncing it correctly. Also include information such as phone numbers or an e-mail address in case the host or producer wants to contact you.

Give your affiliation and position on the topic. Avoid jargon, acronyms, buzz words, and terminology that may be second nature to you but not to your host. Make sure you include a statement about the impact of your information on the audience and why they should care. It's surprising how much of this content hosts use in introductions. Include a list of talking points or areas for discussion. Simplify technical information or complex issues.

Many interviewers will use your information sheet as a starting point, because it offers a shortcut in their preparation process. Hosts generally have other responsibilities, and time is at a premium for them in preparing for your interview. Some hosts may avoid using your information sheet, but most will appreciate your efforts. Do not provide questions, though, since hosts sometimes perceive this as an attempt to control the interview.

■ Anticipate Questions and Develop Responses   Good interviewees anticipate what will be asked and how they will answer questions. First try to find out general topics and questions. The host, reporter, or producer will usually give you some general direction for the interview, although it is unlikely that he or she will share specific questions with you. Try asking for some sample questions to see if you can get a better idea concerning the interview's focus and direction.

Anticipate difficult questions, keeping in mind that tough questions are not necesarily hostile ones. Some of the most difficult questions may come from interviewers who agree with your position but feel they should play devil's advocate to ensure balance and fairness.

On the other hand, some interviewers are known for their hard-hitting or even antagonistic style and questions. Write down every tough question you can and phrase it in the most negative language imaginable. Practice your responses to these questions before the interview, and whenever possible do a videotape practice session. Review the tape not only for your responses but also for your nonverbal reactions.

■ Know How to Contact Your Interviewer   Carry a cell phone and make sure you have a way to contact your interviewer on the day of the interview. You should also know the numbers for roadside assistance services such as AAA in case you have problems with your car. There is no reason to let automotive problems keep you from showing up at the studio.

■ **Think Soundbites**   **Soundbites** are the short statements we see and hear on news stories that capture our attention and are immediately quotable. Your 20-minute interview with a reporter may be reduced to a 6-second soundbite on the evening news. Soundbites have become shorter over the last 40 years. In the early 1970s soundbites ran as long as 45 seconds; now most run about 6 to 7 seconds.

Soundbites are video/audio quotations adding impact to stories. During the 2000 presidential campaign, some political observers compared Democratic vice-presidential candidate Joseph Lieberman with Republican presidential candidate George W. Bush in regard to his political positions. Lieberman responded that comparing him with Bush was like saying that a veterinarian and a taxidermist are alike because in both cases you get your dog back. Statements like this become soundbites.

We usually associate soundbites with field or remote stories known as **packages.** These stories are recorded and edited in advance and sometimes last less than a minute and a half. Soundbites can be lifted from in-studio interviews and used later during news, public affairs, or other programs. Newspapers, radio, and other media may quote memorable statements or use soundbites. And people do remember them. Most of the enduring statements made in political campaigns over the last 20 years ("Read my lips—no new taxes"; "A giant sucking sound"; "It's the economy, stupid") were soundbites.

For these and reasons mentioned earlier in this chapter, the soundbite can be a persuasive tool. In her book *Soundbites: A Business Guide for Working with the Media* former television news anchor, reporter, and now media consultant Kathy Kerchner gives the following criteria for what gets "soundbited" by news and information sources:

■ **Personal emotions and experiences.** Viewers are interested in what others think and feel, so don't be afraid to talk about personal emotions when appropriate. A mother whose child was returned after being kidnapped for several days said she felt "as if she had come back from the dead." When a new stadium opened, a baseball team owner said he "felt like a little boy again."

■ **Specific examples.** Avoid generalities and cite specifics. Kerchner uses the example of former House Minority Leader Newt Gingrich when he said, "You cannot maintain civilization with 12 year olds having children, with 13 year olds killing each other, with 17 year olds dying of AIDS, with 17 year olds getting diplomas they can't even read." Viewers process imagery and specifics better than they do abstract information and concepts.

■ **Contemporary references**. These are statements based on popular culture such as films, commercial slogans, television shows, and so on. After winning a particularly difficult race, a local politician made reference to the popular CBS television show *Survivor* by saying, "Now I know how that last person on the island must have felt."

■ **Analogies.** Analogies are another way to add color and impact to your comments. Kerchner cites an example from the O. J. Simpson trial when a Court TV camera accidentally showed the face of a juror during the coverage. Defense attorney F. Lee Bailey expressed outrage at the mistake, saying, "If they had been flying a plane, they'd have killed 300 people." Bailey made his point in the courtroom and the quotation was carried that night on many television newscasts.

■ **Cliches**. The skillful use of cliches can be effective in emphasizing your point, although you need to be careful that you don't overuse them. A local mayor admitting to being "between a rock and a hard place" regarding a policy helps to humanize the situation by showing the struggle in the decision-making process.

■ **One-liners.** We tend to remember good one-liners for years after they've been spoken. During the 1988 vice-presidential debates when Dan Quayle compared himself to John F. Kennedy, Senator Lloyd Bentsen responded by saying "I knew Jack Kennedy, and Senator, you're no Jack Kennedy." Others modified the statement by saying "You're no (fill in the blank)" for years after the debate.

■ **Absolutes.** These can be the "best," the "most," the "worst," or "the most dangerous." Think in terms of what was discussed earlier in this book regarding qualitative significance.

■ **Proportional numbers.** This is sometimes called humanizing statistics and is similar to the old commercial claims, "Eight out of ten doctors recommend. . . . " Round numbers to a figure that is easy for the audience to remember; for example, instead of saying, "There were 68 competitors at the Olympic track trials," say "Nearly 70 competitors took part in the Olympic track trials." Use percentages when appropriate to clarify statistics.

■ **Quote the opposition.** Borrow a page from politicians and sports coaches who love to quote the opposition to build their case. Has the opposition ever said something about you that was unfair? Has the opposition ever agreed with or praised you? Make sure you are not quoting statements out of context, or else the audience could perceive you as unfair and lacking credibility.

Verify that the person actually said what you're quoting him or her as having said. In an age of Internet news reporting as well as many television and other news services competing against one another, there seem to be more inaccuracies than in past years. Don't put yourself in the position of having to issue a retraction.

■ **Humor.** Humor can be used with any of the previously mentioned techniques. The advantages of humor have been mentioned earlier in the book, but it must be appropriate and in good taste or it could backfire. There's no room for racist, sexist, or other politically incorrect humor. Assess whether you use humor well or whether you should use other emotional appeals instead.

Former San Francisco '49ers coach George Seifert used humor effectively during an interview following a '49ers loss. A reporter asked him if he thought his team had played with enough emotion. Seifert responded by saying that he felt emotion wasn't the problem: "There was a lot of emotion at the Alamo, but everyone died." Ronald Reagan made his age a nonissue during the 1984 presidential debates against Walter Mondale when he said, "I won't make age an issue of this campaign. I promise not to exploit for political purposes my opponent's youth and inexperience."

■ Outline Your Response

Consider each response you give to be a "mini-speech." Develop a positive point or two and then give an example to illustrate the point(s). Anticipate the kinds of questions that will be asked, then outline your responses. Don't wait until you're in the guest chair to think about possible responses to questions.

On the other hand, you want to sound natural and unrehearsed, so strive for a conversational style. Visualize a situation in which you are telling a friend some information or a story that is well known to you. Practice your answers out loud to hear how you sound. Doing this will also help you memorize key facts.

■ Clothing

Clothing and appearance were discussed in previous chapters. Many people like to practice in their performance clothes to get a sense of how they will feel during the interview. If you don't wear business clothes on a daily basis, you may want to practice in these clothes if you will be wearing them on the program.

Your clothing choice may depend on your job or profession; for example, a highway patrol officer who was interviewed concerning road rage wore her uniform for the interview. Zookeepers bringing animals on the set wear their uniforms as well.

■ **Visualize a Good Performance**   Just as athletes visualize themselves making a free throw or clearing the bar, you should visualize a good performance. Be message oriented and think about the goals you want to accomplish during the interview. Interviews are opportunities for you to share information with the audience—opportunities that your competitors may not have. Remember that those involved with the program think that you and your message are interesting or else they would not have extended the invitation.

Following your preparation, you are ready to make the trip to the studio.

At the Studio

Depending on the size of the facility, there may be a **green room** where guests wait until it is time for them to go on the set. Many green rooms have television monitors so that you can see the show in progress or watch production personnel preparing the studio. Watch the monitor to get an idea of the interviewer's style and what is going on in the show; you can then make reference to what the other guests have said during your interview.

You may be offered something to eat or drink while waiting. Know what you can safely eat and drink before performance; be careful of foods that could cause a dry throat or indigestion.

Use the time in the green room to practice some of the suggestions given in Chapter 2 to minimize performance anxiety. Talk to others in the room to warm up your voice, and don't forget to check yourself in a mirror to make sure everything is straight and where it should be. If you have long hair, make sure it is out of your face. Viewers may see little or nothing of your face from certain camera angles if you don't brush or secure your hair in some way.

If your producer or interviewer is available before the segment, try to meet with them and cover any last-minute details. You may need to change some of your points and strategies if the focus of the interview has shifted since you last spoke. Be friendly with everyone involved with the production, keeping comments positive regarding the program and other guests.

■ **Cameras**   Once you're on the set, check to see how many cameras there are and where they are positioned. Most studio interviews use three cameras: the camera behind you will shoot over your shoulder for a close-up of the host, while the camera behind the host will shoot toward you. This technique (known as **cross shooting**) provides good shots of both you and the host and avoids profiles. A third camera is positioned between the other two and takes **cover shots:** wider angle shots of both of you on the set. This camera can move or **truck** to one side or another for different angle shots from time to time.

If there are only two cameras in the studio it is a more challenging task for the director to shoot you and the host. The director is often restricted to shooting close-ups with one camera on you and the other on the host but may decide to truck one of the cameras over to get a cover shot for a bit more variety. Don't anticipate which camera is shooting you. Keep your eye con-

Directors will usually cross-shoot cameras for the best angle shots of performers during interview shows.

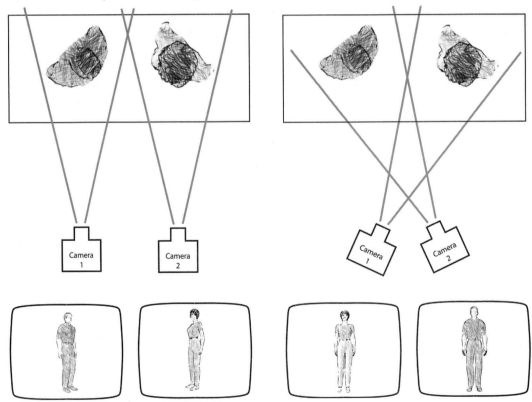

tact and concentration on the host as you would in normal conversation. This will also keep you from being distracted by cameras moving in your line of sight or peripheral vision.

Monitors
You should resist the temptation of sneaking a peek at the studio **monitor** during the shooting. (But if you do catch a glimpse, remember that the shot you see on the monitor is not a mirror image, so an attempt to brush your hair out of your face may find you reaching on the wrong side of your head.)

Look at the monitor if you are describing b-roll that you've brought with you to the studio. Be familiar with your b-roll so that you can anticipate its ending and can make a smooth transition from the monitor back to the host.

During live shows you can look at the monitor during commercial breaks to get an idea when the break is nearing its end and the program is about to continue. This way you're not caught off guard. The floor manager should also give you cues about when the program is resuming.

Sitting
As discussed in Chapter 5, your main goal is to be comfortable without being too comfortable. Some additional tips:

- If you have a choice between a sofa and a chair, choose the chair. Maintaining good posture is difficult when sitting on a sofa because it is easy to sink into it. Find out if a chair is an option.
- See if you feel uncomfortable in the chair because it is too low or too deep. Smaller people can appear to be swallowed by the chair. Studios are notorious for having furniture that still looks good on camera but has seen better days in terms of comfort. Ask for a cushion if you need one.
- Make sure you don't swivel or move the chair back and forth if it has wheels. Be careful of nervous energy being transmitted through your legs and feet, causing chair movement.

Sound Checks
Chapter 6 covered sound check basics and warned against saying, "Testing, one, two, three. . . ." Use the **sound check** to your advantage by giving what might be your first response or a point you want to make. This is another opportunity to warm up your voice while practicing some of your content. Remember to use the same volume during the sound check that you'll use during the interview.

Don't say anything during the sound check that you wouldn't want others to hear. Guests often assume that the videotape is not recording just because the production hasn't started, and there are numerous accounts of embarrassing moments for guests who have said something inappropriate. Don't say anything you wouldn't want quoted after the interview. During the 2000 presidential campaign, George W. Bush was heard referring to a reporter as "a major league A******" into a mic he thought was closed. The comment became fodder for soundbites and late night monologues for days following the event.

Following all your preparation both in and out of the studio, you're finally ready for the interview to begin.

During the Interview

▧ **The Introduction**   Just as for the host, the first ten seconds of the interview are crucial for you as the guest to establish a positive first impression. Most interview segments begin with the host looking at the camera and introducing the guest. During the introduction, the guest is often shot with a close-up. Inexperienced guests make the mistake of looking down or off camera during the intro because they don't think that they are appearing onscreen. Establish eye contact with the host as soon as you know the tape is rolling, and work on the assumption that there could be a close-up of you at any time during the interview.

The same is true with remote and field interviews, when it is often more difficult to maintain eye contact with the interviewer because of distractions. You often see interviewees looking around at other people or events until the interviewee asks them a question. Make eye contact with your interviewer as soon as you know the interview is about to begin.

Mediated interviews, such as ABC's *Nightline*, in which the interviewee may be in a different location, present their own set of challenges. You must maintain eye contact with the camera lens as if it were the eyes of the interviewer. Hearing can be a problem, because you'll be listening through an earpiece or IFB system. During your introduction it is important to make eye contact with the lens because you are visible to viewers at home.

Nonverbal expressiveness should be positive and appropriate to the situation. Some people wait until the first question to seem nonverbally involved with the questioner, missing an opportunity for a good first impression. Anticipate that the host may give you a basic greeting following the introduction, such as "Welcome to the show." Have a short pleasant response prepared in case this happens. Try to anticipate what the first question might be and have your response ready.

■ **The "Heart" of the Interview**   Once the questions begin, you can expect conflict in some interviews. Many news and public affairs directors believe that conflict grabs and maintains audience interest. The conflict may not come from a disagreement with you but instead be issue oriented, stemming from some societal problem such as abuse of the elderly or road rage. It is your job to provide answers that are entertaining and dramatic as well as informative. There are also several specifics you should remember during the questioning:

■ **Maintain control.**   Whatever the interviewer's style or situation, you are responsible for yourself. Don't let yourself feel rushed; maintain your own pace and focus. Keep your main points and the message that you want to communicate in focus. Never become angry or antagonistic toward the interviewer; in volatile situations the audience often sides with the person who seems composed and reasonable.

■ **Trade negative for positive.**   If you get a negative question, don't repeat the negative wording. For example, if the question is, "So I guess your airline is to blame for its poor safety record," don't respond with "No, we don't have a poor safety record." Viewers will remember the negative words of "blame" and "poor." Develop the most positive statement you can while still being truthful.

■ **Buy time to think.**   Guests often feel that they must respond to questions as soon as they are asked and before organizing their thoughts. This feeling often results in incomplete, inaccurate, or garbled responses. Trying to stall or buy time with cliches like "That's a really good question" or "I'm glad you brought that up" doesn't work because hosts and viewers read through them. You don't have to respond immediately. Remember that pauses create anticipation for hosts and viewers, putting you in a powerful position as long as you don't use them too often. Gain a couple of seconds by pausing, another second by using the host's name, and at least two more seconds by saying, "I think what's at issue here is . . ."

Make sure you don't sound condescending to the host and viewers by saying, "As I said earlier . . ." or "I thought I answered that question. . . ." The host may be asking or repeating a question for purposes of review or clarification. Avoid putting the host in an inferior position.

■ **Silence is golden.**   Don't feel the need to keep talking if the host is silent or doesn't ask you a question. It is the host's or reporter's responsibility to keep the interview moving, so don't worry about what you perceive are awkward silences. The host may be trying to get you to say more or make a statement you are not ready to make. When you're finished speaking, stop, and make sure you end on a definite note. Some people with rising inflection at the ends of sentences can fool hosts into thinking that they are going to continue. Make sure the host knows you have concluded, so that he or she can ask the next question.

■ **Use humor when appropriate.** The value of humor was mentioned in the section on soundbites. Humor research shows that it has effective, persuasive appeal because it acts as a yielding factor. In other words, humor gets the audience to let their guard down and accept what you have to say, while defusing stressful or intense moments. It also acts as a breather for the audience. You don't have to be a stand-up comedian; some very serious people make effective use of humor. Spontaneous, timely, and relevant humor makes for a more interesting interview. Don't force humor into the situation, though; it can backfire. Collect funny quotations, stories, or other material with universal appeal for use in a variety of situations. Some of the best use of humor doesn't come from people who are naturally funny, but rather from people who are well read and use humor in a natural way.

■ **Build bridges.** Bridging takes you from a question the reporter has asked to an answer that forwards your agenda. Be careful that you don't ignore the host's question by "answering *a* question and not *the* question." Acknowledge the host's question, make a transitional bridge, then give your agenda-making statement.

For example, during a recent nurses' strike, a spokesperson for the nurses' union was asked, "Isn't it true that many hospital patients will be victims of the strike?" The spokesperson answered by saying, "It's unfortunate that some patients may not get the care they deserve; however, nurses have been underpaid in this city's hospital system for the last five years while also facing long hours and a nursing shortage. This is a chronic problem that impacts the long-term health care in this city." The spokesperson was able to acknowledge the question and make a basic transition to the agenda statement that nurses have been underpaid and that this situation has a long-term impact on health care. Here are some other basic bridges:

"Let me give you a little background information . . . "
"You might think that is the case; however . . ."
"Let's look at the entire picture instead of the small piece . . ."
"Another thing to consider is . . ."
"The real significance of those numbers is . . ."

As you become more experienced as an interviewee, you will develop a natural use of bridges. The main point to remember is to get from where the host is to where you want to go with your response.

■ **Timing.** Media consultants differ as to whether or not guests should worry about time remaining in an interview. Some consultants say that timing is the responsibility of the host and the guest shouldn't be concerned with the clock. Others say that time management by the guest may be an advantage in the interview. Developing a sense of timing or an "internal clock" can assist you in making sure that your most important positive points are communicated to viewers and that you had the maximum impact. At first it may be difficult for you to concentrate on time while answering questions, but with experience you can soon develop the skill of knowing how much time is left in the interview.

During the show's last minute, you must give brief answers to questions. You will probably know that time is short because of a verbal cue from the host such as, "In the few seconds remaining can you tell us . . . ," or because of hand signals or time cards shown by the floor manager. Typical hand signals include the crossing of the arms or the thumb and forefinger forming the letter C for 30 seconds and a fist and arm raised in a "knocking the door" gesture for wrapping up the show. These signals can give you a general idea of time remaining in the show, but remember that time is the host's responsibility. If you look for the floor manager's cues or time cards, make sure you use peripheral vision so you aren't caught looking off camera

Your final statement should be positive and memorable. This is an excellent time to introduce a soundbite so that you create a powerful final impression. Fill as much of the last minute as possible without making it too difficult for the host to get out of the show on time. Doing this usually keeps the host from asking a follow-up question.

Many times at the end of the program viewers see the host and guest talking to each other as the credits roll. The audio operator cuts the mics so that nothing will heard on the set. Take your cue from the host as to what you should do and engage in quiet conversation during these final seconds.

Following the Interview

If you are one of several guests being interviewed during a program, you may have to move quickly off the set to allow the next guest time to get ready for the rest of the show. There may not be much time for you to interact with the host following your segment. If there is time, this is an excellent opportunity to create a positive final impression. Let the host know that you are available for other program opportunities in the future.

Request a videotape of the interview so that you can take it home and critique it. Sometimes production personnel will have a dub of the interview available for you before you leave the studio; in other cases, you may have to wait a few days for a copy to arrive by mail. Once you get your copy of the interview, make sure you critique it for the quality of your answers and your delivery. If you're doing interviews on a regular basis, keep video copies of your work and make comparisons between programs to check your progress. As always, try to look at your work objectively as if someone other than you were on the screen.

Portions of your interview may be edited and used for other sources as soundbites; for example, it is common to see soundbites used later on a newscast. Find out if any of your interview has appeared on another program and see what choices are made concerning edited segments and soundbites. This will help you in the future to determine the kind of answers you give and assess whether or not they are brief, colorful, and to the point. In cases where it is appropriate, send a thank you letter or note to the host and producer for inviting you to appear on the program. You may think that the host and producer should be thanking you for your time (and many times they will), but you have an opportunity here to extend the positive impression you've created. Remember too that you are representing not only yourself but your organization as well.

A Different Kind of Interview: The Video Employment Interview

Most of us have experienced the jitters and tension involved with a job interview. We worry about trying to remember information about employment history and answers we've prepared, while also trying to respond quickly to questions. Imagine having to do all of this while being televised during your interview.

Video job interviews are becoming more popular as part of the total employment interview process. Most experts agree that the final interview with an employer should be face to face. All other interviews will be by phone, videoconference, or on the Internet. Employers are finding that video interviews save time and money both for the company and interviewee.

Companies such as Cisco and ViewCast.com have developed software for Internet employment interviews that reduces some of the choppiness of movement and gestures. Corporate recruiters are saying that the time is here when employers may dial up candidates and interview them in a matter of minutes.

Chapter 12 presents particulars regarding the standard employment interview. Here are some suggestions to help you in the world of "virtual interviews." You should also follow these guidelines if you do Internet or teleconference presentations:

Check Your Space

As with any production, try to check out the space where you will be interviewing. Facilities for the video interview can range from multiple-camera studios to small rooms with one camera. Some office supply stores and copy services such as Kinkos have facilities to rent for video interviews.

Sit in the chair you will be using so that you will be comfortable and look your best during the interview (see Chapter 8 for a discussion of problems with various types of chairs). If there is a monitor and you can see yourself, look at your posture to ensure that you are sitting up straight without looking too stiff. Check to see if there is any other furniture in the camera's line of sight, and see if you can move it. Furniture can be a nonverbal barrier between you and those watching you.

Interviewees often forget to work with their microphones before the interview. Make sure you know what type of mic you will be using and do a sound check just as you would in other video productions. Some facilities have clip-on mics; others have a desk or mic pad (a small, disc-shaped microphone that sits flat on a table). Be conscious of mic placement so that you are close enough to the mic for optimal audio quality.

Videoconferencing facilities often have very sensitive microphones, so limit movement near the mic, such as tapping on a desk or shuffling papers. Noises that one would hardly notice in a live situation are distracting to those listening to video interviews. It's easy for the focus to shift from what you are saying to the sound of rustling papers or tapping fingers. Limit other distracting sounds by closing the door and turning off your pager and cell phone.

The importance of eye-to-lens contact with the camera has been emphasized throughout this book. Make sure you know where the camera that will be shooting you is and strive for maximum eye contact. Avoid looking off camera for long periods of time while you are thinking during a response.

Get to the facility in plenty of time so that you feel comfortable in the interview space. This allows you time to work with equipment and relax a bit. Real-life interviews are stressful, even without the added dimension of video equipment and trying to communicate with people at a distance.

Limit Your Movement   Despite rapid advancements in Internet streaming video and teleconferencing technologies, movement is still a problem on many delivery systems. Gestures often appear choppy and movement is delayed a bit. Limit movement and gestures even more than you would for a regular video performance. Excessive gesturing and movement makes you look out of control on most teleconferencing or streaming video systems. Gestures seem to work best if they are in front of your body instead of to your sides. Work on communicating energy through your eyes and face. If you have the opportunity to practice with the system you will be using, do so. Videotape your practice session and see which gestures seem to work the best for you.

Be Careful of Monitors   There may be a monitor in your interview space so that you can see the people you are talking to at the other location. This can help you in placing faces with voices; however, it can also cause you to look off camera and lose eye contact with your interviewers. Look at the monitor before you begin or early in the interview to see your interviewers; then focus on looking at the camera lens to maximize your eye contact. Concentrate on looking at the lens even when the interviewers are asking questions, instead of looking off camera at the monitor. Review the items discussed in earlier chapters regarding eye contact and use them when interviewing.

Lighting   Lighting, or the lack of it, can be a problem with video interviews. There may be shadows or too much lighting in some areas. Avoid shadows and dimly lighted areas; they will make you appear tired and older. Check to see which area has the best lighting and try to sit there.

You can control lighting by closing curtains and blinds. Rooms with portable lighting instruments or light dimmers provide more flexibility, so experiment with adjusting the lights before your interview. A white tablecloth can reflect light up for even lighting on your face. If the room has intense lights, you may want to bring some powder to cover any shiny areas of your face.

Clothing   People usually remember to "dress for success" when they go to an interview, but they may not realize how the video system "sees" what they wear. Suits and dresses that look great for a live interview may reflect light or have patterns that don't reproduce well. Review Chapter 3 before choosing your clothing for video interviews. The quality of the camera and equipment varies in different facilities, so err on the side of simplicity by avoiding questionable patterns, colors, and jewelry.

A white shirt may reflect too much light on your face, so choose an off-white or light blue shirt or blouse. Remember that pastels and colors in the middle of the gray scale seem to work best on video.

▓ **Watch What You Say before and after the Interview** Remember that you should be careful of what you say and do before and after interviews. Make the assumption that people can see and hear you at all times. When you come into the interview space, assume that the camera is on and the mic live. There are numerous stories of people who have walked into the facility and started saying or doing things that put them in a less than positive light. Don't do anything that you wouldn't want people watching to see, and be prepared before you enter the area. Adjust clothing and brush your hair off camera so that your interviewers will not see you doing this.

Mastering the video interview can give you a major advantage over people who are still trying to learn the basics of the technology. By adjusting your delivery for the medium, you will increase your chances of having an in-person interview. Remember that most final interviews leading to jobs are still done in person.

Rewind and Fade to Black

If you are invited to be a guest on an interview or news program, see it as an opportunity to deliver your message to a large video audience. Find out why you have been invited to appear on the program; then develop the central message and positive points you want listeners to hear. When sitting in the "other" chair as interviewee, try to remember the information discussed in Chapter 8 concerning you as the host or interviewer so that you can anticipate the host's questions and strategies. Take movement, eye contact, and clothing into consideration as well.

Video employment interviews are here to stay as a way of screening applicants while saving time and money. Transfer what you have learned about the way video affects your performance to the video interview to increase your comfort level during such interviews.

These days the question is not whether you will appear on a video interview, but when. The increasing number of cable options, news services, and streaming video sites provides more opportunities for people to deliver their messages to broad and specific audiences. Adjusting delivery to the screen can help determine whether or not the audience perceives you as an effective communicator.

Exercises

1 Have a classmate or a colleague do a practice interview with you concerning one of your areas of expertise. He or she may give you some of the fields to be covered but should not give you the questions in advance. Videotape the interview and compare your perceptions of it with those of your host.

2 Watch local cable news and public access programs and critique the guests. What are some of the most common mistakes they make? If you were a communication consultant, what advice would you give to each interviewee?

3 If you have information of general interest, such as news or details of a special event, check with your local public access station to see if there are opportunities for you to appear on an interview or news program.

INTERVIEW

Vickie Jenkins

Media Consultant with Performance Power

Vickie Jenkins is an award-winning broadcast journalist and strategic consultant with more than 20 years of experience designing and delivering communications programs for companies and global audiences. She facilitates strategic planning sessions; coaches executive teams for their presentations, public speaking engagements, and media interviews; and hosts performance improvement seminars. Her client list includes companies in the fields of technology, medicine, finance, public relations, food, publishing, professional services, energy, and entertainment.

Here's how Vickie describes her general approach to working with clients.

When I work with clients, I need to know their level of media experience before we begin the training . . . whether they've been interviewed before, how that session went, and what their fears are. Then we set the list of performance goals.

I explain that the "Performance Power" discipline needs to be practiced daily . . . not just when they have an interview coming up. The more they use those "perform-ance muscles," the easier it becomes when the camera is actually turned on them. We discuss the psychology of performance and winning techniques used by CEOs, actors, and athletes. I give them a feedback form so they can learn to critique themselves in a more objective way. They need to review their videos as if they were watching someone else on television and evaluate that performance top to bottom.

I have a "holistic approach to communication coaching, which means that my clients learn to prepare both mentally and physically, improving everything from the content of their messages to the delivery of them.

Because I often work as a strategic coach/consultant with companies, I also facilitate the development of their messages. In order to communicate effectively with others, through the media or in person, you must get clear on your message.

Question: Can you give a brief checklist of things you cover with clients; especially first-time interviewees?

Vickie Jenkins: Performance Power covers the following:

- Media experience and feedback
- Performance fears/issues
- Target venue (where do you want to appear—CNN, etc.)
- Content preparation
- Physical and mental preparation
- Practice
- Performance
- Critique/feedback
- Performance-polishing schedule
- Content (talking points, audience interest, memorable message, realism)
- Visual: eye contact, body language, appearance
- Vocal: breathing, voice quality, energy
- Mental: grounding/focusing exercises, success visioning
- Practice: videotaping with real-time Q and A, energy and focus
- Critique: content, body language, energy, interest, focus
- Performance Power polishing: new goals and practice schedule

Q: What do you see as the most common problem(s) for new interviewees?

VJ: What I call "brainlock." Anyone who is out of their "comfort zone" switches to a "fight or flight" response in those circumstances, and that's where they completely lose their train of thought. It's the fear of being outside their comfort zone that makes them "lose it." But once they learn the Performance Power technique and practice, they don't need "fight" or "flight"; they handle the interview with ease.

An athlete doesn't run a race without months of mental and physical practice, and it's the same with great performances on camera. The more they practice, the more they are exercising their "performance muscles" so they won't "lock up."

Q: Are there techniques or advice that makes your consulting firm unique?

VJ: I design each performance coaching program for the client's needs. I don't stand in front of them and lecture, because they only learn by doing the actual performance training themselves . . . on-camera, real-time scenarios. I don't use a standard set of handouts, because those don't address each specific client's concerns. Even if I'm training an entire executive team, I handle each of the members separately, with specifically designed questions, feedback, and performance tips. That's why my coaching works faster and more effectively than a "cookie cutter" approach.

Clients also get my 20-year expertise as a television/radio performer and strategic facilitator/coach, who not only knows how to ask the tough questions to elicit their answers but also has the ability to give them the techniques and confidence it takes to grow with their performance. Some consultants may be good performers, but can't coach others to a better performance. Other consultants are great coaches but lack the hands-on media performer experience. I offer the best of both worlds. I also give my clients performance tools and techniques they can adapt to all types of communication circumstances—in board meetings, public speaking, presentations, and interviews—so it's truly worth the up-front investment.

Q: Can anyone be an effective communicator on television?

VJ: Anyone can be a "more effective" communicator than they are, whether it's on television, radio, in a group, or one-on-one setting, once they learn the Performance Power discipline, which includes preparation, practice, performance, and review. The discipline I teach is practiced on the physical as well as the mental level, and designed to get you relaxed and focused so that you simply speak naturally.

The discipline is the foundation; then you adapt it for each of your specific communication environments, such as a satellite television interview, group discussion on camera, live audience participation, call-ins on television, interview shows, etc., so that speaking on camera is as natural as having a conversation with a colleague.

Q: What advice do you give to clients concerning handling difficult questions?

VJ: Stop ignoring the tough issues. I practice the most difficult questions with my clients because it will do them no good to pretend that the topics will not come up. But just like any other "comfort zone" issue, when clients get used to repeatedly talking about the tough issues they've been avoiding, the questions are easier to respond to. I also teach them how to redirect the conversation by having them offer up new information in their answers.

But I only teach what I call "natural communication," which means you don't waste time posturing, using false language, or "spinning phrases." You give honest answers, admit mistakes, and when you don't know an answer, say so. If clients aren't willing to do that, I don't work with them. Confronting the toughest questions also gives clients a chance to get clear on their messages, eliminate roadblocks to bigger success, and rethink their own values and mission—and that's when true learning takes place.

Q: Other thoughts?

VJ: The only difference between video performing and other forms of communication is that you must adapt your communication style to fit the audience and format needs. If the show's five minutes, keep your answers short. Remember to keep your energy and enthusiasm, and audience interest, going by using your hands, voice, and facial expressions.

Any physical distraction (uncombed hair, flashy clothes/jewelry, fidgeting in your seat, squeaky voice, etc.) will distract the audience from hearing your message.

Get clear on your audience message, practice your messages out loud, warm up physically and mentally, stay "on" throughout the entire performance, and after the performance review all video sessions for performance polishing tips and future practice sessions. When you practice and receive focused feedback from a qualified coach, you will be able to move your performances to a new level each time!

CHAPTER TEN

"And Now the News, Weather, and Sports . . ."

Many aspiring video performers want to be news anchors, reporters, weathercasters, and sports anchors or reporters. There are good reasons those breaking into the industry aspire to work in news (for our purposes, this includes weather and sports). The people we see on national and local newscasts constitute just about the highest percentage of performers on television. And news anchors and reporters at both the national and local level are often among the most admired people in television, according to public opinion polls. Weather forecasters and sports reporters are both national and local celebrities, providing us with information in creative and entertaining ways.

The newsroom is usually a television station's largest and most visible department, accounting for half the station's employees. In addition, departments such as promotions, production, and graphics provide support for the news area.

Local news has become a major profit center for stations, with some of the highest advertising rates being charged for commercials during newscasts. For this reason, well-recognized anchors and reporters are among the highest-paid personnel at local stations.

The public service of providing viewers with information they need to know is also rewarding. While the television news industry has come under fire over the past two decades for providing "infotainment" instead of hard news, consider the following: How often have you turned to television news during a crisis or severe weather when you needed information as soon as possible? In a crisis television news still delivers a valuable public service, and at its best television news rivals other news sources in the quality of information provided. With all its problems, more people still get their news from television than from any other source.

News anchors may appear to be merely attractive front people, reading machines who look into the lens and mouth words written by other people. In most cases, nothing is further from the truth. For one thing, anchors work long, difficult schedules. For another, many anchors have come up through the reporter ranks, so they know how to write the news while also appreciating the efforts of those covering field stories.

As with all television production, teamwork among anchors, reporters, news administration, production personnel, and others is the key to successful newscasts. This chapter provides an overview of the responsibilities and job descriptions of newscast performers, along with advice on how to tailor your performance when delivering news, weather, and sports in both the studio and field.

First, here is a brief survey of the past, present, and future of television news.

The Development of Television News

Chapter 1 included some of the highlights of television news. Early television news was nothing like the visually driven newscasts of today. Basically, television news was radio with still pictures, and the visual elements were few and far between. The technical limitations of television dictated the production values of early newscasts, in which an anchor read news copy on camera for about 15 minutes with a few still pictures, maps, and film clips included when possible. Eventually, more visual elements were used throughout the 1950s and early 1960s; but television news still lacked much of what we see today.

The assassination of President Kennedy in 1963 was the coming of age for television news. As millions of viewers tuned in to watch the events of the weekend following the assassination, this tragic event clearly demonstrated to television executives the importance of news programs. Television networks captured these images despite using heavy, awkward equipment that was made for studio and not field production use. The nonstop coverage until after President Kennedy's funeral demonstrated that television news could rise to the occasion in covering significant events.

News executives and others came to realize that news operations would have to cover stories of this magnitude better and faster as the public became increasingly dependent upon television for news. Other television executives realized that television news, once viewed as a public service, could also be a profit center.

By the early 1970s, portable electronic newsgathering (ENG) equipment had replaced film cameras, allowing faster editing and airing of stories. Remote trucks, helicopters, and other news hardware meant that television news departments could now cover stories all over town in a matter of minutes. On-location reporting soon became the norm, whether or not it was necessary, because stations had the equipment to broadcast "live from the scene."

The 1970s also saw a greater emphasis on news anchors and reporters as personalities, as the public began to make their network choices depending on whether or not they liked the people delivering the news. Consultants surfaced at the local and network news levels, giving advice ranging from clothing and hairstyles for performers, to the color and design of news sets. News formats such as "happy talk" helped stations to differentiate themselves from one another.

CNN brought radio's all-news format to television in the 1980s, providing an alternative news source to networks and local stations. As a result, local stations were able to share their video and live feeds with CNN, receiving coverage of national events from other CNN partner stations in return. The advent of CNN also meant that network and local news operations tended to interrupt their regular programming more frequently and cover breaking stories longer to compete with CNN.

RATINGS POINTER

Become a critical observer of your local television news and note when the station decides to interrupt regular programming for a breaking local news story. What types of stories do they cover in this way, and how long do they stay with them before returning to regular programming?

Channel-surf to find out which other stations are covering the story, compare their respective coverage, and note when each station decides to return to local programming. A breaking news story is also an excellent opportunity to observe reporters and anchors using their impromptu delivery skills—skills any newscaster needs to develop. ★ ★ ★ ★

Other cable information services such as ESPN and The Weather Channel emerged in the late 1970s and throughout the 1980s. Corporate takeovers of ABC, CBS, and NBC resulted in the closing of news bureaus and news personnel layoffs as cost-cutting, profit-increasing measures.

Despite network layoffs, opportunities for those starting in television news increased throughout the 1990s with the growth of local cable news and sports services. Today, Internet streaming video has the ability to enhance television news while also providing archival video of past news stories. Although packaging and personalities will continue to be an element of television news, there is no substitute for credible people delivering information in a clear, concise, and ethical manner. Consider the tragic events of September 11, 2001, and how millions turned to television news during this crisis. People wanted credible information from network anchors and reporters. Many people in front of and behind the camera are involved in bringing you the news.

The Players and Process

The number of people newsrooms employ varies according to the station's **market size;** for example, a station in a **major market** such as Chicago could have two dozen producers, whereas a station in a **small market** might have only one or two. The same criterion applies to the number of reporters and other staff. Some of the players and processes involved in newsgathering include the following:

▨ **News Director and Assignment Editor**   **News directors** are the top executives in television news. Ironically, large-market news directors may not be involved with the day-to-day decision making concerning which stories are covered, because they work on budgets, personnel decisions, and equipment acquisition.

On the other hand, news directors in smaller markets often wear many hats and may even cover some stories and anchor the newscast. The major responsibilities of news directors are budgets, hiring personnel, promotional strategies, editorial policy, and the overall planning of news coverage. News directors are increasingly focused on the business side of running a news department.

The **assignment editor** is the main person in charge of the nerve center of the newsroom, the assignment desk (usually known as "the desk"). The number of people at the desk will vary. You may find news planners and desk assistants along with a number of interns if it is a major market or network news operation. Desks in small-market stations may have only an assignment editor and an intern or two as assistants.

Desk personnel monitor various police and fire scanners along with other news sources such as wire services and CNN. The assignment desk sends reporters and news photographers (photogs) to the scenes of breaking stories, often referred to as **hard news.** In some cases a photographer may go alone to shoot video of a story such as a fire, especially if the fire is in the early hours of the morning when news personnel are at a premium. Copy will be written later in the newsroom to be read by the anchor over b-roll of the fire.

Many news operations now take the "one person band" approach whereby a reporter doubles as a photog, both reporting and shooting the news event. The reporter may shoot the necessary video, interview people at the scene of the event, and then set up the camera and stand in front of it.

The assignment desk also sends reporters to cover **soft news** events such as press conferences, meetings, public and court hearings, parades, and so on. Since these are scheduled public events, the news staff has some advance warning in regard to covering them.

The **news planner** is responsible for selecting events to be covered, a task that requires sorting through numerous press releases, e-mails, and letters from organizations, groups, and individuals wanting coverage. Even smaller markets receive many more requests than could ever be included in a half-hour newscast. News planners have to anticipate which of these requests has the potential for audience attention and appeal. Slow news days or weekends are the times when such events tend to make the evening newscast.

Promotional stories often feature people appearing on that station's or network's programs; for example, when David Letterman went on the road

KGO San Francisco news set.

to produce his show in Los Angeles and Chicago, the local CBS affiliates in those cities included interviews with Letterman on their newscasts. Not surprisingly, some television critics questioned the news value of such stories.

Newsgathering is a dynamic process in which the desk personnel must keep in constant contact with those in the field via pagers and cellular phones. Reporters and photogs may be reassigned to a more important story if the need arises. The desk is constantly in touch with news sources such as police and fire departments, local government officials, and even private citizens who have news tips. Some stations invite individuals to call the station if they have news tips as part of promoting the newscast.

Newsgathering Personnel   Reporters and photogs create the words and pictures that make up a news story. In larger markets writers work behind the scenes doing research and editing. All newsgathering personnel work together to assemble and check facts before writing stories, shoot and edit the video and audio, and compile all these elements into a final news package. Newsgathering personnel understand the importance of functioning as a team, especially under stressful working conditions involving tight deadlines.

Reporters must have excellent oral and writing skills. They often have to present a live story in an extemporaneous style with limited notes or an outline, while making certain that all important facts are included. Reporters have to deliver these stories smoothly without "uhs," "you knows," and other vocalized pauses. The experience of doing a live story on a newscast is similar to a trapeze artist without a net in front of thousands of viewers.

Photogs can be sent with a reporter or alone if a story doesn't require a reporter on location. On very heavy news days, the photog may be sent alone just because the newsgathering staff is spread so thin in covering numerous stories.

Producers   Back at the station, a **producer** starts to put the pieces of the newscast together to decide what the viewers will see and when. Producers work with some input from news management to determine the lead stories, timing, and which stories may be dumped from the newscast.

At larger stations, a producer may be responsible for only one newscast, but at smaller-market stations producers may work with multiple newscasts. In the smallest markets, the producer is also the anchor or reporter. During the newscast the producer communicates with the director to time the program and decide whether stories have to be deleted or if "padding" is needed at the end to extend time. In some cases when there is a major breaking story, the producer must decide (along with news and station management) to extend the newscast's time limits in order to cover it.

News Writers   **News writers** are generally **reporters** working in the field who write much of their own material for live reports or packages. Other copy, such as introductions and rewrites of wire service and network stories, is written by news writers. News writers often provide the glue for the newscast, writing transitions between stories as well as **bumpers,** or lead-ins to commercials.

As you can see, newscasts require numerous people working together under intense deadlines to get the program on the air. All television productions require individuals to function as a team, but none more than a newscast.

Preparation for a Career in News

Aspiring television journalists often wonder what is the best preparation for a career in television journalism. What major is best, and what courses should they take? If you talk to television journalists, you will find that there are almost as many different qualifications and ways to enter the field as there are people. Nevertheless, the advice many television journalists give contains some similarities:

A Broad-Based Liberal Arts Education   Almost all the television journalists interviewed for this chapter stressed the importance of a liberal arts education. Too often students with limited knowledge do not know how to make connections between various subject areas or modern and historical events. In other cases, lack of background in a tradition of ideas causes novices to behave according to the old cliche, "Don't confuse me with the facts, my mind is made up."

One journalist tells the story of a friend's daughter who refused to watch the presidential debates because she didn't like one of the candidates. The daughter wanted to be a television news reporter or anchor. The journalist asked the young woman, "Don't you think you should watch the debate so you can at least form some counterarguments against the candidate you don't like?" She answered, "No, I know I don't like that candidate." The journalist hopes that this young person has no future in television journalism.

In addition to taking wide-ranging general classes, students often wonder which specific courses best prepare them for a career in television news. Your instructors and counselors can help you plan your academic program by suggesting courses within your major and electives. Part of the challenge you face is that a wide variety of academic departments offer the specific courses needed for a television news career. Your major may be communication, journalism, mass communication, speech communication, or any of a number of other departmental titles, Whatever the major, it is important that you gain particular knowledge and skills in order to have adequate preparation in television news. Here are some suggestions for coursework as you plan your academic career:

▦ Any Course That Involves Writing

Over 50 television news professionals, ranging from producers to reporters, were interviewed for this chapter. All of them stressed the importance of writing skills. Many of those interviewed felt that people entering the industry lack good writing skills and that newcomers often have to learn on the job.

Take as many writing courses as you can, ranging from creative to broadcast writing. There is a difference between writing for the eye and writing for the ear (discussed in more detail later in this chapter), so learn to make this distinction. Try to get a position on your campus newspaper even if you don't aspire to be a print journalist. Many of the principles of writing, research, and journalism ethics are the same in print as in television. The better a writer you are, the more valuable you will be to a television news operation.

▦ Political Science

Knowledge of political systems such as city, state, and national governments is crucial for the news reporter and anchor. Understanding international events and political systems is also important for many news personnel. Political science courses help you to understand how various forms of government work. You can apply this knowledge to covering stories in any city, state, or country.

Along with political science, urban and ethnic studies can assist you in looking beyond your own experience and examining people from a variety of backgrounds. We live in an increasingly diverse, highly mobile country. Knowing more about different types of people will help you understand and cover a greater variety of stories.

■ **History**   An archway over one of the entrances of the National Archives Building in Washington, D.C., carries the inscription "Study history." It's commonplace to gripe about Americans' lack of historical knowledge, but the sad fact is that many Americans do not know basic information about U.S. history, let alone world history.

Not only should you have historical facts at your disposal, you should also recognize historical trends. The statement "History repeats itself" is a cliche, but it cannot be ignored. For example, many of the things happening today in the Internet industry are very similar to what was happening in the broadcasting industry early in the last century. Being able to understand and recognize these trends gives you the advantage of comparing recent and past events.

Too often reporters attempt to cover stories without doing the historical research necessary to put them in their proper perspective. Historical knowledge can help with contextual aspects of many stories.

When studying history, don't neglect more recent events of the last 25 years. Many history classes sacrifice discussing recent events in favor of teaching history from the more distant past. Continue adding to your historical knowledge by reading news magazines and newspapers. Online editions of newspapers such as the *New York Times* and the *Washington Post* help you stay current with the news as well as providing you with historical context. Note how print journalists provide historical background for their stories and see if you can transfer these principles to your coverage of news events.

■ **Psychology and Interpersonal Communication**   Knowing how people think and feel will help you both on and off camera. Many times you need to be a counselor, coach, or listening ear when dealing with people you cover in stories. You will encounter a variety of personalities and egos of those in the public eye, as well as average people who suddenly find themselves in the news. The ability to understand these individuals can give you an advantage over reporters who are concerned only with the story and not the people behind it.

Awareness of people's feelings and motivations helps you to be a better interviewer in the field by giving you some insight into why interviewees are pursuing a course of action or behaving the way they are. Your ability to have some empathy with the interviewee will also help you refine your questions and on-camera delivery skills.

Working with your colleagues on location and back in the newsroom also requires interpersonal communication skills. This book has repeatedly stressed the need for teamwork in a variety of production situations and nowhere is it more important than in a television newsroom. Those who can't function well in a team or think of themselves as stars or prima donnas often have short-lived careers.

Art Courses
Courses such as music, painting, photography, and acting not only enhance your education but also contain theories and skills you will use in reporting news. Musical knowledge can help you with music choices you may need to make when reporting feature or news stories. Visual arts courses, such as painting and photography, teach principles such as composition that are directly applicable to shooting news stories.

Acting courses assist with developing concentration, confidence, and other performance skills. Believe it or not, actors and news reporters or anchors share some common goals. Both groups want to be perceived as natural and believable; and actors' training emphasizes these goals.

Computer Courses
Computers are important newsgathering tools whether you use them for simple word processing or for sophisticated graphics production. Basic computer skills are as important in the newsroom as critical thinking skills in evaluating Internet news sources. Those considering careers in television news should take as many computer courses as schedules permit. As with any hardware, don't think in terms of mere button pushing, but rather how you use the computer to communicate your end message.

Communication Courses
No matter what the name of the department (communication, communication studies, speech communication) you should take a variety of courses in this subject area. Interpersonal communication has already been mentioned as a valuable course.

See if voice and diction courses or speech lessons are offered at your institution or organization. These courses help with many of the voice production and articulation skills discussed in Chapter 2. The goal should not be to make you sound overprecise or formal but rather to sound both conversational and polished. Voice and diction courses can also help with accent reduction or regional vocal habits.

One of the most valuable activities you can pursue is competitive *speech and debate,* also called forensics. Debating helps you develop crucial thinking skills and the ability to express a point of view concerning a wide variety of current events and values topics. Speech helps you learn to write for the ear, develop research skills, and improve poise and confidence.

Some speech classes, such as informative and persuasive speaking, require you to memorize long portions of text and deliver it in a polished, conversational manner. Extemporaneous and impromptu speaking are "think on your feet" events with little or no preparation time. The skills you develop from these occasions will help you overcome situations in television news where you have to report breaking news with limited or no notes.

■ **Electronic Media Courses**   Obviously, you should take courses in electronic media, but think about how they will build toward your goal of being a television journalist. Students often look at production courses as being the cornerstone of their media major; however, courses in media writing or media law and ethics will provide more of the information necessary for you to become a complete electronic journalist. Technology changes, but your ability to understand the laws and ethics behind what you report will serve you in the long term.

■ **Personal Observation and Experience**   Many things you do outside the classroom can further your progress toward becoming a television journalist. Begin watching both national and local television more critically and comparing how the networks and local station present the news. What are the similarities and differences between network newscasts? How do the networks compare in news coverage to cable news services such as CNN and Fox News? What are the content and stylistic differences between local newscasts in your city (don't forget to watch local cable news services when doing your analysis)? You will soon notice some trends in news coverage and the state of television journalism. Be careful not to imitate reporters and anchors you see on air, but do notice similar qualities that makes them effective.

Start looking for on-campus opportunities such as working at your campus radio station or newspaper. These places provide excellent starting points for anyone who eventually wants to become a television journalist. Obviously, you should pursue out-of-class productions; for example, some campuses produce a newscast for on-campus or cable viewers.

If you're interested in sports, contact your campus sports information director to see if you can help during campus sporting events. The campus radio station may broadcast games or have other programs involving your team.

Combining these cocurricular activities with a liberal arts academic program helps prepare you for your first television news position. A liberal education not only enables you to become a better critical thinker, it improves your writing skills and your understanding of people. One experienced broadcast educator told his students, "You're not writing stories about television, you're writing about other things." Having broad-based knowledge will help you write about those "other things."

Some Basic Ethical Considerations

There is intense competition today between various television news sources to be the first to get a story on the air, partly because more sources than ever are competing for the same stories. Years ago, there were only three major networks and three to six local television stations with news operations; now there are many more on-air and cable services providing news.

As a result, news programs sometimes sacrifice accuracy to beat the competition. Speed is important, but inaccurate reporting damages both the reporter's and the news operation's credibility. The 2000 presidential election offers a prime example of news operations rushing their projections concerning who had won the vote in various states. As a result, Vice President Gore initially was declared the winner in Florida. When George W. Bush was later declared the winner of the state—and the election—many observers felt that the whole television news industry had "egg on its face." What could be more embarrassing to a news operation than declaring the wrong candidate the winner in a presidential election?

Inaccurate or unethical reporting also causes people to lose their jobs. Newswriting texts contain comprehensive information regarding journalism ethics. The following are some basic considerations:

Privacy   It seems to some viewers that news magazine programs and newscasts are increasingly using hidden cameras and other hard-hitting techniques to cover stories. After watching so many of these stories, you may be concerned about privacy issues and what you should consider when covering stories. The lines can be blurred in regard to privacy, but here are some suggestions that seem to be universal among most journalists:

- You do not need permission to record someone at a press conference. Since this is an event at which reporters are invited to ask questions of the celebrity, executive, or spokesperson, those in charge of this event obviously want coverage and video on newscasts. Remember, however, that there is a difference between being assertive and aggressive when asking difficult questions during the conference. Also, maintain your professionalism when setting up and breaking down your equipment.

- Interviews done in a public place where you identify yourself, your affiliation, and what you are doing are fair game for a telecast. The person has the option of talking to you or declining comment. Uninvited interviews sought after you enter a home or office are another matter, though, and you should check with news management and in some cases a legal department.
- "Ambush" techniques and hidden cameras are gray areas that also require consultation with news management and attorneys.

Also unclear is the extent to which you can pursue public figures such as movie and sports stars. Some news organizations argue that these public figures have given up much of their right to privacy because they are in the public eye. If, however, a film star has a family member who is seriously ill, do you continue to pursue that star for comments?

You've probably seen stories on local newscasts in which a reporter has shoved a microphone into the face of a parent frantic over a missing child, or into the face of someone who has just lost his or her home to fire. Let sensitivity and common sense be your guides for dealing with tragic stories and judging whether or not you can approach people in such difficult circumstances.

■ **Libel**   Libel is the crime of publishing or broadcasting untrue information that damages a person's reputation by holding him or her up to public ridicule, hatred, or scorn. The U.S. Supreme Court has ruled that any public figure filing a libel suit (the plaintiff) must prove that the controversial material was published or broadcast with "actual malice," meaning that the publisher or broadcaster either knew that the information was false or recklessly disregarded whether it was false or not.

Libel law is a fluid proposition, so you need to be current with the courts' interpretation of it. Libel laws also differ from state to state so you will need to familiarize yourself with specific laws wherever you are working.

For our purposes, the best defense against a libel charge is being able to prove the truth. If you are broadcasting a charge of a criminal act or incompetence against an individual, you had better be able to prove it. For example, if you assert that air traffic controllers at your city's airport are incompetent, you should have recorded evidence and reliable eyewitness interviews to back up your claims. Questionable research and evidence could cost your news operation huge legal fees and a possible financial award or settlement with an individual or organization.

For this reason, many television news reporters will avoid terms such as "incompetent" in favor of grouping their facts together and letting the documentation speak for itself. Think in terms of using information that is verifiable to protect yourself from charges of libel.

■ **Controversial statements.** A statement such as "There are four people dead and 25 seriously ill due to food poisoning at Ross's Restaurant" should be attributed to a health official or credible source. You should let viewers know who determined that it was food poisoning from the restaurant that caused the deaths and illnesses

If the event or statement is verifiable, you probably don't need attribution. For example if Mayor Brown visited a children's day care center, you don't need attribution because there is visual evidence of the visit through video and film. But if the mayor stated, "There needs to be more funding for preschool education," the statement must be attributed to the source: Mayor Brown.

Privileged communication is another defense against libel. If you repeat remarks made by members of congress from the legislative chamber or judges in open court, you are protected from libel. In these situations you are simply reporting what these officials said.

Fair comments against public officials or celebrities are not considered libel. People in the public arena take risks in exposing themselves to criticism or negative publicity.

When in doubt concerning privacy and libel laws, consult your news management people or legal staff before airing the story. An area that is less abstract for reporters is attribution.

Attribution   Beginning reporters often fail to tell viewers where they got their information. **Attribution** tells viewers the source of your information. Think of it as a verbal footnote or similar to when a public speaking instructor asks you to cite your source in a speech.

You should use attribution in the following situations:

■ **Opinions.** If you report, "The governor is responsible for some of the environmental hazards in the south side of town," you should attribute the opinion to the source such as "The president of the South Side Citizens' Council stated today. . . ."

■ **Arrests and legal charges.** Attribute any information regarding arrests or legal charges to the official source. "Police have charged" or "according to police spokesperson Jill Doe" are basic phrases that apply when police arrest a suspect. It is critical to include the terms "accused" or "alleged" when referring to someone charged with a crime. Not only do these phrases and words minimize the possibility of future legal problems, they also keep from trying individuals in the court of television.

RATINGS POINTER

Besides some of the traditional ethical considerations mentioned in many newswriting texts, ethical questions now arise regarding the business side of television news as it continues to be a profit center for networks and local stations. This reality creates numerous gray areas in covering a variety of stories. For example, one East Coast major market station featured a series on weight loss and healthy eating that included live shots from a restaurant chain famous for salads and other healthy foods. The chain bought commercial time on the station because the live shots originated from one of its restaurants.

Be aware that the lines between classic journalism ethics and news for profit will continue to blur. ★ ★ ★ ★

Writing for the Ear

You may already know that there are different writing styles for television and print news. Print news uses the passive voice, television the active voice. Television news is what's happening now so almost everything is active. A print lead may look like the following:

> Jill Thomas upset the incumbent Mayor Richard Daniels last night to become the new mayor of Washington. She won the election by less than 1,000 votes.

On the other hand, a television lead may sound more like this:

> There's a major political upset this morning. Jill Thomas is the new mayor of Washington. She beat the incumbent Mayor Richard Daniels by just under 1,000 votes.

When writing for television news, work on making the transition from the passive voice you may have used for a newspaper or organizational newsletter to an active voice.

A good way to practice writing for the ear is to take newspaper articles and rewrite them in the active voice for television. You may find this a tedious exercise, but it is one of the best ways to develop your **writing style for television**. Also, notice that the writing style of online news sources often uses the active voice. ★ ★ ★ ★

Here are some other points to remember when writing for television:

■ **Use Shorter Sentences**   Write the way you speak and use shorter sentences. This will make your **copy** easier to read as well as sound more natural. Some journalists and instructors say that the maximum length of a sentence should be twenty to twenty-five words. You don't always need to consider this a hard-and-fast rule, but it will help you formulate brief, pointed sentences. Shorter sentences also facilitate ad-libbing and sounding conversational.

■ **Don't Overdo Description**   Colorful writing is important, but don't belabor the obvious concerning what the viewer can see on the screen. Use description to extend and build upon what the viewer sees. If you are covering a parade, you probably don't have to write in detail about the costumes people are wearing but you can mention that the parade extended for over a mile because the audience won't see that.

■ **Remember the Difference between Readers and Listeners**   Readers can read more slowly and take time to process information, whereas listeners can't listen more slowly or review information. Keep this distinction in mind when writing for television. Also avoid sound-alike words such as *can* and *can't*. Another reason to use shorter sentences is that longer sentences can cause the listener to lose key ideas.

■ **Use a Limited Vocabulary**   This isn't the same as "dumbing down"; instead, it helps the listener to process and retain information while you're speaking. Avoid language that you might use in a research paper or report. Use more concrete and less conceptual language.

The great broadcast journalist Edward R. Murrow said that when he was writing, he tried to visualize himself having coffee with a college professor on one side and a blue-collar worker on the other. He used language that the worker would understand without insulting the intelligence of the college professor. Murrow was perhaps being unfair to both very intelligent blue-collar workers and less intelligent college professors; however, the concept of using language that aims "down the middle" does help listeners understand your content.

Now that you know all the basics of the newsroom, including writing for television, you are ready to get away from the station to cover **field productions** live or on tape.

In the Field: Live and on Tape

You'll have opportunities to report news both live and in taped **packages.** During a typical day you may work on one or two stories, appearing on newscasts for three minutes or less. Sometimes you work many hours on a story, only to have it bumped from that night's newscast due to other breaking news or time limitations. Other times, you may be the reporter fortunate enough to break a major story and report from the scene.

Live shots come by either microwave or satellite transmission. As previously mentioned, many stations and networks feel that live reports on location increase the interest level in a story as well as the credibility of the news operation.

"Going live" may be beneficial for the news operation and viewers, but it also causes difficulties for the reporter and crew. There is the additional pressure of avoiding mistakes and performing without a net. Reporters must gather information quickly, check for accuracy, and present their material flawlessly. Distractions, including people, objects, and weather, can create more problems for reporters and tech support.

Live reports often start and end with **stand-ups** in which you see the reporter looking at viewers while delivering information. After a few seconds of stand-up there may be b-roll video of events on the scene, or the camera may pan away from the reporter to show what is happening. This serves as a visual sandwich between the stand-ups. Stand-ups, common to both live reports and packages, deserve a closer look.

Stand and Deliver:
The Art of Doing Stand-ups

Some people in the news industry wonder why reporters bother with stand-ups. In an age of so many other visual options, are stand-ups really necessary? They may not be, but they do have their advantages. First, they can add to the credibility of the reporter and the news operation. Hearing a reporter is one thing, but putting a face to the voice is something else, especially when we see that reporter on a regular basis.

Stand-ups can also add to the visual impact of the package if they are done in a creative way. Using props or your surroundings can make the stand-up more appealing.

There may be times when you want to make a point to the viewer and looking at the camera lens and delivering the information is the best way to do so. You may also want to use a stand-up when you want to highlight that the point you are making is important, the essence of the story.

RATINGS POINTER

Former KDKA Pittsburgh and KPIX San Francisco general assignment and business reporter Craig Miller offers the following advice on the best use of stand-ups:

- You can use stand-ups as a transitional device to get from one part of the story to the next. Don't use stand-ups just to get your face onscreen.
- Use props or demonstrate something if it is appropriate to do so.
- Keep your hands free by using a lavaliere instead of a stick microphone. It's difficult to do anything creative while holding a stick mic. News directors will sometimes fight you on this because they want to see the station's **flag** (the logo with the stations call letters and channel) on the mic. Miller always tries to do important interviews with no mic visible in front of the interviewee's face.
- Think in terms of creative stand-ups. Miller says that producers still recall a stand-up from a story he did concerning a leveraged buyout of the Safeway supermarket chain. The stand-up had Miller walking down the aisle of a Safeway store saying, "So why are these stores so attractive with all their inventory, overhead, and tiny profit margins of one or two cents on the dollar? Why would this be a juicy takeover target? Well, the answer may not be on any of these shelves. The answer may be underneath my feet." At that point the camera tilted down to the floor to make the point that the real estate was the most valuable aspect of the takeover. This stand-up had no gimmicks or props but still made a point.
- Don't walk during a stand-up just for the sake of walking. Miller calls this an "unmotivated trot." Think instead of what you can do that is plot advancing, that serves such a function in the narrative flow that the audience didn't even realize it was a stand-up. ★ ★ ★ ★

Background can also aid with creative stand-ups. Several years ago KRON San Francisco entertainment reporter Henry Tannenbaum did a series on San Francisco morning radio called "The Radio Wake-Up Wars." One report included information that AM radio was popular in San Francisco because the signal bounces over the hills instead of into them. During one of Tannebaum's stand-ups he said, "The reason for AM's popularity in San Francisco is as old as the hills; in fact, it is the hills." The camera zoomed over Tannebaum's shoulder to the hills in the background.

Some people wonder if it is ethical to do a stand-up in a location different from the one you are talking about in your story. For example, if you are doing an investigative report on a medical topic, can you shoot your stand-up in the hallway of your station if the background is generic tile and looks like a hospital? The ethical lines are somewhat blurred here. NBC reporters often use a Presbyterian church next door to the network's Washington, D.C., bureau as a background for stand-ups because it has white columns and in one reporter's opinion, "just looks bureaucratic and governmentese."

Most reporters agree, however, that if you're doing a live shot, you should report from the actual location. You should try to use the actual location in packages as well; however, you may "cheat" and use a generic location if you are under time constraints.

Stand-ups during live reports often conclude with questions from the anchor back at the studio. Be prepared to respond to impromptu questions that elicit more background information. One of the challenges during the Q and A session is that you have to listen to the anchor through your IFB earpiece in which you can also hear the director's commands.

Also, if you are communicating by satellite, there can be a delay of a second or two after the anchor speaks before you hear his or her voice (watch for this delay on newscasts when the field reporter seems to hesitate for a beat or two). This puts added pressure on you to respond as quickly as possible to make the delay less noticeable. There may be times when you hear your own voice coming back to you similar to an echo. Despite these distractions, you are expected to give your reports in a smooth, conversational manner.

RATINGS POINTER

Giving information to viewers while listening to a director or other person through your IFB requires concentration. You can develop a high level of concentration by practicing reporting a live story while listening to a talk radio station in your ear. You'll find after several practice sessions that you can listen to the radio while reporting your story. ★ ★ ★ ★

Field Interviews

On-location interviews are an important part of both live and package reports. Besides the techniques covered in Chapter 8, **field interviews** involve several other elements.

First, decide whom you should interview. Make sure the interviewee is credible and has information that will add to the quality of the report. Some people will want to appear on camera, but have little to say that provides insight into what has happened, whereas others who have valuable information may be camera shy or afraid of being quoted out of context.

You may have to act as a counselor or psychologist to persuade these people to appear on camera. Work on getting hesitant interviewees to ignore the camera and talk to you. Empathy with the interviewee goes a long way in persuading a reluctant person to appear on camera.

Have the interviewee stand slightly upstage from you instead of standing beside you. This adds to the interest of the shot and allows the photog the opportunity to zoom in for close-ups of the interviewee, or zoom out for over-the-shoulder shots toward the interviewee.

Whenever possible, try to conduct the interview in a location without a lot of distractions going on behind the interviewee. The focus should be on the person and not the surrounding activity. Close-ups can help limit distractions, but make the job easier for your photog by choosing a neutral background for the interview. Check, too, for objects in the background that might cause composition problems for your photog, such as a tree limb or street sign that appears to grow out of the interviewee's head.

Since video space is exaggerated, stand close to the interviewee so that there is no space between you on the screen. Beginning reporters often stand too far away from the other person, creating the impression that each person

Place your interviewee slightly upstage for added shot interest.

Too much space between reporter and interviewee.

Proper space between reporter and interviewee.

is glued to the sides of the screen. You may want to tell the interviewee why you need to stand closer to them than you would in regular conversation.

Remember never to hand the microphone to the interviewee, because you then lose control of the interview. Also, inexperienced interviewees are often unaware of proper microphone techniques and can display nervous habits when holding the mic.

Shooting on Tape: Videotaped Packages

Videotaped packages are the other field stories seen on newscasts. Most of these stories last just over a minute, but they can require hours of hard work. Besides stand-ups, other pieces are involved in putting a package together. First, the ingredients, then the recipe:

■ **Soundbites.** Soundbites were described in Chapter 8 as video quotations for which we see and hear a person on camera. Soundbites are for color and emphasis, not for background information (you can do a better job of condensing background information yourself). Keep soundbites brief and remember that the average bite is now seven seconds.

■ **Natural sound.** Sound that comes from people and things on the scene is **natural sound.** Look for opportunities to use natural sound that adds interest and color to your packages; especially at the beginnings and ends of stories. Remember that audio is often the most neglected aspect of video production. Effective use of natural sound can be the difference between a good package and an excellent one.

■ **Cover video.** These images provide an orientation for viewers by showing where the story is shot. **Cover video** usually means medium or long shots used at the beginning or end of a story.

■ **Cutaways.** Closely related to cover video are **cutaways,** brief shots that act as the glue or continuity between shots within the package. Cutaways, are useful in piecing soundbites together so that you avoid **jump cuts,** edits in which the composition of two shots is almost the same and you edit them together, causing the image to move or jump abruptly on the screen.

Cutaways can also be **reaction shots** of you listening to the interviewee. If you're shooting the interview with one camera (as is usually the case) the photog will have to shoot reaction shots of you following the interview. In these shots you look as if you are listening to the person. Don't fake or overdramatize your reactions; keep them true to the original reactions you displayed during the interview.

Work with your photog in getting several cutaway shots when you're on location; look for buildings, street signs, crowd shots, and anything that gives the viewer some sense of what's happening at the event.

■ **Voiceovers.** Your narration and telling of the facts behind the story is a **voiceover.** Voiceovers often accompany cutaways and provide audio bridges between soundbites and other segments.

■ **Fonts/character generator.** Back at the station, you will probably add printed information and other visual support via a character generator and computer graphics. Basic information such as names and titles, along with more sophisticated graphics such as charts and graphs, is added during the editing process.

Example of two shots causing a jump edit.

R A T I N G S   P O I N T E R

You can make it easier to edit your package by *slating* each take you do in the field. Do this verbally by identifying the location of the take and counting backward from five to zero. For example: "City Hall, take 2. Five, four, three, two, one. . . ." This will save time in locating specific segments you want to include. ★ ★ ★ ★

Putting the Package Together

Packages can be edited in a variety of ways. As you become experienced, you will discover creative storytelling and editing techniques.

Here are some basics for packages, along with a time line for you to follow.

- Unless it is an in-depth or special report, most packages are between 1 minute and 1 minute, 20 seconds long. The first 20 seconds are various cover video shots giving the viewer a visual orientation of the story with voiceover from the reporter. The reporter tries to cover most of the "Five W's and H" (who, what, when, where, why, and how) during this time.

- The first soundbite usually comes about 20 seconds into the story (sometimes sooner). As was mentioned earlier, soundbites average about 7 to 10 seconds. Longer soundbites may include cutaway shots to provide more visual information and interest for viewers.

- Next come more cutaways and a voiceover providing more in-depth information, bridging to the second soundbite. You may use a stand-up for a bridge as well. In either case, this segment lasts about 10 to 15 seconds.

- Another soundbite will usually come at about the 40-second mark.

- More cutaway shots and voiceover for 10 to 15 seconds

- A third soundbite.

- A stand-up or cutaways with voiceover for about 10 seconds to conclude the package.

Time line of a typical news story.

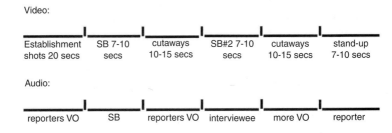

Video:

| Establishment shots 20 secs | SB 7-10 secs | cutaways 10-15 secs | SB#2 7-10 secs | cutaways 10-15 secs | stand-up 7-10 secs |

Audio:

| reporters VO | SB | reporters VO | interviewee | more VO | reporter |

RATINGS POINTER

Watch your local news and see how closely reporters follow this formula and time allocation for their packages. Also, watch the nine or ten o'clock local news (depending on your time zone) to see if they broadcast longer packages because they're doing an hour-long newscast. ★ ★ ★ ★

Special Area Reporters

These reporters have expertise in a specific area such as business, consumer affairs, science and technology, health, agriculture, and entertainment. In many cases these reporters did not start out as television performers but were newspaper writers or worked in the profession associated with their specialty (for example, many health reporters are medical doctors).

Special area reporters are valued for their knowledge and ability to simplify complex information. If you want to be a special area reporter, you should have at least a minor in the area you wish to report and knowledge from print and electronic sources. If you're already in the workplace, contact local television stations or cable operations to see if they can use your expertise. Small- and medium-market stations are often looking for reporters with specialties, while cable has expanded the opportunities for people who have special knowledge and are effective communicators.

Special area reporters may work in the field or do their segments in the studio with the anchors.

News Anchors

Other chapters in this text have covered items such as nonverbal communication, phrasing, and reading from prompters, all things good anchors need to know. This section covers other material unique to the role of news **anchor.**

Not too many years ago, news anchors were older white males with deep, authoritative voices who read the news. Now both men and women from various racial and ethnic groups are employed as anchors at both the network and local levels. Anchors are people who can read copy from a teleprompter in a conversational style and also **ad-lib** when necessary. They are usually well groomed, stylish, effective communicators.

Students often want to become anchors because of recognition and financial gain; however, it is important to remember that most anchors start out as general assignment reporters and work their way to the anchor desk over time. Gone are the days when an attractive person stared into the camera and read what someone else had written (although there are a few cases in which this still occurs). Most anchors are knowledgeable about current events and are good writers.

The few minutes we see an anchor onscreen represent only the tip of the iceberg. The anchor has many responsibilities:

- Preparing one or two daily newscasts. Some local stations do one hour-long newscast. A noontime anchor will probably double as a general assignment reporter. A small-market anchor may also be the news director.
- Appearing on weekend, holiday, and late-night newscasts.
- Writing as much as half of the copy read on air.
- Reporting from the field and traveling out of town for special reports.
- Doing special assignments reports.
- Working with news management to determine story selection.
- Serving as a representative for the station at public appearances and special events.
- Coordinating news content with a co-anchor and others such as weather, sports, and special area reporters.
- Suggesting graphics and other visual support for stories.

At news services such as CNN or local cable news channels, anchors may have a shift of several hours and function as the glue between all the segments aired during that block. Some anchors also do one-minute updates throughout the day.

You'll find that anchors' jobs can be similar to those of air traffic controllers in that they must juggle multiple tasks. They gather news from a variety of sources, including wire services and cooperative services such as a network, CNN, or sister station. They also check with reporters and other anchors on the progress of developing stories. And they meet throughout the day with news management to determine event coverage and which stories make it to air.

Often, you'll write a rundown of the day's top stories along with voiceovers for b-roll and **tell stories** in which you appear onscreen reading a story with no accompanying video and perhaps only a corner graphic as visual support. Anchors also write **teasers** and **tosses** (bumpers). Teasers are the messages heard right before the commercial break that keep the audience watching the newscast after (and the sponsors hope *during*) the commercials. In most cases they are read with accompanying b-roll that previews the story. Tosses are introductions to other segments hosted by business, health, weather, and sports reporters. Tosses are written out so the director knows when to change cameras and go to a different segment, but they are delivered in a conversational style. The overall style will determine whether the toss is businesslike or more "happy talk."

The news script is often written in all capital letters with the video information such as b-roll and graphics on the left side and what the anchor reads on the right. Most stations have teleprompters; the hard copy of the script is insurance in case something goes wrong with the prompter. The script is often color-coded so that the anchor can keep the pages in order and also, as was mentioned earlier, to prevent the glare produced by white paper.

■ The Anchor on Air
Anchors must seem in control even when there is late-breaking news or chaos around them. Concentration is the key element in being a good anchor, because so much is going on in the studio and control room. The original script for the newscast will undergo changes on the fly, so if you become an anchor, you will have to adapt to your producer's split-second decisions.

There may be a breaking story requiring you to deviate from the original script to go to a field reporter or other remote source such as a CNN or network feed. Production assistants or runners will bring you copy throughout the newscast, sometimes handing the material to you while the camera is on your co-anchor. The producer or director will give you information regarding what to add or delete from your copy via the IFB earpiece. Again, concentration is important because often you must listen to instructions while delivering your copy. Floor managers will also communicate time cues and let you know whether to speed up or slow down. Commercials provide some time for all to regroup. During a commercial you can talk directly with the floor manager, producer, and director.

The end of the newscast may require you to stretch with some additional copy or delete whole stories. Directors and producers have some control over timing the end of the program by either speeding up or slowing down the rolling of the credits; however, editing copy near the end of the newscast is a more desirable way to ensure that things end on time. In most cases it is not hard to stretch a newscast, because there are usually more stories than can be covered in 30 or 60 minutes.

When reading from a prompter, keep in mind some additional details besides the information offered in previous chapters:

- Your vocal pitch goes up when your volume increases, so try to lower your volume. Let the microphone do the work and don't overproject by talking to the camera or floor manager. Some speech coaches actually have the anchor whisper his or her copy, then increase the volume gradually for the best pitch quality.

- Your vocal pitch goes up when you are tense. Work on controlled breathing and the suggestions given in Chapter 4.

- Focus on the message, not yourself. Analyze the meaning of the message and make distinctions between tragic and lighthearted stories. Let the audience hear the mood in your voice and don't forget your nonverbal communication.

- Make sure your copy has phonetic spellings of difficult names and words. Wire services provide a list of these pronunciations on a daily basis.

- If your prompter fails, your thumb can be your friend. When reading the prompter, slide your thumb down the side of your hard copy. This will help you find your place in the script in case of prompter failure. Avoid looking surprised if the prompter goes down; it happens.

- Break contact with the camera lens and prompter by looking at your script (especially between stories). This makes your eye contact more natural instead of looking as if you're staring at the viewer.

- Develop a clear signal between you and the floor manager regarding camera changes. These changes are usually noted in the script and reinforced with signals given by the floor manager (waving a hand under the camera lens, then pointing to the hot camera). Make your turns to the camera smooth and controlled. If you're caught looking at the wrong camera don't panic; make a confident turn to the "hot" camera. In many cases the mistake is not your fault but an error in the control room.

- Overdo your energy. Experiment with your reading style and push a bit with your facial expressions and vocal energy. What seems like overdoing it for you may represent the optimum energy level for the viewers at home. Remember that your perception of energy is different from how you appear onscreen.

RATINGS POINTER

Some anchors will draw pictures in the margins of their scripts as mood prompts for stories (smiling faces for upbeat stories or frowning faces for serious stories). Develop whatever prompts you need to help you convey mood. ★ ★ ★ ★

Energy must be controlled so that you are not moving back and forth onscreen. There are often corner graphics, key IDs, and other visual information that make your screen space seem smaller. Anchors who move too much seem to bump into the graphics, As always, communicate energy through your eyes, facial expressiveness, and voice.

More about Robotics Some basics concerning robotic cameras were covered in Chapter 7. Robotic cameras are often used in newscasts because most of the camera shots are simple due to limited movement by the anchors.

These cameras are not without their problems and challenges for anchors. Since there are no humans operating the cameras, the floor manager is sometimes the only person in the studio. For simple newscasts and updates, there may be no floor manager, so the anchor must rely upon the camera's tally light or commands given through the earpiece to know when to start reading.

Some older robotic systems can seem to have minds of their own as cameras sometimes pan away from the performer to another area while "hot." Try to adjust to any camera problems that may occur by moving with the camera if possible, or looking down at your script if the camera has moved so that you cannot see the prompter.

Don't be distracted by robotic cameras that may be moving into position for other shots. Some systems are on tracks that allow cameras to move about the studio for different shots. It can be disconcerting for anchors not familiar with robotic systems to see a camera suddenly take off to another area of the studio on its own. Keep your focus and concentration on the camera shooting you.

The Anchor as a Real Person Despite advances in technology and ENG hardware, viewers make decisions about which news to watch based on the messenger. If you analyze the content of local or network newscasts, you'll see that most are similar in the story selection and order; in fact, often the same story is on two or more stations at the same time.

Ultimately, viewers will watch your newscast if they perceive you are interested in them and their community. Good anchors are familiar with the important issues and interests of the community and are, in a sense, the most visible ambassadors for their stations or networks. As an anchor, learn all you can about the people and issues in your community so that you can connect with your audience. Review the information about community profiling in Chapter 3, and use it to develop your style as an anchor.

In an era of intense news competition and more source availability, the human factor is more important than ever in the public's selection of news sources.

Weather

For many viewers, the weather forecast is the most important part of the news. Some local stations now try to counterprogram their late night newscasts by airing the weather segment early in the program.

Years ago, the weather forecaster may have also been a staff announcer, children's show host, or someone with other duties at a local station with little training in meteorology who drew on a weather map with a marker and gave a summary of a report by the U.S. National Weather Service. Today, most stations have a trained meteorologist gathering information from a variety of sources (although the weather may be a simple forecast from the anchor, especially on weekends and holidays).

If you visit a local station you will usually see an area to the side of the news set with a solid blue or green chroma-key wall. This is where the weather reporter delivers the forecast. You will also notice two television monitors on each side of where the reporter is standing. These monitors are the only way the reporter can see the same visual information the audience sees. Weather maps and other graphics appear via chroma-key, where any area of blue or green is eliminated and replaced by the visuals. As mentioned earlier, chroma-key is an electronic instead of projection process. The weather reporter sees no image projected on the wall, only on the studio monitors.

The only way the weather reporter knows if he or she is pointing at Los Angeles or Chicago on the national map is to look at the monitor to see hand placement. Locating where you are and how you should gesture can be confusing, because the monitor doesn't provide you with a mirror image; sometimes even experienced weather reporters forget which way they should move. It often takes many hours of practice before beginning weather reporters feel comfortable with the mechanics and techniques involved with chroma-key.

RATINGS POINTER

Chicago's Fox weather reporter Steve Perez Schill has a trick for when he forgets which way he should move or gesture when working with chroma-key. When he's confused about movement, he will move one of his arms slightly or twitch an elbow in the direction he thinks he should move. If that is the right direction on the monitor, he makes his move in that direction; if not, he knows he should move In the opposite direction. For example, if Steve sees that there should be a motion to a northern jet stream on the map but is confused as to which hand to use, he moves an arm where he thinks the jet stream is to see if he's moving in the right direction. This trick helps you orient yourself if you've lost track of direction and where things are on the chroma-key map. ★ ★ ★ ★

Another problem with using chroma-key is that it is very easy for you to become dependent on the monitors, constantly looking at them instead of the camera lens. Remember that you want to refer the information to the viewers at home and not to the studio monitors. Practice making frequent contact with the camera lens so that you connect with viewers.

Clothing was mentioned earlier as another potential problem with chroma-key. Check out the colors you're wearing to make sure part of the chroma-key map or other information doesn't reproduce on some article of your clothing. You may want to bring any questionable colors into the studio for a color test with the chroma-key system.

Weathercaster with chroma-key map.

Hitting your marks was also mentioned as important with proper lighting and camera techniques. Nowhere is this rule more important than in weather reporting. Your chroma-key wall has to be properly lighted (usually even, flat lighting works best) for proper image reproduction and to avoid intense shadows. Also, you are confined to a small area onscreen, so if you move too much you will move out of the frame. Learn to work within the area marked on the studio floor for your performance.

RATINGS POINTER

Advances in chroma-key technology have eliminated some problems such as shadows and poor reproduction. A system called the *Ultimate* provides sharp, high-quality images. Foreground people or objects casting shadows on a blue background can be mixed in such a way that the shadows appear natural instead of overly dark. The *Ultimate* system makes the weather reporter look as if he or she is standing in front of a real map in the studio instead of a chroma-key image. ★ ★ ★ ★

There are some obvious differences in content between national weather forecasts seen on CNN or the Weather Channel and your local station. National cable services or network programs such as *Today* and *Good Morning America* focus on giving brief information about each region of the country, whereas local forecasts are concerned primarily with the city of origin. National forecasts can even include international travel forecasts along with weather conditions throughout the United States.

Local forecasts consider whether or not people in a given city need to carry an umbrella tomorrow or if there will be rain for the big game this Saturday. They also provide some national conditions, especially for holidays such as Thanksgiving when people travel. More national weather conditions have been included on recent local newscasts because we are a mobile society, with people routinely traveling across the country as part of their jobs.

Remember, however, that if you are a local weather reporter, you will focus on local conditions. Other exceptions to this besides travel are letting people know about weather that affects their pocketbooks (for example, a hard freeze that destroys a significant number of crops, thereby driving up the price of fruit and vegetables) or violent conditions for which you may have interesting b-roll (an excellent example of this was b-roll taken with a home camcorder of a tornado touching down in downtown Miami).

Basically, being a weather reporter requires you to anticipate the needs of the audience in regard to how weather affects their lives. Information concerning a sudden frost or snow coming to a ski resort is weather news that the audience can use. As a weather reporter, you are unlike others on a newscast; you are predicting what you think will happen instead of telling what has already happened so there are times when you will be wrong. Spencer Christian mentioned in Chapter 3 that part of the secret of being an effective weather reporter is explaining to the audience why you were wrong and how Mother Nature threw you a curve. No matter how much you know about weather, you will never be right 100 percent of the time.

Sports

Many sports fans at one time or another have wanted to be sports reporters on the evening news or play-by-play announcers. Being a fan certainly helps in pursuing a career in television sports journalism, but the fan must also incorporate the previously discussed aspects of journalism and interviewing in order to be successful.

Television sports journalists must study hours of tape before doing their sportscast or play-by-play as well as familiarizing themselves with the personnel from many teams. An understanding of the history of various sports, strategies (the "Xs and Os") behind plays, and evolving trends are all important aspects of sports reporting. Doing a major event such as *Monday Night Football* requires the same type of study of the players and strategies as studying for a major exam.

As with other on-air positions, there is intense competition for television sports reporting and play-by-play opportunities, with hundreds of resume tapes coming to a station or sports team for one position. The good news is that there are more opportunities than ever for jobs in television sports, because there are more teams televising their games and more sports channels due to cable. A few years ago, major league teams and major college programs televised their games; now minor league teams and smaller colleges are often seen on regional sports networks.

■ **Preparation**   It's not enough to be a fan; you must be a fanatic, and a knowledgeable one at that. Many television sports personnel have read about and participated in sports since childhood. They understand the histories and strategies of most sports and can explain this information in a conversational style. Some sources that can help get you up to speed with your sports knowledge include the following:

■ **Print sources.**   Sports sections of newspapers and sports magazines such as *Sports Illustrated* often provide you with more in-depth information than simply watching a nightly recap of scores.

That said, there are some excellent sources of electronic sports journalism, including *Sports Center* on ESPN and numerous sports radio stations around the country. Be careful when relying upon information from sports talk radio stations. Use critical thinking skills to judge whether or not the talk show host is providing credible information or merely trying to initiate controversy.

■ **Internet websites.** These have revolutionized sports research and reporting. Professional and college teams have their own sites providing current information about players, trades, injuries, and the outcomes of games. You can also download broadcasts of games from these sites. In many cases, team websites are replacing team newspapers and other print reports because they can offer up-to-the-minute information.

■ **Press releases.** Teams still use these to communicate breaking events. It's not difficult to get on the mailing list for a team's press releases, especially if you're involved with a campus radio or television station.

■ **Videotapes of games.** The more you watch, the more you learn and can develop a critical eye for the game. If you want to be a play-by-play announcer, turn down the sound and do your own. Warn friends, family members, or roommates what you're doing so they don't question your mental health.

■ **Conversations with players and coaches.** Nothings beats primary research. Conversations with the participants can help you gain new knowledge and insights into the game.

■ **The Sports Anchor and Reporter** Sports personnel at most television stations act as both in-studio anchors and field reporters. It is not unusual for someone to do three two- to five-minute sportscasts Monday through Friday and other sports features on the weekend, such as a team interview show. Sometimes the weekend sports anchor does field reports several days during the week or may anchor early sportscasts Monday through Friday. In any event, television sports personnel must be able to work in the studio and remotely.

The sports anchor will give scores and talk over highlights of games. Sometimes the anchor is getting the scores during the sportscast through the IFB or notes handed to him or her off camera. Anchors will sometimes do their sportscasts on location at a stadium or arena before the game. They must watch monitors to see all the scores, highlights, and other visuals while delivering their information, often without the aid of a teleprompter. Remote sportscasts often include short interviews with players and coaches sandwiched between the scores and highlights.

When doing field reports, or remotes as an anchor or reporter, it is important to remember the information discussed earlier in the chapter regarding interviews and other aspects of working outside the studio.

Play-by-Play Announcer   Being a play-by-play announcer means performing "without a net" for two or three hours because there is no script. You may have spotters, producers, or other assistants, but ultimately it is your performance that creates an exciting experience for viewers. Books such as Gary Bender's *The Call of the Game* and John R. Catsis's *Sports Broadcasting* can give you specific information about play-by-play announcing, ranging from how to keep statistics to creating football depth charts. Curt Smith's *Voices of the Game* and *The Storytellers* are excellent books about baseball play-by-play announcers on both radio and television. What follows is a basic foundation for calling television play-by-play:

■ **Let the pictures do the talking.** There is a tendency for television play-by-play announcers to describe the obvious to viewers when the visuals can speak for themselves. Don't make the mistake of doing radio play-by-play on television; let viewers enjoy the visuals and ambient sound, An excellent example of how to do this was when St. Louis Cardinals slugger Mark McGwire set the home run record in 1998. After hitting the record breaker, the announcer didn't speak for several minutes after his initial home run call, making the visuals and crowd noise seem even more intense during this historic sports moment.

Sports television has become a close-up medium, especially during dramatic moments in a game. Don't spoil the moment with talk that distracts the viewer from the drama.

■ **Tell the audience what they can't see or isn't obvious to them.** The camera can't catch everything, so you need to be the viewer's eyes in the announcer's booth. Tell viewers where outfielders are playing a hitter if that isn't on the screen. If there was a key block away from the ball during a football game, let the viewer know. In many cases the director will catch up to you with visual support either live or replay to show the action.

■ **Point to particulars in replays.** Use replays to show why a play succeeded or failed. Replays are wonderful teaching tools.

■ **Simplify the "Xs and Os."** Don't try to impress viewers with your knowledge of strategy and jargon. Work on explaining and simplifying the finer points of the game. John Madden is successful because he appears to be a regular guy who knows something about football. Viewers feel they know him. Treat your audience as friends who happen to be watching you describe a game.

■ **Get the story behind the game and players.** Sports has become narrative. Good play-by-play announcers not only describe the action on the field but also explain the backgrounds of players and teams. Viewers enjoy hearing the stories behind their favorite players and how they became stars. An excellent example of this was the revelation during the 2000 Super Bowl that Super Bowl MVP quarterback Kurt Warner had been a supermarket stock clerk in his recent past.

■ **Do your homework concerning statistics, records, and player numbers.** Again, this is like studying for a major exam. You need to know player averages, statistics, and team statistics. Spotters can help with numbers during football games, but the more players' numbers you know, the less dependent you'll be on the spotter. If you can't readily identify a player, cover until you can make the identification. Keep mistakes to a minimum and correct them as soon as possible during your play-by-play. Team and conference websites provide statistics and other information. Develop a positive relationship with the sports information director or media relations person of the team you're covering. This person will be invaluable in helping you prepare for a game.

■ **Work with your color person before the game.** Make decisions concerning who will bring up certain key points, including who says what during the pre-game show. Reach an agreement on how you will pronounce difficult names. You may want to call a practice game with your color person before doing a real telecast.

■ **Let the humor come from the situation instead of imposing it on the game.** Television sports is becoming more entertainment oriented to attract the casual fan. Some announcers seem to have their humor planned, wedging it into the game at any opportunity. Most viewers can tell if humor is spontaneous or contrived, and natural humor usually wins out over canned material.

■ **Avoid cliches and catchphrases stolen from other announcers.** Describing an exciting game as a "real barnburner" will probably elicit groans and laughter from your viewers. Stealing a famous home run call or signature phrase from another announcer will cause even more negative audience reactions. Develop your own word choice and use of language. Sports cliches are constantly evolving, so listen to other announcers to see if certain terms are overused, for example, the phrase "having so many weapons" to describe a football team with a potent offense.

■ **Watch your monitors.** There's a temptation for play-by-play announcers to watch the field or court and not watch what the home viewer is seeing on the monitor. You must watch the monitor so that you can refer to what the viewer sees. Refer to actions you see off the field as well as on. WGN's famous baseball television director Arnie Harris is known for crowd shots and colorful hat shots in the stands. Play-by-play announcers watching the monitor can refer to these shots, thereby adding color to the game.

Make sure you constantly check your monitor for statistics, graphics, replays, and other visual information you need to relay to viewers. Your producer will often alert you concerning when this information will appear.

■ **Don't guess if you don't know.** Wait until you know that the ball has cleared the fence for a home run or you see the official's signal for a touchdown. Don't speculate on the severity of players' injuries. Make sure you're able to verify information about injuries and that you receive injury updates from credible sources such as team trainers or sports information directors.

Your play-by-play career will start with a minor league team or smaller college, although more opportunities are surfacing with regional sports cable operations. In any event a love of sports and long hours will help advance your career as a television sports journalist.

Rewind and Fade to Black

Intense competition continues in the television news industry due to new on-air and cable services as well as new delivery systems such as the Internet. Television news is no longer just a service to the community; it is also a profit center for stations and networks. This reality presents challenges and ethical questions for those involved with television journalism.

The line between hard news and entertainment has blurred over the last few years. You will no doubt encounter situations in which you're asked to cover a story with questionable news value. Be prepared to deal with competition and ethical issues as you pursue a career in television journalism.

There is still intense competition on an individual level as people graduating from journalism or communication departments vie for jobs in news, weather, and sports. Remember that students should complement these majors with a good liberal arts education. Television news departments are looking for people who have broad-based knowledge, writing skills, and the ability to think fast and communicate information under pressure. These skills have been invaluable for television journalists since the days of Edward R. Murrow and will continue to be useful in the age of cyber-communication.

Technology will change, and the newscasts of 2010 will look different from those of today, but future successful journalists will be good and accurate storytellers. Former CBS news executive Burton Benjamin once said:

> The good journalist is a treasure, and they won't be able to clone him [or her] in a laboratory. The problem that television faces, in my opinion, is for the creativity to keep up with the racing technology. I don't care whether or not a story is coming to you via satellite, has been written by a computer and transmitted by a correspondent with an antenna implanted in his [or her] head.
>
> If he/she can't write, he/she can't write by satellite or quill pen. If he/she can't report, he/she can't report. And all the technology in the world will not save him [or her]. There is so much at stake today that if we simply go with the technology, we are going to be in trouble. There was never a time when . . . reporters who can write, report, analyze, and ask the right questions were needed more.

Exercises

1 Compare and contrast the content and styles of network newscasts such as CBS, NBC, and ABC. What stories do they cover, and what are the respective styles of the anchors? Do the same with local and cable newscasts. Watch at least three newscasts per network, station, or cable service.

2 Observe how various stations use live shots. Do they add to the reporting of the story, or do they seem to be a gimmick? Watch stand-ups and see if they are done in a creative manner.

3 Choose stories at random from your local newspaper. Study each story for 15 minutes to familiarize yourself with the information. Take notes if you need to, but fill no more than one sheet of legal paper on a clipboard. Look into a camera and give a one-minute report concerning each story while maintaining good eye-to-lens contact.

4 Videotape yourself reading from a teleprompter (if you don't have a tele- prompter, write out three stories on cue cards and read from them). When you replay the tape, study your eyes to see if they shift back and forth or if they appear natural.

5 Prepare a weather forecast based on basic information found in your news- paper. Don't worry if you don't have chroma-key; you can work off a regular map. If you want to be a sports anchor, prepare a three-minute sportscast with scores from your local paper. Record highlights from ESPN or another source, edit them together, and include them in your sportscast.

INTERVIEW

Lori Hillman
Former *CBS Evening News* Producer

Question: As a producer, what are your expectations of a performer during the production process?

Lori Hillman: The most important thing is to go into the story together, it's team- work. The only difference between a pro- ducer and a reporter who is skilled at writ- ing is that one is in front of the camera and the other is not. The person in front of the camera should have production skills in addition to performance skills. This means you need to be really charismatic and connect with the viewer. If you can't do that, there is really no need to be in front of the camera.

Q: You've worked with Dan Rather and Bill Moyers. What would you say are their strengths as communicators.

LH: My experience with Dan Rather is that he is a master of presenting the mate- rial. He is a master of being in front of the camera and he loves what he does. . . . He is quite committed to the product.

I worked much more directly with Bill Moyers and that was an amazing experi- ence. He embraces everyone he comes in contact with—from the person in the bank to the person in the coffee store. He's a very curious person and he cares about how all sorts of people see the world. I helped him back in 1984 with his cam- paign commentaries, and he would ask me about how I felt concerning all sorts of issues: What does a young educated per- son think about a variety of issues? I think he is someone who takes it to heart; I think he listens to people. I think he's much less concerned about the glitz of television than the content. I think he saw television at that time as the best way to reach a wide audience. I don't think he was taken with the phenomenon of being on television. The written word is very important to him and he is a curious thinker. He was not into being a star on television. . . . Moyers sees television as a tool to reach people. . . . I think his heart lies in the story and writing the information. . . . He can get outside of his own belief system and way of thinking about things. That's why his commentaries were so interesting.

Q: What can a performer do to make the producer's job easier?

LH: Know the story, care about the story. The way television is produced today, things are run very much like a business. . . . A producer will often research, write, and report the story, and screen the tape, and the on-camera reporter will record the voiceovers—it happens all the time. It's a way to get product out. That's what makes television different from print, you need someone with those on-camera skills to package the story. In print, whoever does the research writes and reports the story—that's the person's byline you see. In television, it's the person with on-camera skills. . . . There's a lot of that now because with budget constraints a reporter and producer can't go together to cover a story. You divide the labor. I worked on many stories where I've done the research, writing, screening of tape, and supervising of the editing, and the reporter does a stand-up or a voiceover. . . . My most rewarding experiences have been when the reporter and I have worked as a team. Those experiences seem to be richer. Sometimes two heads can be better than one. When the right people and the right story come together it can be incredi-

ble. My experience was that this process happened less at the network than at the local level. . . . I don't want to suggest that reporters are sitting back in their offices with their feet up while the producers are busy. Reporters are out doing other stories. This is a way to increase the volume and get more stories on television.

Q: Couldn't there be a time factor in regard to breaking news and getting a story on air?

LH: That's exactly right! Another situation could be that I was working on a longer news story and the reporter I was working with had to go out on a breaking story. There are only so many reporters in the organization. So there may be five breaking stories and only three correspondents. Well, a correspondent is not going to sit down and work with me on a story that may be airing in two weeks; he or she is going to be out covering that breaking story. The cases where the producer does all the work and the reporter does none of it are exceptional; that's not the general rule.

Q: Wouldn't it also be the fact that news organizations are now smaller?

LH: Absolutely. When I started at CBS in the early 1980s, the producer and correspondent went off and shot, wrote, and edited everything together. It was a luxury in a way, but not terribly efficient. . . . I think where you get into trouble, and it doesn't happen very much, is when a correspondent knows nothing about the story that he or she is reporting. Again, that doesn't happen too much.

Q: Are there things that a producer can do to improve a bad story?

LH: Yes. For example, when a reporter is recording a voiceover and it sounds flat, you have to really be a voice coach. Usually a reporter is getting help on the side if he or she is new and that shouldn't happen on the network level, but it does. If a voiceover isn't delivered well, it is a disaster and no one will listen. A producer can help, even though most producers are not voice coaches by training. If I'm writing a story, I'm hearing how it should be voiced in my head. There are reporters who understand how I'm writing and, in turn, I write for them so we are totally in sync. . . . With voiceovers, there are certain words that need to be punched and intonation needs to be a certain way. With better reporters, a producer doesn't need to do too much coaching.

Q: It sounds as if it's the same relationship a political speechwriter has with a politician in that they need to know the person's vocal habits.

LH: That's exactly right. I work with someone now where we have almost a shorthand experience where everything I write sounds almost totally like the way I intended it to sound . . . I never have to say, "Punch this word," or "Read it like this."

Q: You say that you are not a voice coach. Is the advice you give primary gut instinct?

LH: There's no science to this. Most people will agree that a well-produced piece is a well-produced piece. A lot of it is an innate sense of how all this should come together . . . it's how you put the puzzle together. You either have a knack at this or you don't. You can be a good reporter but a terrible television reporter. Writing and packaging television stories is so different from writing for print. You either get it or you don't.

Q: Have we lost the art of being good storytellers?

LH: I see a lot of resume tapes of people coming out of college. I think that at the network level the commitment to journalism is different. I think that a lot of these are beginning reporters who want to be on television. You can't be at the network level without some knowledge and skills because you have to think on your feet; but I see a lot of young people who just want to be on television. I think that for many the journalism and content of a story is not as important as it used to be. I could be wrong, but that's my impression. Even with dot.com and all, it is still a glamour position to be on television and I think the business is still attracting people who want that.

Q: What story do you remember where everything clicked between you and the on-camera reporter?

LH: Two stories come to mind. One was at CBS in New York where we did a story about homeless kids living underneath Grand Central Station in the tunnels. We were the first television group to take a camera down there. There had been a couple of print stories. . . . Those were the days when there was a lot more money for risk. You could go to your news director and pitch a story and he or she would say, "Go see what you can do." There were no guarantees on stories like those, but our bosses would let us go after them anyway.

That story was incredible. I spent one full night in the tunnels with the kids and the correspondent, Harold Dow, and the camera crew. Then I spent a couple other nights shooting other elements of the story. This report told an incredibly bleak story of what these kids were up to underneath Grand Central Station. Some were lying near the third rail; if you hit that, it's all over. These kids were willing to work with us because they were connected to a homeless advocate who knew us. It was the kind of thing that we couldn't believe what we were capturing. As depressing as it was, I think it was an important story to tell and I think we told it in an effective, powerful way.

The other story that was amazing was one I produced at KPIX, San Francisco, as executive producer of special projects, I found a little clip in a humane society brochure that talked about exotic animals in Texas being auctioned off, mistreated, and put on enclosed hunting ranges. I thought this was interesting and showed it to my news director and he said "Go." We did a little prep work, but not a lot. We found out when the auction was, but you can't call up people and say, "Hey, we want to come and shoot the mistreatment of animals." Loren Nancarrow, the reporter, Mary Bauer, the cameraperson, and I spent about ten days in the Texas hill country. We got some of the most incredible video I've ever seen in my life. It was horrible, but if you're trying to tell a television story, it was about as good as it gets.

We went to the auction and they gave us access to anything we wanted because they think what they do is fine and they let us shoot whatever we wanted. We went to a hunting ranch and shot a hunt. There are fences around these ranches. We also met a very wealthy couple who had a pair of bears in their backyard that were caged. We did a five-part series and ended up winning several awards, including a local Emmy. *60 Minutes* ended up wanting to use some of our footage.

This story was so different from anything we had done because we discovered a whole industry we hadn't known about. We were learning about this activity and getting some of the best b-roll I've ever seen, and great interviews. We would come back to the hotel and we couldn't believe what we had. It was the most exciting story, and it wasn't a war or anything like

that. . . . I've interviewed important people and done important stories, but this one was enlightening.

I've never been so in sync with a team as I was with our reporter and cameraperson. We got back to San Francisco and it continued. Loren and I wrote scripts, Mary was totally involved, we each tried so hard. We were all wanting to do as much as we could to go the extra mile. No one was complaining, "When's lunch?" "I'm tired, I don't want to carry this anymore," which can happen a lot. There are situations where the crew waits to be directed by the producer. For example, if the producer doesn't say, "We need to shoot that sign," it may not get done.

Our trip to Texas wasn't anything like that. . . . It was the kind of story that shot and wrote itself. That's when you know you have a good story and that you have all the material you need to work with. We also had a news director who was really excited. It was enterprising reporting and not much had been done on the subject.

Q: What piece of advice would you give to those who want to be television news reporters.

LH: Mainly, I think that if you want to be on television as a journalist you have to first be a journalist and be attractive and have a nice voice, second. It's important to have those things because that's the way our culture is. If you don't like being called "talent," which can be used as a derogatory term, you need to be a journalist. That means you have to understand what reporting and writing are about, how to cover a story, and what questions to ask. You need to care about the content. I think that's really important for new people who want to get into news. The best on-camera people are the ones who care about the news.

INTERVIEW

Steve Perez Schill
Weathercaster for WFLD Chicago Fox

Steve Perez Schill has been a weathercaster for over twenty years in markets ranging from Eureka, California, to Chicago. He is part of WFLD's *Nine O'Clock News* in Chicago, where he has three weather segments during the hour-long newscast. In this interview, Steve talks about creating a weathercast and how to progress in a performance career.

Question: You had a variety of work experiences before becoming a weather-caster.

Steve Perez Schill: I was in high school and I didn't know what to do so I joined the army . . . got out of the army and still didn't know what I wanted to do so I went to college on the G.I. Bill. I went to Diablo Valley College (near San Francisco) to do my general education classes and took a speech class. At that point in my life, that's what I wanted to do, become a speech teacher at a community college. . . . Went to Humboldt State University and took speech classes along with radio and television classes. Then I started doing some commercial work, along with a live, phone-in television talk show. While I was doing that, I started to teach and coach speech at Pima College.

I also started teaching at Humboldt. While I was doing all those jobs, another opportunity opened up in weather. I was sharing an office with the weathercaster and he told me he was leaving. He said, "Steve, I think you would be really good at this." I didn't know a lot about weather at that time, but I auditioned. I had to stand in front of the chroma-key blue screen and I didn't know what I was doing but I got the job. . . . I was paid $300 a month to do

the same job I'm doing now, only double the hours. . . . My weather education came from the National Weather Service. . . . Here at Fox we have five computers that help me do the job. Back then we had none. I had to drive to the National Weather Service office, pick up the information, and ask them, "You're calling for fog. How does fog form?" They would sit with me and give me books and have me read information. So for over three years, that's where my primary weather education came from. . . . On the way to Chicago, I went to Bakersfield, CA; Portland, OR; Tucson, AZ; San Jose, CA; then to Chicago.

Q: You mentioned that you were a teacher. Does that experience help you in explaining the weather each night?

SPS: Absolutely! The things like eye contact and gestures, but perhaps the most important thing is audience analysis. Who is the audience? Much of this information we get from demographic analysis. But I have a wide spectrum of people and for some this information is difficult to absorb. However, the bottom line is not that difficult. The bottom line is that its going to be sunny and the temperature is going to be 65 degrees; that's what they are waiting for. . . . How do we take all that information and condense it down to two and a half minutes? I have to make a judgment from all the computer information I have; what does the audience need to know and how does that support my end contention?

I like to build what I call a surface map. I will very simply put in the highs and lows and fronts and put them into place, move them to where I think they are going to be, and simply put in a few words that tell why it is going to be warmer. . . . You will also see this through the graphics. So basically the job is to take complex information and support it with graphics that detail the forecast. We are taking that information and showing the folks why it is going to be warmer.

Q: Describe your communication with the director and the control room after you have created the weathercast.

SPS: If there is any severe weather, the producers and I will confer to figure out strategies. What kind of information should I be offering right at the top? Usually, I'll do a rundown along with a list of graphics, and I'll photocopy that and give it to the director. It lets them know where I'm going every night so they don't dump out of a graphic early and come back to me.

Q: And of course you're giving verbal cues to them so they know where you are going in the weathercast.

SPS: Oh sure! Things like, "And tomorrow . . ." and so on.

Q: We've talked about the substance, how about style? How does your style differ from other weathercasters in this market?

SPS: I really see myself as just your average guy. Now I'm making a lot more money, but for over three quarters of my career I wasn't making very much. I still have that average "Joe Blow" mentality.

Every night I try to include that average person on the street by including them as a weather spotter. I'll call somebody in the Chicago area, ask them what they are doing, and get the temperature at their house. Then I'll mention the name on the air. I try to personalize it as much as possible.

Going back to my surface maps, I like to simplify things as much as possible. Take the mystery out of weather. Sometimes it's very complicated because there [are] a lot of things going on and you really don't do the weather justice. More often than not it is really pretty simple. I like to goof around as much as possible as long as it doesn't interfere with the message . . . I never plan jokes. If it happens, it happens. I like to stay as loose as possible and interact with the anchors.

Q: How long did it take you to get comfortable with using chroma-key?

SPS: Everything is backwards when using chroma-key. It's like looking in a mirror. There are times even twenty-two years later when I have trouble with it. When I'm looking into the camera, I'm not looking at a teleprompter, they switch the camera and I'm looking into something that they call "on air" (instead of a script, whatever is currently on air is shown in front of the camera lens). I can see myself and the graphics behind me. So I could look directly into the camera lens and point at the graphics the whole time but that would be uncomfortable because I would be staring directly into the eyes of the viewers the whole time.

We have two monitors, and every weatherperson has this. They are not looking in back of them, they are looking to the side. They have two monitors so if they want to switch from one side to the other they can do so. So I'm actually able to look at the monitors and switch back to the camera and still work with the information. (Steve's trick of moving an arm in the direction you think you want to go on the map was mentioned earlier in this chapter).

Q: In regard to movement, do you have to move slower or make your gestures smaller because you're working in a small area?

SPS: There are times when I don't want to be onscreen; I want to get out of the way of the map and let the information speak for itself. There are times when there are things going on across the nation and people don't want me standing in the way. If I have numbers, such as highs for the day, or if there is something going on in Arizona and California, and I'm standing in front of those states because my primary focus is the Midwest, that could be a problem. There is one map, the Weatherspotter Map, where I focus on current conditions and at the end I focus on one particular community and I mention a person's name such as "Julie and her friends playing cards out in Oaklawn tell me that it's currently 67 degrees at her house." I'll step back and let that map reveal itself. Often, I'll have technical information relative to that Weatherspotter because it may be a nonprofit organization that has something going on so I want to get it right (the date, time, and place of a special event).

There are times when I notice that just my hands are sticking out into the screen and that can be a problem so I have to pull back a little bit. There is one person who always stands on the same side of the map so that no matter what he's talking about on the West Coast, he stays on that

side and backs up. Pretty soon all you see is a hand on the screen. I would say please do not back up, but switch around. Turn around and work with the information and center it up as much as possible.

Q: What are some tips you give to people in putting together a resume tape?

SPS: I hate to watch myself. I was forced into editing resume tapes and I just hated the process. Finally I said to myself, I'm going to offer one of my editors some money to go through past tapes for me and pick out what they think is the very best and edit it. If you can find a producer or someone who really knows what he or she is doing, and offer them a gift, your unending friendship, money, whatever you can afford to give up to advise you on a tape, that's what I would do.

[Note: Chapter 12 discusses the specifics concerning resume tapes. You can also get advice on good segments to include on your tape from instructors, colleagues, and trusted friends.]

Q: Any final piece of advice for those who are starting their careers as video performers?

SPS: If this is something you really want to do, you just have to go out and start doing it, whether it's at a radio station, college television station, a very small market, or an internship. Internships are the smartest way to go. We've had interns here at Fox in Chicago, the number three market in the nation, who have walked from an internship to a reporter's position without having to go through the things I went through. . . . The main thing is, if you make a mistake don't be hard on yourself. Just go with it and you'll improve.

CHAPTER ELEVEN

Commercials and Public Service Announcements

We know that commercials are the lifeblood of most television stations because they pay the bills and salaries. Even public television, once commercial free, now airs extended promotional announcements for products and services. Commercials can influence our buying choices even if we resent viewing them. How many times have you watched a movie of which the first 30 minutes are uninterrupted, but the final 45 minutes are backloaded so that there are commercials every few minutes? The station or network bets that you are now hooked into watching the film and will endure commercials in order to see how it ends.

You know most of these facts about commercials. What you may not know are some of the following:

- The average household in the United States has at least one television set turned on four to six hours a day. Some surveys indicate a decline in television viewing as people shift to using computers for online entertainment, information, and games or watch videocassettes and DVDs on their television sets; however, it's safe to say that most people spend a significant amount of free time in front of a screen of some kind.

- A significant portion of each television hour is devoted to commercials, promotions, and public service announcements. Depending on the time of day, 12 minutes or more of each hour can be taken up with selling you something. Continuous commercial messages are part of streaming video online productions.

- Despite zipping and zapping, surveys indicate that from birth to age 21 an average person in the United States sees between 250,000 and 500,000 commercials. Television networks, sponsors, and advertising agencies are skewing their messages to young people because they have not yet made brand choices or developed brand loyalty. This is especially true of networks such as Fox and WB.

- Big-budget commercials such as those seen during the Super Bowl may cost as much or more per minute to produce as major theatrical films. A sponsor purchasing commercial time on the Super Bowl or popular prime-time shows may pay millions of dollars per minute.

Performance in commercials, along with production values, has changed over the years. This chapter gives you an overview of past and present commercial performances along with current commercial types and techniques. It also briefly reviews some principles from earlier chapters such as screen space, movement, working with props, and phrasing and emphasis as they apply to commercial performance.

The Evolution of Television Commercials

Early television commercials were live in most cases, often featuring a performer holding a product while making a pitch to the audience. Network programs often had only one sponsor and the sponsor's name was part of the show's title (*Texaco Star Theater with Milton Berle*). Commercials were done live at the network and local levels. It was not unusual to see a commercial set off to the side of the news set at a local station, as live commercials were also aired during newscasts.

Most local stations employed a wider variety of performers than they do today. For example, people known as **booth announcers** did all the station identifications and promotional announcements. They often performed in live commercials as part of their responsibilities. Local stations also produced more of their own programs. Performers in programs such as children's shows would often double as commercial spokespersons. Daytime shows produced for homemakers featured elaborate live productions and demonstrations. As with all live television, things could go wrong during a commercial when the product didn't do what it supposed to or the performer used it the wrong way.

Film and videotape eliminated many live commercials, allowing for retakes and shooting on location. In many cases, performers now functioned as actors portraying characters. Appeals in commercials have changed over the years as commercials now sell products using emotional rather than logical appeals, For example, early car commercials focused on factual information such as engine size, leg room, and gas mileage, whereas recent car spots are more emotional and experiential. They show people driving cars through beautiful scenery and often have implied sexual content. Today's commercial performers are no longer just the credible spokespersons of the past; in many cases they must show emotional attachment to the product and communicate to viewers that they enjoy using it.

Commercials Are More than Selling

The obvious goal of commercials is getting viewers to buy products. This may be the so-called bottom line from which the sponsor judges a commercial's success by an increase in sales, but commercials also create positive experiences, associations, and attitudes. A commercial for a cruise line can create a sense of wanting to get away from one's responsibilities and day-to-day pressures.

Commercials can also create a feeling of "dis-comfort" in viewers: that if they don't purchase a product or service, negative consequences could follow. Several years ago American Express ran a successful campaign showing couples on vacation who had lost all their cash because their purses or wallets had been lost or stolen. Many people could readily identify with the consequences of losing all their cash on vacation—the trip might be ruined. However, we were reassured, if you have American Express traveler's checks there is no need to fear, because they can be replaced in a couple of hours and the vacation can continue.

This campaign succeeded not only because of the product but because of the situation and feelings surrounding it. The actors had to communicate the fear and discomfort of losing money in a strange place.

RATINGS POINTER

One of the first people to examine the emotional impact of commercials was Tony Schwartz, who produced numerous commercials and public service announcements, including one for President Lyndon Johnson that proved to be one of the most controversial political spots of all time: "The Daisy Spot" hinted that Johnson's opponent, Senator Barry Goldwater, might use nuclear weapons against U.S. enemies.

One of Schwartz's key principles is *evoked recall.* He believes that it is easier to get a response out of a person than to put a message into them. If you surround your product with positive experiences and colorful packaging, the product jumps off the shelf and "buys" the person. We see this technique used with commercials for a variety of products ranging from cars to colas, in which actors are seen using and enjoying the product. The message to viewers is that if you buy this product, these good things will happen to you.

The focus of many commercials today is the performer as typical person instead of typical salesperson. ★ ★ ★ ★

Performers must be able to adapt to the varied techniques needed to sell products in today's advertising environment. Research firms such as Look-Look, Inc. examine trends and preferences of younger viewers. Look-Look has discovered that young people don't like hype and that they want to discover products on their own. Such research influences advertising agencies in the commercial appeals they use.

While commercials are always evolving, there are a number of standard types that continue to be popular.

Types of Commercials

Watch an evening of television and you'll see at least one example of each of the following commercials:

- a spokesperson
- a slice of life
- a narrative
- a voiceover

You'll see additional ads using various special effects, but these seem to be the most common types using performers.

▎**The Spokesperson** Commercials using spokespersons have been around since the beginning of television. In many cases the spokesperson is a well-known celebrity or athlete; in other cases he or she may be a representative or president of a company. The spokesperson can also be an anonymous performer playing the role of an expert or convinced consumer. We don't see many spokesperson commercials today because advertising agencies favor more visual techniques and special effects; however, a number of local commercial and public service announcements still use spokespersons.

In any event, the spokesperson looks directly at the camera lens making the pitch to viewers. Credibility and a warm, friendly style are the keys to these spots. Infomercials and shopping networks both rely heavily upon spokespersons.

■ **Infomercials.** Broadcast since the early 1980s, **infomercials** have their roots in extended talks and sales pitches from early radio that sometimes lasted half an hour. Infomercials often appear late at night or on weekends. Basically, the sponsor buys the time, usually 30 minutes, from the station just as if purchasing a 30- or 60-second commercial spot. Infomercials often feature a celebrity or product inventor, although they can also include other performers.

These can be challenging productions because they include demonstrations of the product as well as information for viewers. Some infomercials include studio audiences; the performer must relate to those in the studio as well as to home viewers. The host may have to go into the studio audience and talk to people just as a talk show host does.

Infomercials are also challenging for performers because much of the information must be presented ad-lib. The opening and closing may be scripted, but much of the content during demonstrations and pitches is delivered with few or no cue cards. Performers must be very familiar with the product in order to be effective.

■ **Shopping channels.** A variety of shopping channels have become popular on cable television over the last 20 years. These services allow viewers to see products and then buy or bid on them at home. Performers face many of the same challenges on shopping networks as on infomercials.

During one shift a performer presents many products, so there is no time for fully scripted sales pitches. Performers often work from a product fact sheet or with limited notes. Demonstrations and interviews are also usually included. Hosts interview product creators or fashion experts as part of the pitch. Famous athletes sometimes appear on sports collectible segments. Telephone call-ins are also a part of the process. The host must maintain good eye-to-lens contact while talking to various people who call with questions or comments.

Limited, controlled movement is always a consideration for video performers, but especially so for those hosting shopping segments. Usually graphics share screen space with the performer giving information such as product name, description, price, quantity, and how much time is left to purchase the product. Broad movements cause the host to "bump" into the surrounding graphics. Hosts on home shopping channels must limit gestures and movement more than they normally would for most video productions.

Slice of Life   These commercials feature a 30- or 60-second story in which viewers see a person faced with some problem such as dirty floors or bad breath. The solution to the problem usually comes about halfway through the spot when the product is introduced. After the product is used, floors are cleaner or breath fresher, and things end on an upbeat note.

Performers in **slice-of-life commercials** must demonstrate in a convincing way first that they are worried or concerned about the problem facing them and then they are upbeat and happy because the product has solved the problem. This contrast requires a major mood shift for the performer. Most slice-of-life commercials have more than one character, so the performers have to relate to each other instead of to the camera lens.

Narrative   Narrative commercials differ from slice-of-life spots in that they are 30- or 60-second mini-dramas that can make us laugh or cry. These spots have some of the highest production values in the industry and are often the most memorable. Some feature film directors got their start directing commercials.

One award-winning narrative commercial from several years ago was from the "Got Milk?" campaign (in fact, most of the commercials from this campaign are narrative spots). This spot features a man as the curator of a museum housing artifacts from the duel between Alexander Hamilton and Aaron Burr. The man is sitting behind his desk surrounded with Hamilton and Burr artifacts, making a peanut butter sandwich and listening to a classical music radio station. The music is interrupted by an announcer asking a question for a $10,000 prize: "Who shot Alexander Hamilton?" The curator immediately calls the station with the answer, but there is a problem: He has just taken a bite of his sandwich, peanut butter is stuck to the roof of his mouth, and he can barely speak. He is able to say, "Aaan Buhhh" but the announcer can't understand him.

The solution to the problem is on the curator's desk; a carton of milk. Unfortunately, the carton is nearly empty and the curator can't get enough milk in his glass to wash down the sandwich. The announcer finally says, "I'm sorry, your time is up," and hangs up on the whimpering curator. The final graphic on the screen asks, "Got Milk?"

There is clearly drama in this 60-second spot: Is the curator going to be able to answer the question in time to win the $10,000? The tension is heightened by cutaway shots of the various pictures and artifacts surrounding the curator when he is on the phone. The irony of the spot is that the curator knows the answer better than anyone—if he only had some milk, he would be able to give it.

Narrative spots are designed to entertain viewers and keep them watching while selling the product. Some critics believe that well-produced narrative commercials are more entertaining than some programs.

Acting in Commercials

Early in this book we made a distinction between performance and acting. Slice-of-life and narrative commercials require you to be someone other than yourself, so they demand some acting skills. This chapter cannot address everything you need to know about acting for commercials. Entire books have been devoted to developing these skills. However, this section does cover some of the basics of acting in commercials, while making a distinction between commercial acting and performance delivery. If you're serious about commercial acting, you should take drama courses and try to transfer acting skills to projects in your television production classes. You'll notice that there are some major differences between acting on stage and for video, but there are also a number of theories and skills you can transfer from stage to screen. Here are some rudimentary guidelines on acting for the screen to get you started:

■ **Developing a Commercial Cliche** In most commercials, an actor is not playing a character as in a play or film; instead, he or she is playing a cliche, or a profile of a typical person. For example, let's say you're a 25-year-old woman and you're asked to play a 22-year-old recent college graduate in a car dealership commercial. You will be playing someone close to your age, but can you make the audience believe that you have just graduated from college?

There's a great deal of difference between someone who has already been in the work force for three years and someone just graduating from college. Your job in this commercial is to communicate some of the excitement and uncertainty associated with buying a new car. If the audience believes you are a recent graduate, you've done your job well.

There are a number of commercial cliches or types, including but not limited to the following:

- the businesswoman
- the female executive
- the homemaker
- the soccer mom
- the fashion model
- the grandmother
- the outdoorswoman
- the "silly woman"
- the "goofy guy"

- the father
- the businessman
- the male executive
- the athlete
- the blue-collar worker
- the grandfather
- the male model
- the neighbor

Can you think of some others we see on a regular basis?

RATINGS POINTER

Watch television for an evening and pay attention to the commercials. How many character cliches do you see? Are there some of these that you might be capable of playing? ★ ★ ★ ★

Sometimes people have difficulty determining what cliche(s) they are. Don't be afraid to ask friends and instructors what types they think you could portray. You may be surprised at others' perceptions of what you could do. Commercial class assignments are a great way to experiment with playing certain cliches.

When playing a cliche, you must go beyond merely being yourself; you must develop physical, social, and psychological qualities in much the same way that an actor develops a character for stage or film. The following categories and questions will assist you with your analysis. Remember, you should answer these questions as you think the character would answer them:

■ **Physical qualities.** As you might guess, physical qualities are the look and sound of the character or type you are developing. Actors often call this "developing their base." Ask the following questions about physical qualities:

- How old am I?
- How does my posture express my age, health, and feeling about myself?

- What is the pitch, volume, tempo, resonance, or quality of my voice and what do I think of it?

- Is my articulation careless or precise? Do I have a dialect?

- How energetic or vital am I?

- Are my gestures complete or incomplete? Vigorous or weak? Compulsive or controlled?

- How do I walk, sit, and stand? What is the rate of my walk?

- Do I have objects with me, and if so how do I handle them?

- What do I like to wear? What do I have to wear?

■ **Social qualities.** These qualities influence how the character or type relates to his or her world. Ask these questions regarding social qualities:

- How do I feel when I get up in the morning?

- What is my relationship to my environment and do I like it?

- What is my educational background? How intelligent am I?

- How much money do I have? How important is money to me?

- What is my nationality? Am I proud of it?

- What is my occupation? Do I like it? Why did I choose this job?

- What are my political attitudes?

- Do I have any spiritual beliefs? If so, what are they?

- Who would I choose to be if I could be anyone else?

- Who were some of my childhood heroes?

- Who are my parents? What do I like and dislike about them? What can I still hear them saying to me?

- What do I like and dislike about my family?

- Who are my friends and what kind of people am I attracted to? Who are people I dislike and why?

- What ideas do I like and dislike?

- What hobbies or interests do I have?

- Am I single or married? If single, am I dating anyone? Who are the types of people I'm attracted to?

- Do I have children? If so, what are some of the things I like about having children? What are some of my concerns about being a parent?

- How do I feel about the location where the commercial is taking place?

■ **Psychological qualities.** These are qualities contributing to the mental state of the type or character you are portraying and what makes them tick. Ask these questions relating to the psychological state of the character:

- What choices do I face, and what decisions will I be making?
- How do some of my physical traits impact my psychological traits?
- How do some of my social traits affect my psychological traits?
- What makes me angry? What relaxes me?
- What worries me?
- What are some of my driving ambitions?
- What are some of my gut instincts?
- Do I think things out or do I do them impulsively?
- What do I really want out of life? What do I need?
- What do I like and dislike about myself?
- What are my greatest fears?
- Do other people like me? If so, why? If not, why not?

You may think that these are too many questions to ask in preparation for a 30- or 60-second commercial. Depending upon the featured product or service, you may not have to answer all of them, but the more complete the profile you have of the type or character you're playing, the more believable your performance will be. Determine what things motivate the character and why he or she is making certain decisions in the commercial. Let's look at three types of commercials to see how we can create a comprehensive character profile.

EXAMPLE 1   Commercial for a local automobile dealership promoting recent college graduate discounts. The central character is a 22-year-old female college graduate:

- *Physical qualities*. We know the gender and age of the character. This woman is probably intelligent and energetic. She moves with confidence and stands erect. Gestures and movement are sure and she is not withdrawn or small. She has a strong, confident voice but at times shows a hint of concern about making the right decisions. She wears nice, casual clothes such as slacks and a blouse or sweater depending on the season. She may carry a purse.

- *Social qualities.* She's excited about a new job and some new responsibilities. She hasn't been on the job long enough to get involved with negative office politics, so she wakes up every morning eager to go to work. She is a young urban professional. We know that she is a college graduate and probably did well in school. She is making a good starting salary but has some of the normal concerns about just starting out and having to make a lot of purchases to furnish an apartment. She may also have some student loans she has to pay off. She grew up in a generally positive family environment but worries about what her parents will think about her choice of a new car. She has a wide variety of interests, including a love of the outdoors. She is single but probably dating, and she also wants the person she's dating to approve of her car choice. She enjoys where she lives and the town where the commercial takes place.

- *Psychological qualities.* The obvious choice here is which car to buy. Her physical and social qualities help contribute to her overall positive self-esteem; however, it is a major investment and the first time she has purchased a car without assistance from her parents. She also wants her choice to be endorsed by her friends and close relatives. She may remember times that she has been to an auto dealership with her parents and seen high-pressure tactics from salespeople. She doesn't look forward to dealing with heavy-handed salespeople; this can take some of the fun and excitement out of the experience. She wants to be seen as a credible young professional and doesn't want someone taking advantage of her. Overall, she has a positive impression of herself, but this is one of those experiences that can lead to self-doubt. The recent graduate discount promotion this dealership is running sends a message to her that this dealer may care about her and her needs.

EXAMPLE 2   Commercial for an extra-strength pain killer featuring a 30-something male construction worker who suffers from occasional job-related aches and pains:

- *Physical qualities.* We know that this person has probably been a construction worker for 10 to 15 years who may have started on jobs right out of high school. He has always enjoyed being outdoors and seeing the construction process, from digging the foundation to the finished building. He could be from any racial or ethnic group. He is a veteran of on-site work and knows what he is doing. He is probably a little bigger than average, and his complexion reflects the fact that he has worked outdoors. He has a strong upper body due to physical labor, and a strong vocal quality with maybe a little rasp. He doesn't need to speak with any regional dialect and is used to talking and yelling over equipment noise. His gestures and movement are definite. He stands erect and walks with authority. His walk may be a little slow and controlled due to the nature of his work, suggesting past aches and pains. He could have tools or a blueprint in hand as props. He wears flannel shirt, jeans, boots, and hardhat—typical construction worker clothing.

- *Social qualities.* He likes getting up in the morning and going to work and enjoys the construction site environment and coworkers. He graduated from high school and has good common sense and "school of hard knocks" knowledge. His father was probably also a construction worker. He makes a comfortable living and is mostly concerned with making enough money for family needs, his children's future, and fun on weekends. He respects others if they work hard and wants respect in return. He had a mostly positive childhood and his heroes were professional athletes. He still enjoys watching sports on television on weekends. He has two children, is happily married, and enjoys family activities on weekends.

- *Psychological traits.* Overall he feels pretty good about himself due to his physical and social traits. He gets angry when he sees people not working or not accepting responsibility for their actions. He wants to do quality work and be recognized for his accomplishments on the job. Other people like him both on the job and in social situations. He doesn't do much on impulse, usually thinking things out. He has some doubts and fears about the occasional pain he feels and how many more years he will be able to work. Also, pain slows his ability to do quality work. An effective pain reliever could eliminate these worries and allow him to get on with his work and weekend activities.

EXAMPLE 3 A commercial for AAA featuring a 30-something mother talking about a time when she was driving with her child during a storm and her car broke down. There are segments in which she is telling her story directly to the camera and a flashback scene showing the breakdown and the AAA tow truck coming to the rescue. A five-year-old child is with her in both sequences:

- *Physical qualities.* The mother character's posture is somewhat relaxed when talking directly to the camera. She may be seated in the car with her arm on the window as she addresses the camera. She is attractive and energetic (a soccer mom type) and of average height and weight. She is relaxed with her movement and gestures when telling her story but more restricted in posture and other nonverbal elements when she and her child are in the car during the storm. She doesn't have any objects with her when she is addressing the camera. She probably has a raincoat and umbrella during the storm sequence. Her child may have a small toy of some kind.

- **Social qualities.** She likes her family, but some days finds it difficult to get her family organized and off to work or preschool. She likes where she lives, is a college graduate, and works part-time when her child is at preschool. She had a pleasant childhood with reliable parents and wants to be the same kind of parent for her young son. She desires financial security; she doesn't need to have money for the sake of money but wants to provide a quality education for her son. She and her husband enjoy the creature comforts of typical young families. She has good friendships in the neighborhood and cares about political issues that affect families, such as education and health. She loves her spouse and her family life, but is often tired at the end of the day. She likes outdoor activities that involve the entire family, but also enjoys going to movies on occasion with her spouse and leaving the child with a babysitter.

- **Psychological qualities.** On a daily basis the mother faces many choices that have an impact on her family. She acts angry or upset when she makes the wrong choice or forgets to do something. She also likes to plan ahead. Her chief ambitions are to be the best mother and wife she can be while also contributing to the financial welfare of the family through her part-time job. Overall, she has a positive impression of herself, but faces the usual self-doubts of anyone who is trying to keep all the balls in the air. Safety is a consideration for her and a key emotion in this commercial. The mother has to communicate relief and confidence when recalling the outcome of the breakdown, and fear during the flashback of the breakdown itself.

As you can see, there are a number of questions to ask and answer in creating believable characters for commercials. It's the same work as developing a character for a play or film, even though it's a shorter production.

If you are serious about acting in commercials, you will probably need to find an agent to represent you in finding work. You can find agents through friends who may already be in the business. Good commercial acting classes and television performance classes at colleges and universities also have connections with agents and sometimes invite agents to see students' in-class work. Chapter 12 provides more information concerning agents and unions.

Auditions

In most cases commercials that involve character types require auditions. Books such as Squire Fridell's *Acting in Television Commercials for Fun and Profit* give detailed information concerning the audition process. What follows are some audition basics:

▪ **The Slate**   You will perform your audition for the commercial director, several technicians, and a video camera. Sometimes there are no other people in the room and you must do your audition in front of camera while others watch you from a control booth or other area.

The **slate** refers to the production slate, which you call out by looking into the camera lens and verbally identifying yourself on tape before beginning the actual commercial reading. Many inexperienced commercial actors lose an opportunity to make a good first impression by not doing their slates properly. Give yourself an advantage over other actors by following these guidelines:

The commercial director or tape operator will give you a signal to begin with one of a number of commands ("action," "go," "speed") or perhaps by pointing at you as a floor manager gives an opening cue. As soon as you get your cue, look at the center of the lens, smile, wait a couple of beats, and give your name in a friendly but firm manner.

Make sure you speak clearly, slowly, and loudly. It's amazing how often actors mumble or rush giving their own names. Remember, people are already forming impressions of you during these first few seconds. The slate gives them a glimpse of your personality before you start the reading.

▪ **Question and Answer Session**   Either before or after you read the commercial script, people in the room may ask you questions about yourself. In many cases the tape is running while they are talking to you, because they want to play back your responses. Sample questions you may be asked include, "Tell me a little about yourself," "Tell us about your trip here this morning," "What do you like to do when you have nothing to do?" They may also ask you whether or not you are familiar with the commercial product or campaign. Whenever possible, try to do some research on the product before you audition. You can do this by reading trade magazines such as *Advertising Age* or by visiting the websites of advertising agencies. Some websites allow you to download commercials and watch them in streaming video.

If you know that the question-and-answer session is being recorded, look directly at the camera lens when giving your responses and not at those asking the questions. Looking at people when responding makes you look silly when they watch the tape's playback.

RATINGS POINTER

Looking at a camera lens when giving answers may take some practice. It's natural to look at people when they ask us questions. Practice this technique at home with a camcorder: have several friends ask you questions while you're being recorded. Watch the playback and see if you have good eye-to-lens contact. Notice too how much better the final impression is than if you look at those asking the questions. ★ ★ ★ ★

Other Considerations

- *Listen to the person in charge of the audition.* Make sure you try to follow any advice or directions he or she gives you. Auditions usually take place on a tight schedule so there is no time for directors or technicians to repeat information you should have heard the first time. Some actors are so busy being "on" that they don't hear important information. Be professional and save your performance energy for when the tape is rolling.

- *If you don't understand something in the script, don't be afraid to ask the person in charge for clarification.* Most directors are happy to answer questions before the taping and would rather have you get it right the first time than do a taping with the wrong interpretation or mispronounced words.

- *Be as familiar with the script as possible.* Sometimes the script will be faxed or e-mailed to you in advance; other times the first time you see it is in the audition waiting room. Memorize the opening and closing of the script and deliver them directly to the camera lens.

- *If you're auditioning with another person, make sure you look at and react to your fellow performer when he or she reads lines.* You'll find that this helps your reading and motivation as well as making you look more natural during the playback. Make sure you look down at your script during your partner's last line so that you can pick up your line without pausing. Pauses between readers make you look awkward.

- *Work with real props whenever possible.* If the script requires you to hold a can of the product, use a real can. Practicing with real props before the audition can increase your confidence and comfort level when you have to hold a can or package during the audition.

- *If you make a minor mistake, continue with your reading.* Don't let it throw you. In many cases those in charge will let you read again. Try to review the mistake verbally so that you don't repeat it. If you get off to a bad start, ask if you can start over.

- *Try to control distracting facial expressions or gestures.* Some people punctuate statements with a smirk or raised eyebrows. Close-ups will accentuate any nonverbal mannerisms.

- *Always end your reading on a definite and energetic note.* Remember that the closing is as important as the intro. If they ask you to read again, look at this as a positive opportunity (they wouldn't ask you for a second reading if they weren't interested). Maintain your energy level the second time. This is also a time when the director may ask you to try a different interpretation with your reading. Try to follow directions, making the adjustments as best you can.

- *Following the taping, be friendly but professional.* This is your final impression on those involved in the audition and one of the intangibles that could land you the spot.

If you don't get the job don't take it personally. You should feel good about getting to audition, and there will be other opportunities.

Voiceovers

Voiceover performance doesn't require you to be in front of the camera, but it does require many of the interpretive reading skills discussed in Chapter 4, such as phrasing, emphasis, and word color. Voiceovers require many of the techniques used in old-time radio dramas that enable you to communicate meaning without the aid of nonverbal expressions. Your objective is to bring the copy to life, making it interesting and persuasive to listeners.

Many local stations and cable operations produce their own commercials using production crews to shoot on-location video of a business. This video is edited together along with special effects, graphic material, and the announcer's voiceover. Sometimes we see the performer at the beginning and end of the spot, especially if he or she is a popular local personality.

Voiceovers are produced in several ways. One way is to record the voiceover first and then edit all the visual material to the audio. Another way is to shoot and edit all the video first and then have the announcer read to the visuals. In some cases the announcer will time his or her reading to the images seen on a monitor. A third way is to edit and compress the voiceover to the visuals. Voice compression editing can adjust the rate of the announcer's reading and assist with proper timing of the spot.

Sometimes an **animatic** or video storyboard with audio is produced before the commercial is actually shot. Animatics contain the still images of the storyboard edited to the audio track. This gives clients a better impression of the pacing and sound of a commercial before the spot is produced.

Voiceover artists are in demand not only for television productions, but also for radio commercials, film narrations, and CD-ROM voiceovers. Besides the interpretive reading elements discussed earlier in this book, other points to consider when reading voiceovers include the following:

■ **Read to time.** There is no such thing as a 32-second or 63-second commercial. You must read your copy in the specified time. Keep in mind that 60-second commercials are really 59 seconds and 30-second commercials are 29 seconds. Reading to time is challenging because you must read faster than normal; sponsors want to get as much information into the commercial as possible.

Practice reading scripts and other printed material at a faster rate to develop your skills in compressing copy. Start with shorter scripts, working on reading a 10-second script in 10 seconds; then move on to 20- and 30-second scripts, and so on. You'll find that practice helps you develop an internal clock so that you don't have to rely so much on a stopwatch.

Several things besides practice will help you read faster. First, you can't neglect phrasing and emphasis just because you're reading faster. You can still pause, but your pauses must be shorter. Make sure you maintain vocal variety rather than settle into a monotone. Reading ahead in your copy will also help you sound natural when picking up speed. Try to read at least a sentence ahead to get a better idea of the script's meaning and emotional tone. Doing this also contributes to natural phrasing and emphasis.

Just as in singing, breathing is an important part of reading faster. Look for and mark places in your script where you take a breath. Proper breath control will help you read faster. It can also make you sound more natural and relaxed even when you're pushing the rate.

If you are reading with music background, the phrasing and changes in the music will give you valuable cues as to timing and where you should be in the script at a given point. Listen to the music several times to get a sense of how it flows with the script and how you should time your reading.

■ **Work for a natural delivery.** The days of the baritone-voiced pitch-man are pretty much over. We hear a wide variety of voices and reading styles in commercials and public service announcements. Most of these readers sound as if they are talking to us instead of at us. The following tips will help you sound and look natural:

- *Be careful of overprecise or unnatural pronunciation.* For some reason beginning readers often become too precise in their pronunciation; saying *thee* for *the* or using a long *a* for the article *a*. There's also a tendency to be overprecise with some *t*s found in words like *water* or *often*. The goal is to sound polished and natural.

- *Know your character and his or her motivation.* You've seen the questions that you should ask in order to develop your character. Poorly developed characters result in unnatural-sounding commercials.

- *Make your movements natural when appearing onscreen.* Some voiceovers require you to appear onscreen for a short period of time. Your gestures and movement must be timed to coincide with what you're saying. Practice all movement before the commercial shoot. Movement that seems natural to you in everyday communication can suddenly seem awkward when you're in front of a camera. If the commercial requires camera changes, work for a controlled turn when you switch to a different camera, just as news anchors do.

RATINGS POINTER

There's an old actor's exercise that can help you with timing gestures. You say the phrase, "Beyond the street, a tower; beyond the tower, a moon; beyond the moon, the stars; beyond the stars, what?" You must visualize each object and gesture to it. "See" each object for a split second before you gesture. Work on placement and timing of your gestures and well as smooth movement. ★ ★ ★ ★

Here are some other points to keep in mind when doing voiceovers:

- *Have a profile of the audience in mind before you start your reading.* Who are the people the commercial is targeting? Have an image of one such person in your mind's eye as you read the script. Some performers will even take a photograph of a person with them to help them visualize someone they are talking to.

- *Determine an attitude for your reading.* Are you supposed to be "warm and fuzzy" or more of a "wise guy"? If you have to play a char-

Beyond the street . . .

. . . a tower; beyond
the tower . . .

. . . a moon;

. . . beyond the moon,
the stars;

. . . beyond the stars,
what?

acter or persona for a commercial, you will probably determine the commercial's attitude before working on characterization. Attitude is the foundation for characterization.

- ***What emotions are supposed to be communicated from the script?*** If you are playing a bank customer who is upset about too many service charges, the frustration needs to come out in your voice. Try to put yourself in the position of the character you are portraying. You've probably had similar real-life experiences you can draw on to help communicate emotions.

Public Service Announcements

Most television stations still air public service announcements (PSAs) throughout the day and night; they are no longer required to run them but they do so to create and maintain a positive image in the community. PSAs are brief messages for service groups, such as Boy and Girl Scouts, or causes, such as walks or races that raise money to fight disease. Stations provide the time for these spots free of charge.

Some sponsors run announcements that are similar to PSAs but pay for the time. For example, Coors Brewery has run spots encouraging people not to let friends drive drunk. These spots often appear during holiday seasons when people may be more inclined to drink.

Credibility is the key with public service announcements; the audience must believe that you consider this particular group or cause important. If possible, try to do some background research on the group providing the PSA so that you will feel some attachment to them. Direct eye contact with the camera is important to make the audience believe that you think the message is important.

Rewind and Fade to Black

Commercial production techniques and appeals are changing, but humans are still an important aspect of selling products and ideas. Commercial acting and voiceover work is lucrative for those who can persuade audiences in 60 seconds or less. Educators and agents can help you make contacts to start your career.

In the meantime, use commercial assignments in class or promotional announcements on your job as opportunities to practice and perfect your skills. When you present a commercial in class, dress the part. If you are selling the services of a bank or financial planner, professional dress is in order; sports or casual clothing should be worn if you're doing a commercial for a sporting goods store.

Don't do parody commercials or spots for false products and services like those seen on *Saturday Night Live.* These may be fun, but they don't help you develop the skills you need in order to become effective commercial talent. Save dubs of in-class commercials and consider using good examples of your work on a video resume tape.

Practice reading aloud whenever you can. Work with video equipment or, if none is available, an audiocassette recorder. Look for opportunities to volunteer your talents to your school or community groups. These experiences provide practice and possible items for your resume.

Don't be obsessed with the quality of your voice. As mentioned earlier, most of us don't like to hear ourselves on tape. Work instead on communicating and developing believable emotions and characters. Evaluate your nonverbals to see if gestures and movement are natural. Practice looking at the camera while walking instead of looking in the direction you're walking.

Most important of all, don't be afraid to take chances and fail. This advice sounds threatening to many beginning commercial performers, but the time to take chances and discover your talents is now. Keep a log of the times you give a good performance. Take note of character types you can portray as believable. Instructors, fellow students, and colleagues will help you with your evaluation.

In order to sell products or ideas, you have to sell yourself first. Chapter 12 will help you do this.

Exercises

1 See if you can produce and perform a voiceover for a department or group on your campus. For example, see if one of the athletic teams will allow you to edit together highlights from games and do a promotional voiceover spot for the team. Some cable companies show such promotional announcements.

2 Visit websites of commercial talent agencies. What kinds of courses do they offer? What are the skills they say you will develop?

3 Find a voiceover script and some instrumental music for the background. Practice your timing by reading to certain phrasing and portions of the music. Is your timing consistent with certain portions of the music?

4 Record television commercials that have voiceovers. Transcribe the voiceover, turn down the sound when you play back the tape, and practice doing your own voiceover.

5 Visit local cable operators and see if they need talent for their locally produced commercials. You may be surprised how often they will offer you the chance to be in a commercial (sometimes for pay).

INTERVIEW

George Maguire
Commercial Performer

It's an old cliche, but George Maguire has been a star of stage, screen, and television. He has appeared in major films such as *Fight Club* and *The Game* as well as television series such as *Nash Bridges.* George has also appeared on Broadway and in regional theaters throughout the United States. He is currently a drama instructor at Solano Community College and in charge of its Actors' Training Program. In this interview, George talks about his performance work in commercials.

Question: People often talk about developing a character type, such as "the wise guy" as opposed to a character.

George Maguire: Yes. There's definitely something called "Play the cliche" of the wise guy or any other character type at the audition. There are a variety of cliches, and anyone who teaches commercial acting will tell you to play the cliche and go for it, because that's what directors want to see and that's what sells.

Q: Let's say that a student is wondering what type or cliche he or she can play. How does one discover what cliches he or she can do?

GM: Play as many as you can. Now that I'm 54 years old, I'm usually asked to play the father or the fisherman. I have outfits. I have a closet filled with Goodwill clothing that I get very inexpensively; I also have some very expensive clothing so that I know what to go for when I'm called in for certain things. Often it is the clothing and your own sense of professionalism that is going to get you the job.

I do have racks of clothing that are there specifically for my commercial and film auditions.

Q: Do the majority of people who come to audition come dressed as the character?

GM: I would say well over half.

Q: So the people who don't come dressed as the character are at a disadvantage?

GM: Yes, a definite disadvantage. At a high professional level, I'd say that about 75 percent come in with some kind of character look. Obviously, if you're going to play a mortician, you're not going to come in wearing a sweater. Every man you see will come in wearing a suit.

Q: Some people suggest bringing in basic props or even the product in the commercial.

GM: They have it. In fact, I'd say with the exception of a pair of glasses I own to play the "Orville Redenbacher" look, I don't do it. Every time I tried to use props as a young actor they would tell me to "put that down." If it's a product you're auditioning for, like cereal, they will have that product there. If it's a Coca-Cola commercial, the Coca-Cola is there. They provide everything. If you're playing a fisherman, the fishing rod is there. You don't bring in anything.

Q: How about the first few minutes of the audition? What should people expect and what should they do?

GM: Let's talk about the waiting area before the audition. What I don't do is schmooze with my fellow actors. My entire purpose when I leave my office with my 8 × 10 is to get that job. When I walk into the room I know that there are other men from their mid-forties to late sixties that are my competition. My entire purpose, even though some of them are very good friends, is to get their job. I may say "Hi!" but I don't spend time talking to them. It breeds a familiarity that I don't want to have when I walk into the room.

That's what I do before. Then I walk into the audition room and I get the text if it's there. . . . Sometimes they have a storyboard posted, so you take a look at that and see how the commercial will look. If I get the text I can pretty much memorize the commercial before my audition, because commercials are usually 15- to 30-second spots. Rarely do we do a 60-second spot, so it's not difficult to remember six or seven lines.

Q: So you can have eye-to-lens contact all the time.

GM: Right. If that's what they want. Sometimes they don't want you to play eye-to-lens; they want you to play camera right or camera left. And you have the ability to ask, "Should I play right to the camera?" Ask them after your slate, "Do you want me to play to the camera or do you want me to play to you?"

Q: How should people act during the slate?

GM: If it's an upbeat commercial I give my name in an upbeat way: "Hi, I'm George Maguire." If it's a more serious spot, I use a more serious measured tone when giving my name. Then they will ask you to do a left and right profile before starting the commercial. . . . Immediately in the slate I am myself while also playing the character type they want. It's a preview for what they will be seeing when I read for the commercial.

Q: Do they also ask questions of you during the slate?

GM: Yes. That happens a lot for commercials. I've done some auditions recently where I had to play a fisherman and I was asked to tell stories of something that I like to do when I'm not acting: tell us your favorite hobby; what sports do you enjoy doing, and mine is whitewater rafting. I can talk forever about that. . . . You should always have a story about yourself and never should that story be about acting. Commercial work is about hiring real people who do real things. I'm asked about two-thirds of the time when I do commercial work to have a story. I also change the story all the time.

Q: Do you ever try to match the story with the product?

GM: Not really. I start concentrating on matching the story with the commercial and I can't focus on the story. You pretty much know what they are going to ask of you when you audition for a commercial, and in most cases it's something like, "Tell me about yourself." The other thing is to have some sort of a joke ready and make sure the joke is clean because you never know who is going to be watching these things. I've had that happen many times where they have me tell a little joke, so you better have one.

Q: Do you recall an audition where you said, "That's the best I can do. I know I got the job"?

GM: Yes. And it often happens in reverse where I feel that I haven't done well and I still get the job. I did a Diet Coke commercial for the Super Bowl a few years ago and I felt very confident when I left the audition and I got the job. I have an interesting face, and I can pretty much tell if they like what I have to offer when I walk in the door or if they don't. If I don't get the job, it's because they are looking for another "look." Sometimes they are looking for someone older.

Q: It sounds as if it's important that you don't take rejection personally because they are auditioning for a certain "look."

GM: The only time I take things personally is when they are rude. This rarely happens, although it has happened to me once or twice. It could be that they are having a lousy day and I am the brunt of their lousy day.

Q: What are several quick tips you give to people who want to perform in commercials?

GM: Have an excellent 8 × 10 of yourself. The tools that you have are vital. The resume is also important, and once you start doing commercial work you will build your resume, but it's all about your 8 × 10. Spend the money. No, your brother cannot take a good picture of you. Spend the money and make sure that the picture is who you are.

The next thing is to be positive. No matter what's going on in your personal life, you have to leave that once you walk out of the door of your home. You must concentrate on one thing: I'm going to get that job. You must be positive even if the commercial has a serious tone.

Have the clothes that are appropriate for the spot. Often, I will see a young actor not do that. There's a certain sense of hipness for some young actors. If you have any piercings, don't have them unless it is called for in the audition. I have seen that harm many actors when there is too much hanging on their faces. The same thing is true with multicolored hair dyes. You've just limited yourself and cut off about 90 percent of the jobs you could have. They want the all-American look, no matter what is your background.

Q: Is there anything unusual you have to watch out for during an audition?

GM: There was a commercial for Sugar Pops. When you are doing a food audition, you have to be careful not to eat the product or you will get a sugar high that is unbelievable. With the Diet Coke commercial, I don't like Diet Coke or diet anything. If you have a caffeine dependency, you're going to be pretty high by ten o'clock in the morning. You have to be careful not to eat or drink the product. Sometimes they will even have a little vomit bag there for you to spit it out.

My favorite is Sandy Duncan during Wheat Thins commercials. Have you ever seen her actually eat one? She puts it in her mouth, touches it with her teeth, and the camera cuts. I don't think the woman has eaten a Wheat Thin in her life, but she has been the spokesperson forever. Food commercials are fun.

Q: Any final thoughts?

GM: Commercial work is challenging and competitive. It's all about your sense of self-confidence without being arrogant. Just be who you are and have a great time. You also have to know when your look is changing. The look you have at 19 is definitely going to be different at 23. You can't play the same thing and often actors will make that mistake.

Make sure you update your 8 × 10 every three to four years. Be one step ahead of the competition.

Audition headshot photo for George Maguire.

CHAPTER TWELVE

Finding Work as a Video Performer

After many hours of study, practice, and performance, you're probably wondering, "Where's the payoff?" Obviously, if you have worked hard to become a video performer, you want an opportunity to practice what you've learned and start earning a regular salary. This chapter will give you information concerning how to prepare standard resumes and resume tapes, make contacts, interview, and apply for internships. All of these are necessary steps in landing a position as a video performer.

Instructors and video professionals have probably warned you that there is intense competition for performance jobs in the television industry. More colleges, universities, and specialty schools than ever are turning out graduates. The good news is that there are currently many opportunities for hardworking, creative performers due to the emergence of more stations, cable services, and new technologies. There are also new ways of networking or making contact with employers through job fairs and the Internet.

Getting your first job requires assertiveness and attention to details; however, this is a very exciting time to seek employment in the video industry. Corporate mergers, technologies, and new ways of using video are redefining the role of the video performer.

It is important to remember that several generations of people in the industry have gone through the same process in finding and surviving a first job before you. These people had to work with less than state-of-the-art equipment when they were students and with the pressures of putting together resumes and resume tapes while trying to graduate from their respective programs. In most cases, industry professionals are good people willing to help newcomers during internships and networking. While they may be helpful, it is important to remember that your former supervisors are not running an employment agency. Ultimately, whether or not you get the job depends on your abilities and hard work.

Before you continue pursuing a video performance career, it is important to do some serious self-evaluation concerning your strengths and weaknesses. This will help you determine your chances of making it as a video performer.

Self-Evaluation

Before getting down to specifics concerning your performance strengths and weaknesses, ask yourself some general questions about whether or not a career as a video performer is right for you. Once you've addressed these questions and issues, move on and assess specific aspects of your work.

Being a video performer can be lucrative, but for every news anchor or commercial actor making a six-figure income, there are dozens who are barely making it from paycheck to paycheck. Don't expect to make lots of money in the early stages of your career. If you're doing this just for the money, you should probably think of other options.

Can you meet deadlines and perform under pressure? Some people are creative when time is on their side but fall apart when faced with deadlines. Video performers of all kinds work under intense pressure and time constraints. Be honest with yourself as to whether or not you can perform well when time is short.

Criticism is part of all aspects of video performance. Do you have thick skin or do you object when someone criticizes you? In most cases, the criticism isn't personal; it's just a matter of trying to produce quality work under intense time constraints. If you are able to take criticism and integrate it into your performance, you can be an effective performer.

Are you willing to move to other regions of the country? Most beginning performers must leave their hometowns and move to other areas for their first jobs. Don't think that you'll be able to land a job in your hometown, especially if it is a major market. Be prepared to travel to small- and medium-market stations in the early stages.

Most of all you need to consider whether or not you'll be happy as a video performer or whether some other aspect of the television industry would be a better fit for your talents. Many people who thought they wanted performance careers have found better positions in areas such as sales, promotions, and research. Make sure you understand all your industry options before settling on performance.

Organizations that can assist you with obtaining information concerning the television industry include the honorary broadcasting society Alpha Epsilon Rho, the International Radio and Television Society (IRTS), the Association for Women in Communication (AWC), and student chapters of the Radio and Television News Directors Association. All these groups give you insights into the television industry that go beyond the classroom, while guiding you to special programs and speakers. They also provide some excellent opportunities for networking. Many people now working in the industry are or were members of these organizations.

If you're still interested in performance after answering these questions, you can move on to specific elements of your self-evaluation.

Specific Evaluation Elements   Some people have difficulty watching themselves on videotape no matter how many times they have done so. As suggested earlier, try to distance yourself from the fact that you are watching "you" on the screen; pretend instead that you are watching another person. This will help you form a more objective self-evaluation. Remember that we are usually our own worst critics when viewing tapes.

On the positive side, we often surprise ourselves with how good a performance looks on tape compared to our perception of how we performed live. Small mistakes or imperfections are often not nearly as bad as we originally thought.

Self-critique is important, but getting others' opinions is better. Work with your classmates, coworkers, and other peers to check your strengths and weaknesses. Most important, work with instructors and try to get comments from television professionals concerning your tapes. Keep a file of comments and see which ones seem to be consistent among your critiques.

Don't wait until late in your academic career to start evaluating your work. Start with seemingly minor projects, keeping comments from your instructor and others. One of the major mistakes students make is not saving video examples of their work throughout their academic careers. As a result, classroom videotapes usually get erased and the student is left scrambling before graduation to find examples of work for a resume video. Save everything you can from class projects.

Once you have collected samples of your work, you can assess the following:

Vocal aspects. Listen to your tape to determine how you use your voice and how well it communicates meaning to viewers. Answer yes or no to the following questions:

- Does my voice have good vocal variety as opposed to sounding monotonous?

- Am I able to control my pitch, or does it go too high when I get excited or try to emphasize words or phrases? Do I need to lower my natural pitch a bit? Does my pitch go up at the ends of my sentences so that they sound like questions instead of statements?

- Do I sound conversational, or does my voice fall into predictable vocal patterns?

- Are there any other problems with my voice? Is there raspiness or hoarseness? Is my voice tight or pinched? Do I sound as if I'm talking through my nose or have a cold?

- How is my breathing? Am I breathing from my diaphragm or from my chest? Am I running out of breath before getting through complete phrases? Do I still need to work on my breathing (don't forget that breathing from your diaphragm is a natural way to lower your pitch without straining your throat)?

- Is my reading rate appropriate? Am I able to read fast and still sound natural? Do I need to pick up my rate (many beginning performers need to work on reading a little faster)?

- Is my diction clean without being overprecise? Do I pronounce words properly? Is there anything that might be distracting about my diction, such as a regional dialect?

- Do I seem to understand the interpretive aspects of reading copy? Am I able to convey a mood and change the mood within the copy? Does the mood seem believable or overdramatized? When reading news stories, do I make a clear transition between the moods in stories?

- Am I able to group words together into natural phrases? Is the phrasing choppy? Do I have a tendency to pause at all punctuation marks?

- Do I sound as if I am trying to communicate meaning to viewers rather than coming across like a reading machine? Is there anything I or a friendly critic can isolate that will make me sound more natural and involved with my vocal aspects?

■ **Visual aspects.** Remembering that over half of what we communicate comes through nonverbal means, check your tape for these items:

- Are my gestures and movement controlled, or are they too broad for video?

- Do I have good eye-to-lens contact?

- Are my nonverbal expressions consistent with what I'm reading? Do my facial expressions help communicate the meaning of the message?

- Do I control head movements to avoid excessive bobbing or moving out of the frame?

- Is my body posture appropriate to my performance? Is it natural without being too stiff? Am I too casual?

- Are my clothes and hair appropriate to my performance? Do the colors or patterns of my clothes present any technical problems for the video system?

These questions will help you "break down" your performance in much the same way that coaches use videotape to analyze what went right and wrong in a game. Be specific in your self-critique. If you find a number of items that need work, focus on improving one or two at a time; then move on to others.

If you are doing self-critiques and working in a systematic way, there is no reason for you to get discouraged: you are doing the hard work of becoming a quality video performer. Ask yourself the question, "Am I doing the best I can given my skills and experience level?" If the answer is yes, you should feel good about what you're doing.

Moving On: The Resume

As for most other jobs, you will need a printed **resume** listing your skills, work history, education, and other important facts about you. It has often been said that a good resume won't automatically get you a job, but a bad resume will probably lose you a job. A good resume can help get your "foot in the door."

There are numerous resources and guidelines for resumes, but ultimately you should aim to create a resume that is tailored for a specific situation. College career placement centers can provide valuable information about writing resumes; however, it is best to compare this information with that provided by video professionals and service groups. Try to network and get examples of good resumes from video professionals. You can do this through media job fairs or television service organizations such as Alpha Epsilon Rho or the AWC.

Books such as Yana Parker's *Damn Good Resume Guide* provide valuable information regarding resume basics. Use information from this and other general resume guides and adapt your resume to the television industry. Here are some basic points to consider when preparing broadcast performer resumes:

■ **Choosing a Resume Type**   Two of the most common resume types are the **chronological resume** and the **functional resume** (sometimes called the **competency-based resume**). These days **scannable resumes** are also becoming popular. Use the chronological resume if you have work experience and you're continuing as a broadcast performer (especially if you have an unbroken employment record). Someone who has been a video performer for several years will usually choose a chronological resume. As you've probably guessed, chronological resumes list your past jobs, starting with the most recent.

The competency-based resume works best for those graduating from college or a professional program, people making a career change, or those who don't have a record of continuous employment. A competency-based resume allows you to organize your information by skills—for example, news reporting, news anchoring, ENG camera, video editing—and to highlight these skills in an organized, easy-to-read format.

Experts differ as to how specific you should be in listing model numbers of equipment you can operate. Some tell you to include every model number; others advise that since technology is changing so fast, it really doesn't matter. Many in the industry say that they are looking for creative people who can write and communicate ideas; they will train you in the technical aspects but they can't teach creativity. One thing you should stress is the type of editing you can do. If you can do both linear and non-linear editing, make sure you state this.

Examples of chronological and competency-based resumes appear later in this chapter. Later in your career, you may decide to compile what is called a *bio* instead of a resume. Bios are narratives relating your work experience to date. Most performers work at several stations before they decide to use bios instead of resumes.

Students often ask if they can include information about college work such as producing a cable television program or sporting event. This is valuable experience to mention, but make sure you clearly label it as college experience or a college cable or radio station. Also, make a distinction in your resume between a regular paid position and an unpaid internship at a television station. Employers value such experience but take a dim view of those who try to pass internships off as regular professional positions.

RATINGS POINTER

It is estimated that as many as 40 percent of resumes contain inaccurate or false information. Make sure you give an accurate representation of your skills and work history. Lines of communication are short and employers can check your history through technological means or personal contact. You won't get a second chance to explain false information or inaccuracies on your resume. Also, for jobs such as news anchor or reporter, falsification sends a metamessage to the employer regarding your ethics and attention to detail. ★★★★

■ **Items to Include on Your Resume**   You should include the following headings on resumes:

■ **Personal information.** Basic information such as your name, address, telephone number, and e-mail address should be included at the top of the resume. For an on-camera performance position you should also include height, weight, hair and eye color, and a photograph. You do not have to disclose your marital status, parental status, or racial and ethnic background. You may be thinking, "Well, won't they be able to see this based on the photographs?" Not in all cases. Keep in mind that discrimination based on racial or ethnic background is against the law.

Do not include hobbies and special interests, unless they apply to a production you might be doing; memberships in social clubs or organizations; or college transcripts (unless requested by the employer).

■ **Career objective.** Most resume experts suggest that you list a career objective or "job target" after your personal information. This sentence specifies the kind of work you are looking for and makes it easier for the employer to see if you are a good fit for the advertised position. Some people think that listing a career objective is too limiting for multitalented applicants who may be suited for a variety of jobs. The way to get around this problem is to list different career objectives depending on the positions for which you may apply. Make sure you tailor each career objective to the advertised position.

The career objective should be brief, preferably a sentence or phrase such as, "A position as a news reporter and/or camera operator and video editor." Even if the reporter position is the main job you want to pursue, it is still wise to list the camera and editing skills if the station employs the "one person band" technique of reporting, shooting, and editing stories.

■ **Skills or a chronological list of jobs.** Next comes the body or "meat" of your resume in which you describe the jobs you've had or your skills (depending on which resume format you've chosen). Again, if you're doing a chronological resume, list your jobs starting with the most recent and working backwards. For the functional resume use a number of skills headings such as reporting, production and editing, and so on.

With either format, make sure you use action words to describe your skills and accomplishments. Use verbs such as "*wrote, produced,* and *edited* features for *Campus Video Magazine* cable access program"; or "*Served* as volunteer for WXXX election night coverage." When listing your accomplishments, be sure to include job promotions and instances when you suggested changes or innovative programs. You should also mention positive evaluations you have received for your work. Don't be afraid to sell yourself by noting recognition for good work. If you don't include this, the employer will probably never know how good you are.

RATINGS POINTER

Try using some of these action verbs in your resume when referring to your work experience, skills, or accomplishments: *edited, wrote, produced, interviewed, performed, created, analyzed, prepared, supervised, planned, scheduled, organized, developed, promoted, programmed, maintained, facilitated, coordinated, operated, compiled, implemented, managed, researched, introduced, redefined, resolved.* ★ ★ ★ ★

Sometimes you can include skills that are unrelated to video performance on your resume. For example, writing for your campus or local newspaper is an obvious accomplishment to include if you are applying for any position involving writing skills. Roles in dramatic productions or participation in activities such as speech and debate should also be included, since these activities are wonderful preparation for video performance. Also, employers are likely to have been involved with these activities when they were in college, thus providing you with a good link or icebreaker if you get to interview with them.

■ **Education and training.** List your college degree(s) and any other specialized training you may have received, for example, being part of a special actors' workshop or taking a computer or editing course at a technical school. Make sure to include your college major. If you graduated with honors or received a special graduate's award, you should note this as well (if you don't toot your own horn, no one else will).

■ **Honors and affiliations.** Many applicants include honors and professional affiliations under a single heading. This section is the place to mention an award for one of your productions at an on-campus video festival or a speaker's award at a debating tournament. You should also mention here your membership in any professional organizations and note relevant accomplishments in nonprofessional organizations such as student body president, class secretary, and so on.

■ **Special skills.** You can include here any additional skills that may help you as a video performer such as knowledge of a foreign language (make sure you specify which one(s) you can speak or read) or exceptional computer skills.

■ **References.** Some career counselors tell you not to list references and to include instead the statement "references available upon request." The thinking here is that if you apply to a number of stations, your referees will be flooded by phone calls from prospective employers (a nice situation for you but a potential inconvenience for them).

We believe, however, that at the end of your resume you should list three to six referees who are familiar with your work. Include names, addresses, affiliations, phone numbers, and e-mail addresses. Make sure all the information is current: Nothing is more frustrating for potential employers than to call for a reference and get the wrong phone number.

Get permission from your referees in advance and tell them the time frame when they may be called. You may send out dozens of resumes, but in most cases only a few will elicit calls for references. Thank your referees with a card or letter following the job search. Some job seekers even send a small gift or token of appreciation along with the thank you. References should be instructors or other professionals familiar with your performance ability. Don't use family members, relatives, or friends who are not industry professionals.

Use standard word-processing fonts such as Helvetica, Geneva, or Times Roman and stay away from fonts that would be better suited to a party invitation. Usually, 12-point font size with 1.5 spacing is the best to use. Duplicate your resumes on white, off-white, or buff paper with matching envelopes. Word processing makes it easy for almost anyone to create a professional-looking resume, but if you have doubts about your ability to produce a quality resume, consult your career center or a professional resume service.

Charles M. Turner
420 East College
DeKalb, IL 60115
815-555-8888 cmturner@netcom. net

OBJECTIVE

Position as a general assignment reporter and weekend anchor.

EMPLOYMENT

1999–present

News reporter for WTVO, Rockford, IL. Covering local stories; live field reports; can write and edit news packages. Specializing in city government reporting.

1998–1999

Internship with WMBD, Peoria, IL. Collected and edited wire copy and rewrote stories. Served as an associate producer for *Good Morning in Peoria.*

1997–1999

Volunteer with PBS pledge drives for WTVP, Peoria, IL. Worked in various crew positions and edited promotional video for pledge breaks.

HONORS

Dean's list, junior and senior years; student director of Channel 8 student-produced cable newscast. Graduated cum laude, 1999.

EDUCATION

B.A. in communication, emphasis Radio-TV-Film, Northern Illinois University, 1999. Course work included newsgathering and reporting, video editing, and video performance.

REFERENCES

Dr. Jane Stowell, Northern Illinois University, DeKalb, IL 60115 (815-778-1234)

Dr. Joseph Taylor, Northern Illinois University, DeKalb, IL 60115 (815-778-1244)

Ms. Judith Santacaterina, Northern Illinois University, DeKalb, IL 60115 (815- 778-1247)

Sample **chronological resume** for a student looking for his second position out of college.

Tracy Jacobs
42 B Street
Vallejo, CA 94590
(707-555-1234) tjacobs@aol.com

OBJECTIVE	Entry-level position in a television sports department.
EXPERIENCE	Play-by-play announcer for Northern California Community College football and basketball games on Pinole Cable Access.
	Assistant public relations coordinator for Solano Steelheads minor league baseball team. Wrote copy for Steelheads' press releases.
	Host of sports radio program on KDIA, Vallejo, CA, covering college and high school sports.
COMPETENCIES	Ability to do sports play-by-play of baseball, basketball, and football. Ability to write and edit sports packages for local newscast. Knowledge of nonlinear editing systems. Bilingual in Spanish.
AWARDS	John Davis scholarship for excellence in broadcasting. Outstanding radio-television major at California State University, Sacramento. All-county selection as halfback for Hogan High School Football Team.
REFERENCES	Mr. David Snell, Coordinator, Vallejo Cable Access, Vallejo, CA 94590 (707-555-1589)
	Mr. Greg Poff, Instructor, Solano College, Fairfield, CA 94585 (707-555-8990)
	Dr. Jill Owens, Professor, California State University, Sacramento, 94595 (916-555-9012)

Sample **competency-based resume** for a student who may have less paid experience but still has valuable performance experience.

> **RATINGS POINTER**
>
> There are those who believe that creative, attention-getting resumes and gimmicks are in order when applying for a video performance job. Some people use colored paper and envelopes or different resume formats in order to stand out from the competition. One applicant used a menu format for his resume with the headings "Appetizers" for his education and training, "Main Courses" for work experience, and "Desserts" for awards and other accomplishments. Other applicants have sent gifts along with resumes. Most experts agree that you should "play it straight" and stay away from offbeat resumes and gimmicks. In one case a news director received a basket of fruit from an applicant along with her resume and tape. A hungry newsroom employee devoured the fruit within an hour but the applicant never got the job. Lori Hillman, a former producer with *The CBS Evening News with Dan Rather*, tells of one applicant who sent popcorn with his resume tape along with a note saying "For your viewing enjoyment." The snack drew snickers from those who saw the tape. ★ ★ ★ ★

■ Cover Letters

The **cover letter** accompanying your resume can create a positive first impression. Think of it as a commercial for the potential employer to read your resume and watch your tape. You want the tone of the letter to be friendly but professional. Keep the following things in mind when writing your cover letter:

- Make sure you address the letter to the person who can hire you. Stay away from generic titles such as "To Whom It May Concern" or "Dear Sir/Madam." You may find the name of the contact person in the job announcement. Television station websites often list the names of key personnel. You can also call the station and ask for the name of the news or personnel director.

- Your cover letter is business correspondence, so use a format that includes a heading, inside address, greeting, body, and closing signature. Make sure you double-check the address of the station for the inside and envelope addresses.

- Make your letter no more than three or four paragraphs. Stay on your key points and don't ramble. Remember that you only have a few seconds to persuade the reader to consider you for the job.

- Show that you know something about the station and the city or town. Potential employers love to see that you've done your homework. Stay positive, though; don't write "I see from the last ratings book that you had the lowest-rated newscast," even if this is true. Tell the reader what interests you about working at this station apart from getting a regular paycheck. Look for common ground and make connections with the station and city.

- Focus on what makes you special. There's an old slogan in advertising known as the *unique selling proposition*. When you have a number of brand names of the same product, like soap, you have to explain to buyers what makes your soap different from the competition. Do the same thing when selling yourself to potential employers. Many cover letters and resumes say the same things and present applicants with the same skills: reporting, camera operator, editing, and so on. Use your cover letter to stress qualities that make you different from the typical applicant.

- Specify what you want. Don't try to be a Jack or Jill of all trades, hoping that you will fit into some position at the station. Write your cover letter for a specific position and state why you are qualified for it.

- Make sure you sign your name. It's amazing how many applicants forget to do this. Black ink looks the most professional.

- Match the cover letter, paper, font, and font size to your resume.

- Don't mention salary requirements.

- **Never send a handwritten cover letter.** Type your envelope as well.

- Don't print your cover letter on the letterhead of your college station, internship station, or any other station where you are currently working. This sends a message to potential employers that you are looking for a job on someone else's time. Will you do the same thing at your next station?

Your cover letter should look as if it is written for that specific station and not as if you are bombarding stations around the nation with the same letter and resume. If you include station information and other specifics, you will have an advantage over applicants who appear to be "shotgunning" their information to dozens of stations.

If you are writing to an agent, your letter can be brief because he or she will be most interested in your resume tape. Summarize your qualifications and how the agent can contact you.

Make sure you use the "spell check" function on your word processor, but be aware that it cannot catch every error. You must also carefully proofread both the resume and cover letter; your eyes are the best means for checking your work.

Some potential employers sort resumes and cover letters into two piles—those with errors and those without. In many cases the resumes with errors are not even considered. The reasoning here is that applicants who can't be accurate with something as important as their personal information are unlikely to be accurate in their work at the station. Don't give potential employers an excuse for not looking at your materials. Other common resume problems include inappropriate length (keep resume to one page), lack of specifics, failure to list job accomplishments, irrelevant information, and name dropping.

Potential employers don't care if you were the drum major for your high school band. Mention only experience that will help you do the job, for example, involvement with your campus television or radio station, newspaper, or the speech and debating team teaches skills that are transferable to video performance.

Most potential employers also couldn't care less if your father is the news director at KZZZ. Don't try to impress them with people you know. Mention other people if they made you aware of the position and have some link to the station where you are applying. Sometimes during an internship someone working at the station may hear about a position at one of their former stations and pass the word on to you. The person will often invite you to use his or her name. Take the person up on the offer.

RATINGS POINTER

Another method of screening resumes is computer scanning. Cover letters and resumes are scanned by a computer that looks for key words and phrases the potential employer considers important. Those resumes with the most key words, or "hits," receive top consideration. To create a resume for this technology, follow these guidelines:

- Examine the job notice carefully. Make sure your cover letter and resume include information contained within the notice, such as important skills and abilities. If the notice mentions "communication skills," make sure you include this phrase in your materials. Echo the wording used in the notice.
- Use concrete words. Stay away from descriptive language. Precision is the key.
- Mention industry organizations and acronyms. For example, ENG and EFP will probably be included in any scanning involving production equipment. Mention industry organizations to which you belong. Since many people in the industry are familiar with IRTS, this organization could be included in the scan.

- If you think a station will be scanning your resume, ask if they prefer that you send it via e-mail.
- Unless time is an issue, avoid faxing your resume. Faxed resumes often cause problems with the scanning process, and you might lose many key words in a scan.
- Use black ink on white paper. Make sure you use a high-quality printer for the original, and send a clean copy with no marks or smudges. Use 10- to 14-point font size.
- Don't allow letters or lines to touch each other. Avoid underlining, italics, and boldface. Also stay away from fancy layouts, shading, and boxes. Crisp, clean copy is best.
- Solid bullets are OK but don't take a chance with other fonts or wingdings. Keep it simple. Remember, you're trying to impress a machine, not a human.
- Prepare two versions of your resume: one that's scannable and the other a nonscan. You can send both versions to a station and label each with a Post-it note (scan copy and nonscan).
- Work with your campus career placement center or a resume writing service when you prepare a scannable resume. These services can give you valuable advice and in some cases can test-scan your resume for potential hits or problems. ★ ★ ★ ★

■ **Photographs**   Potential employers are split over whether or not you should send photographs along with your resume and resume videotape. Some say that they can see what you look like on tape and don't need the photos; others like having photos of you working in various situations.

If you're applying for a news position you can choose to send photos along with your other materials. Some news directors will toss them (sorry, but true); others will keep them on file with your other materials. Make sure they are high-quality photos that show you working. You don't necessarily need to have them shot by a professional photographer. Send 4 × 6 and not 8 × 10 pictures for news positions.

If you are interested in commercial work, you definitely need to send 8 × 10 photos, especially when dealing with an agent. Some commercial performers prepare a **composite photo,** that is, one sheet with four different poses or situations demonstrating the various character types the performer can portray. Composites should be shot by a professional photographer for the best results. You really do get what you pay for.

The Resume Tape

Resumes, cover letters, and photographs may get your foot in the door with potential employers, but it's the **resume tape** that will get you in the station to stay; it is the most important piece of your employment package, because it quickly demonstrates your onscreen presence and other talents.

The resume tape should be an ongoing project, constantly updated with your best and most recent work. Industry insiders advise having two tapes: a personal archive of your best work and an edited tape ready to mail.

You will receive various tips for putting together a resume tape from instructors, friends, websites, and those already working in the industry. What follows in this section is consensus advice from news directors, reporters, commercial talent, and other credible industry sources. One of the best guides to resume tapes, *How to Prepare and Improve Your Television Audition Tape,* is available from Don Fitzpatrick and Associates of San Francisco. Numerous students and seasoned professionals have used this guide as their resume tape blueprint.

Details ranging from which tape format you should use to how to follow up with potential employers are all important pieces of your application package:

■ **Tape Format**   Video performers often wonder which tape format to use to send to potential employers. The answer seems to be VHS. Recent industry surveys indicate that most news directors and others making personnel decisions prefer VHS because they have easy access to it: almost everyone has a VHS machine in the office. Those who prefer Beta or other formats seem to be videographers or other technical types who prefer Beta's better quality.

On the positive side, VHS is less expensive to buy and mail than other formats—an important consideration when sending tapes to numerous stations. The downside is the quality of VHS versus Beta. Make sure you dub your resume tapes from the original tape and not from a copy so that you don't lose a generation. Use the highest-quality (High Grade) VHS tape for best results.

Some ads and job notices will tell you what tape format they want at a given station. If the ad doesn't tell you the format, you can always call the station to see what they prefer.

■ **Packaging Your Tape**   Part of your overall presentation is making sure your tape is packaged in a professional-looking manner. Put your tape in a plastic tape box instead of leaving it in its cardboard package. This creates a better impression while also protecting your tape during shipping.

Label the front of your tape box with your name, address, telephone number, and e-mail address. You should also label the tape itself with at least your name. Make sure to use printed labels instead of handwritten ones. Label the ends and the sides of the box with your last name. There should be no doubt about the name of the person who sent the tape. Put a small printed card or sheet of paper with your name and a rundown of the resume tape's contents inside the tape box. People such as Don Fitzpatrick advise you not to record the rundown on the tape itself because it is too difficult to read (the person has to pause or rewind the tape).

When mailing the tape, don't send it in a shredded-fiber, padded envelope. When the envelope is opened, these fibers fly everywhere and can get into the VCR where your tape will be played, causing damage to the machine. Use bubble-wrap envelopes instead.

Content

As with printed resumes, there are different opinions concerning resume tapes. One thing is certain: News directors, agents, and others have limited time to make hiring decisions. There may be 50 or more tapes on their desks at a given time. They want to see the applicant's best work and see it fast. You have 15 to 30 seconds to grab the attention of the person watching your tape. No matter what you think of think of the so-called 30-second rule, it is a reality of the business.

Make it as easy as possible for the person watching your tape to know who you are by including a slate with your name, address, telephone number, and e-mail address. Make sure all information is current; there are numerous stories of potential employers trying to track down applicants, only to be frustrated by outdated information on the printed resume or tape. Also, don't put a temporary address or phone number on the slate. The following suggestions are for specific jobs. If you are a student or recent graduate, you may not be able to include all these items on your tape, but keep them in mind for future reference.

Resume Tape Don'ts

There are several items potential employers don't want or need to see on your tape:

- ***Don't put color bars and tone at the beginning of your tape.*** These are used by broadcast engineers to adjust video and audio levels, but they are a waste of time for the person viewing your tape. Start your tape with black, then your slate. Remember that time is of the essence and you don't want to waste the potential employer's time with even a few seconds of bars and tone.

- ***Edit out the opening of the newscast.*** News directors don't want to see all the fancy graphics a news consulting firm recommended for your station's opening, they want to see you. If you include bars and tone plus the opening, you have wasted almost a minute of the news director's time (remember the 30-second rule).

- ***If you're an anchor, don't try to edit seven different newscasts together and pass it off as one.*** News directors will see your change of clothes and know that these are several different shows edited together. This sends the message that you can't get through a single program without a mistake.

■ **Reporters**   Many people now use a montage approach at the beginning of their resume tape, showing a minute or two of quick excerpts from various stories, commercials, or other performance work, depending on the job they want. Think of the montage as a quick sample of your best work.

If you are applying for a reporting position, you should have several stand-ups and live shots at the beginning of your tape, followed by three or four complete packages. The montage lets the news director see how you perform in a variety of situations in two minutes or less. Some people have added music or other special effects to their montages. Weigh the advantages and disadvantages of going to an "MTV approach"—you can't go wrong if you keep it simple.

Some news executives won't look at the rest of the tape if they don't see a stand-up on the first story or two, so make sure you include one early in the montage. Remember the advice concerning creative stand-ups given in Chapter 10 and feature these on your tape.

Following the montage, there should be a compilation of several types of stories. Try to include a story for which you do the intro from the news set. This sends a message that your story was important enough for you to come out of the field and into the studio to report it. People see *you* and not the anchor on the news set. If you can't do an intro from the news set, include a hard news package showing you in the story's first 30 seconds. The key here is enhancing your credibility by demonstrating to those watching the tape that you have the ability to report important stories.

Include a live shot with your resume tape. News executives want to see how you think on your feet and report while going live. Chapter 10 discussed some of the problems with an overdependence by news operations on live shots, but the fact remains that most operations have the equipment and feel the need to go live on a regular basis.

Include portions of a longer news series or documentary if you have them. Later, when you have your first job, you will want to include any series you cover during a **sweeps** period. Sweeps periods are the months during which the ratings of the newscast determine the station's advertising rates for the next two months (currently February, May, August, and November).

Don Fitzpatrick and Associates warns that you should be careful in using music on your resume tape and with individual packages. Some executives believe that music is a gimmick used to cover an applicant's poor reporting skills. Fitzpatrick says you should ask the following questions before using music:

- Why are you using the music?
- Is it appropriate?
- Is it necessary for understanding the story?
- Will it make a *schmaltzy* story even *schmaltzier?*
- Do the pictures tell the story?
- Does the writing tell the story?

Watch local and national newscasts along with network news-magazines to compare how and if they use music. You will notice that some stations and networks use music while others don't.

Include a softer or feature story at the end of your tape to show your versatility. Stay away from producing a tape filled with feature stories if you want to be a hard news reporter; on the other hand, include a full menu of feature stories if you want to be a feature reporter.

Include any video of you anchoring; you can place this at the end of the tape. Experts are divided over whether or not you should include an anchoring excerpt, because news directors looking for reporters don't want to see someone's anchor excerpts; but in a marketplace where versatility is an asset, a brief anchor segment could help you land a job. Remember that many weekend anchors are general assignment reporters during the week.

RATINGS POINTER

Beginners, and even some veterans, wonder which are the best types of stories to include on the resume tape. One suggestion is to include stories unique to your city or town that will attract immediate attention. For example, there was a story in San Francisco of a group of engineering students who suspended a VW Bug from a net off the side of the Golden Gate Bridge. Besides being a unique story, this offered strong visual appeal and some excellent writing opportunities for reporters.

When covering local issues, don't make the assumption that those watching the tape will be familiar with the story. Choose stories that give enough information for viewers to understand the context. ★ ★ ★ ★

Anchors   You probably won't get an anchor position as your first news job. In most cases, anchors are promoted from the ranks of general assignment reporters. Still, if you've had some anchoring experience with an on-campus or cable newscast, you can prepare an anchor resume tape. In some cases, students fresh out of college have landed anchor jobs at local cable news operations or small-market weekend anchor positions.

For beginners, it is probably best to put reporting segments at the beginning of your tape, followed by examples of your anchor work. Later, you can prepare a tape with just your anchor work.

Start your tape with shots of you covering breaking news. Select recent segments of your anchoring and edit out everything else, including packages, weather (unless it's a weekend anchor position where you have to do the weather), sports, and commercials. Edit out your co-anchor reading stories, but do keep some examples of interaction between you. News executives like to see how anchors interact with each other. Keep some examples of interaction with the sports- and weathercasters.

Include a variety of stories to showcase your reading ability. The majority of the stories should be serious in tone, but include at least one lighter story to demonstrate your range. Your tape should include two or three complete newscasts of about two minutes each (it's pretty amazing to consider that with packages, segments from your co-anchor, weather, sports, and commercials, you're on for only about two to three minutes during a 30-minute newscast).

Weathercasters   Weathercasts are a little easier to edit because they are shorter, self-contained segments of three minutes or less. You should include two weathercasts on your tape—one from a heavy weather day and one from a light weather day—so that news directors can see how you handle both situations.

Make sure not to edit more than two weathercasts together so that potential employers won't see several different clothing changes and hairstyles. It should be clear that you can get through an entire weathercast without mistakes.

You may want to include a remote weathercast and some reporting on your tape. Newscasts increasingly include more segments on how the weather affects economic and environmental issues. Keep the tape between seven and ten minutes long.

■ **Sportscasters**   The basics of a weathercaster video also apply to sports reporters and anchors. Show one or two complete sportscasts with no change in clothes or hairstyle. Include some examples of field reporting, live shots, and anchoring.

One factor that may distinguish you from your competition is good reporting skills. Your ability to break and develop sports stories or take a story about the local little league and make it interesting makes you more marketable than an interview you did with a famous athlete. Most athlete interviews tend to be boring and not very original; use them on your tape only if you were able to discover some new information or if the interview is distinctive in some other way.

Should sportscasters begin their tapes with a montage approach? The montage can be an exciting way to get into the tape, but don't sacrifice showing your reporting and reading skills by spending all your efforts on a slickly produced montage better suited to the big screen on the scoreboard of a major league game.

Music can be used on a sports tape during the montage, but make sure it enhances the visuals and is not a gimmick. Many consultants suggest you err on the conservative side by not having music in the background when showing reporting segments.

Finally, if there is something you do during your sportscast or in reporting that is distinctive and creative, include this on the tape. Vernon Glenn of KRON's "Mr. Involvement" segments (when Vernon tries to participate in a certain sport or activity) are excellent examples of creative sports reporting. Show that you can do something besides read scores or analyze the local football team's offensive line.

■ **Other Programs**   The number of talk and specialty shows is increasing at both the local and national levels. Many of the same resume tape principles apply for those wishing to do programming other than news. You can include a montage of various feature and interview segments you've done, along with two or three complete interview or feature segments. If there is a cohost, show yourself ad-libbing with him or her at least once on your tape. You can also show stand-ups and live shots.

Many news reporters and anchors are crossing over to more entertainment-oriented programs. If your experience is in news and all you have is material from newscasts, go with feature stories and lighter items. Program directors are looking for good reporting, writing, and ad-libbing skills.

Play to your strengths when considering jobs in programming. Many news reporters with expertise in areas such as high-tech or home improvement have made the move from news to specialty programs. Also, locally produced magazine programs such as *PM Magazine* offer other performance opportunities.

■ **The Resume Tape Follow-Up** You've sent a well-edited resume tape along with your cover letter and printed resume. Do you contact the station's news or personnel director to follow up—and if so, when? Follow-up is great, but you have to give your potential employer time to receive and review your tape.

First, don't send your tape via Federal Express or other overnight service unless requested to do so. In many cases the tape will arrive on the desk of the news director or other reviewer at the station and stay there for a week. Those who will watch your tape are busy with their other responsibilities such as getting programs on air. Sending your materials to the station overnight is an expense you don't need.

Give your potential employers at least a week to ten days before asking whether they have received your tape and where they are in the hiring process. Remember that there are probably a hundred other tapes that will be reviewed along with yours.

Unsolicited tapes may go unreviewed for months or forever. You can send an unsolicited tape to a station where you really want to work, but be strategic as to how many unsolicited tapes you send, because the process can be very expensive. Think in terms of submitting unsolicited tapes to a few places where you really want to work instead of sending them to dozens of stations.

The key concept regarding follow-up is to be assertive while also being realistic about timetables and the other responsibilities of all who may see your tape. Try not to take rejection personally: there are only so many jobs, and even good candidates are not the right fit for every station's style and format.

Internships

A major step in landing a job as a video performer is an internship; that is an opportunity for you to work at a television station while receiving college credit. Many internships require the student to work 15 to 20 hours a week, sometimes more. You can think of this as a part-time job, although in many cases you will receive no pay. Some internships offer an hourly wage or daily stipend, but recent surveys indicate that a majority offer only college credit.

Internships may not be financially rewarding, but the true value comes from the experience you gain and the contacts you make. You may not appear on camera due to union restrictions, but you can still learn a great deal from working with professionals in a high-pressured environment. Some of the specific benefits of internships include the following:

- *An opportunity for "hands-on" experience.* No matter how good your classroom experience has been, there is no substitute for daily work at a television station. You will note a major difference between preparing for your classroom productions and preparing for a station's newscast or other programs. Some students do two or more internships during their academic careers to sample work experiences in different departments and thereby discover the best fit with their abilities. Working in different departments is a good resume builder.

- *Applying for internships helps prepare you for future job searches.* You will prepare a resume, cover letter, and perhaps a resume tape when applying for an internship. In many cases you will also have to interview for the position. These skills transfer when you apply for your first paid position.

- *You may be able to update your resume tape with segments you've done during the internship.* A tape of class projects is a good start, but nothing will impress future employers more than seeing work you've done during an internship at a television station. Remember that your resume tape is always a work in progress.

- *Internships help you develop as a professional.* You see workplace expectations and develop a sense of responsibility. If you make a mistake during a class project, only a few people will see it; not carrying out responsibilities during an internship can affect a production thousands of viewers will see. If you're not feeling well, you often have the option of missing a college class. During an internship, not showing up on days when you don't feel 100 percent can result in a negative impression and evaluation.

- *You develop confidence.* The internship experience can demystify many of the processes and practices of a television station. Many students leave internships better prepared and more confident during job searches knowing they can do the job.

- *Professionals provide you with feedback concerning your performance.* Most industry people working with students provide constructive feedback and suggestions for improvement. Many of these people have been through their own internships, so there is a sense of "giving back" to others what they gained. These professionals also help you make connections between what you learned in the classroom and the workplace. Flexibility and openness to new ideas are important during an internship; you don't want to get into the habit of saying, "This is the way I learned it or did it in class." Every station has slightly different procedures and terminology, so you want to adapt to its style.

- *You gain contacts and networking opportunities.* Someone you work with during an internship may become a mentor, assisting you with job searches and career advice. Station personnel may alert you to positions at other local stations or stations in different markets. Some surveys show that one in six people working at a television station started there as an intern. You may not be fortunate enough to land a job at the station where you interned, but you will have established valuable contacts and relationships to assist you with early career development.

One benefit of internships that may not be perceived as positive is finding out that being a television performer is something you don't want to do. After internships, students sometimes change their minds concerning performance careers; they find that they are uncomfortable with the pressures, hours, or lifestyle of those working in television. Don't feel bad if this turns out to be true for you; finding out what you don't want to do is just as important as discovering your life's work. There are other jobs in television and other allied industries that may be a better match for you.

Internship Requirements   Requirements for internships vary with educational institutions and stations. Some positions require you to be a college junior or senior with a certain grade point average (GPA); others have no such requirements. You can find out internship requirements for various stations by calling their personnel departments or visiting their websites. The director of internships at your college or university will also have information concerning internship requirements.

Recently, stations seem to be less concerned about class standing and other requirements. Many students from community colleges and high schools have landed internships at local stations after taking only a class or two in television or a related field. Stations have become more concerned about attributes such as creativity and reliability rather than technical knowledge and "button pushing"; still, having a good academic background in many of the areas previously discussed in this book provides you with a foundation for a positive internship experience.

Establish a good work ethic and positive relationships with faculty members in your major, because you often need a faculty member to recommend you for an internship.

Internship Credit   In most cases the pay you get from an internship is college credit. Students often have to be enrolled in a college internship class before they can work at a station. One of the major concerns here is liability insurance—is the student covered if something happens on the job? Students enrolled in an internship class are usually covered through the college's policy.

Students can receive a full semester or quarter of college credit depending on how many hours they work. Check with your campus internship director to find out how much credit you can receive for the amount of work expected at the station.

Getting an Internship   Campus internship directors can help you with notices and information about internships, but getting one is often up to you. A first step is sending your application and other information to the personnel director or person in charge of internships. This is where many students end their searches, expecting the station to call them back in a few days. Being assertive and proactive is the key. Call the contact person after a few weeks to see if he or she has received your materials and to find out the time line for decision making.

Some students have reported success in calling the station and talking directly to the internship supervisor, asking if they can drop by and deliver their application materials. Some supervisors will appreciate your assertiveness whereas others won't, so you have to be sensitive to each situation.

Other students have contacted the department where they wanted to work, such as news, sports, or local talk show. This approach can help you get the internship you want instead of being put in a pool where you may end up with responsibilities that don't match your interests.

Start your internship search at least six months in advance. Many students wait until a few weeks before they want to intern before contacting stations' internship supervisors. Often, all of the positions have been filled or only a few less desirable spots remain. Selling yourself early and often increases your chances of getting the internship you want.

Once You're In   Working as a station's intern can be like taking Human Relations 101. There will be times when you are asked to do menial tasks such as answering the phone, photocopying, and getting coffee. At other times you may be involved with a breaking news story on the road with an intriguing remote production. Whatever the request, make sure you maintain a pleasant attitude and do the job to the best of your abilities. Internships are getting better in the sense that there is less "gofer" work than there used to be and station personnel really do try to teach interns some meaningful skills; but remember that teaching is not the first responsibility of station personnel—getting shows on the air is.

Volunteer to do tasks before you are asked. The reporter who has been editing a piece for two hours without a break will usually appreciate your offer to get him or her some coffee or bottled water.

Even when doing menial tasks, you still absorb the language, procedures, and atmosphere of the station. If you are pleasant and reliable, people will notice and involve you in more interesting projects. Don't be afraid to introduce yourself to others around the station. Once you have finished your daily intern responsibilities, ask if you can sit in during production meetings or taping sessions to see what is going on.

Too many interns leave the station after they do their shifts. These people are soon forgotten by station personnel at the end of the semester. Look for ways to get more "face time" around the station so that people get to know you. Remember, they can help you network to find positions at other stations.

Above all, ask questions and find out all you can, comparing the information to what you have learned in classes. Learn about equipment or computer programs you may not have on campus. Technology is constantly changing, so no matter how good your campus experience, you probably won't have the state-of-the-art equipment of most television stations. Look on the internship experience as building upon existing knowledge and skills.

Following the Internship   After a semester or two it is easy to forget those who helped you during the internship experience. You're so involved in finishing graduation requirements and putting together application materials that you may forget to say thanks to those you've worked with at the station. Make sure you acknowledge those who have assisted you during the internship with a thank you card or letter. Remember that these people have taken time away from their work to teach practical skills and help you understand the dynamics of a television station.

Maintain contact with those you worked for because they can help you with leads to positions or serve as references. The lines of communication are short in the television industry. People find out about jobs and tell others about job openings across the country in a matter of minutes. Make sure you are part of the grapevine by staying in touch with your past supervisors.

Ultimately, finding a job after the internship is up to you. Don't put your contacts in the unfair or uncomfortable position of trying to find you a job. If you've done quality work and respect your contacts, they will be your biggest advocates in the job search process.

Job Interviews

No matter how talented you are, knowing how to present yourself in an employment interview can be the factor that lands you an internship or job. Applicants often spend hours editing a resume tape and other application materials, only to lose out on a job because of a poor interview. Sometimes this failure is due to a lack of preparation: People think that there is no way to prepare for the interview, so they simply show up and try to answer questions without anticipating what might be asked. Interviews can be intimidating, but there are a number of things you can do to make them more positive experiences while increasing your probability of success. If you arm yourself with these suggestions, you will be in a similar position to a football team that has access to its opponent's playbook and knows the formations and plays that team will run. Consider the following when getting ready to interview:

Networking or Informational Interviews   Not too many years ago, networking or **informational interviews** were the rage. Job hunters called potential employers and asked them for a few minutes of their time to gather information about a job or company. The theory was that the job hunter not only found out about jobs and organizations but also had an opportunity to network and make contacts with potential employers.

Over the past few years there has been a mild backlash. Many employers felt that they were spending a large portion of their days with job hunters during informational interviews, taking time away from their responsibilities. Networking and informational interviews can still be valuable in the job search process; however, sensitivity and common sense are what can make them work. Calling someone "cold" or showing up unannounced at his or her office is probably not a good idea. Making use of names given to you by friends or other contacts can be an effective means of getting an informational interview. College instructors can also give you names of people who may spend time with you.

During the informational interview, you can ask the interviewer to review your materials and comment on their strengths and weaknesses. This is also an opportunity to get more information about the television industry while warming up for real job interviews.

Before the Interview   Interviews allow you an opportunity to present your best self. In order to do this you should do certain things before going to the station for the interview:

Find out as much about the station as possible before you go. The Internet now makes this easy, since many stations have their own websites providing information about personnel and programs. There are also online newsletters for television in many markets, such as DCRTV (Washington, D.C.) and NYRTV (New York City), providing daily reports about local stations.

You can also access industry websites such as Shop Talk and local newspapers to see what is happening at various stations. If the station is a network affiliate, you may want to check the network's annual report to review some of the salient issues for the company over the last year. For example, if you are applying to a Fox affiliate, you can get the annual report of Fox's parent company, Newscorp. The more homework you've done, the better your chances for success.

Anticipate questions that may be asked. There are general categories of questions that are asked in almost any interview no matter what the job. If you know these, you can anticipate questions that may be asked in these categories.

Questions concerning *planning and organization* are often asked. You may be asked how you would structure your workday or handle multiple tasks. Work habits and time management questions are also included in this category.

You will also be asked about your *assertiveness and enthusiasm.* Television is not for those who lack assertiveness. Questions may be asked about how you will report certain stories or pursue guests for interview programs. Your overall enthusiasm and dynamism during the interview will also be noted.

Interpersonal communication skills will be addressed. This text has stressed throughout the importance of teamwork, and potential employers want to make sure you can work with others in high-pressured situations.

The ability to handle pressure is one of the key elements of being an excellent video performer. Interviewers want to have some idea whether you can function in stressful situations. They may ask how you handle stress.

Your *accomplishments and record of success* will be of interest to the interviewer. Many times we feel awkward talking about our talents or things we've done well. There's nothing wrong with talking about your abilities and success stories. Be your own best advocate. Make sure you have some accomplishments to talk about that show why the interviewer should hire you. Have several stories ready that highlight your successes and relate them to the television industry.

Maturity is another attribute measured through skillful questioning. How you have handled major disappointments or adversity can tell the interviewer a great deal about your character. Everyone has experienced setbacks: it's how you have dealt with them that can be impressive to potential employers. This is also a time for you to share with the interviewer how you have dealt with various challenges or difficult productions.

What would you change about yourself or *what is your greatest weakness* is often referred to as the "Why I shouldn't hire you" question. Everyone is working for improvement in some area. Be honest with your interviewer and tell him or her what you perceive as being a weakness and how you are working to improve it.

The interviewer will probably ask other types of questions, but if you prepare for these categories, you will be well on the way to a good interview performance. Write out several questions for each one of the categories in advance and prepare a mental outline of how to answer them. You want to give polished responses without sounding overrehearsed or canned.

Anticipate that the interviewer will ask if you have any questions. Have at least one question ready relating to station operations, procedures, or opportunities. Many interviewees lose a chance to impress potential employers with their knowledge of the station by not asking a question when invited to do so. You've done your homework concerning the station, so now is the time to demonstrate what you've learned. The question(s) you ask may be used as part of the interview evaluation process.

Don't ask questions about salary or benefits during the question time. If you are offered a job there will be plenty of time to discuss these items. If you are applying for a position at a small-market station, you can in most cases expect a lower salary than in major markets (more about this later).

Do some practice interview sessions with someone who can simulate a serious interview. Make these sessions as realistic as possible. Friends, colleagues, or instructors may serve as practice interviewers.

Have a datebook, organizer, Palm Pilot, or other means of recording time, dates, and addresses of interviews. Do a dry run to the station before your interview so that you know the travel time, location, parking, and traffic problems or road construction. Online services such as Mapquest and Yahoo! Maps can assist you with directions.

If your interview is in another city, get information about the city through its chamber of commerce, online sources, or library resource materials. Familiarize yourself with pertinent issues and interests. Various motor clubs and travel agents can help with transportation and lodging near the station where you will interview.

The day before your interview, consider what you will wear. Pack the day before if your interview is in a another city. You will have enough stress on the day of the interview without having to decide. Err on the side of conservative dress. Make sure that all clothing is cleaned and pressed and your shoes are shined.

Make sure you take copies of your resume and other application materials with you. Station personnel are often very busy, so make their job easier by having your application materials with you.

RATINGS POINTER

A quick time-out here to mention answering machines/services, e-mail, pagers, and cell phones. Potential employers need quick access to job applicants when there is an opening. They don't have time to call two or three locations in order to find you. Make sure that all information on your printed resume and tape is current and that you can be reached even if you can't stay by the phone. An answering machine or service is essential when applying for jobs so you can return calls the same day.

Make sure the message you leave identifies who you are and sounds professional. Some potential employers are turned off by listening to a minute of your favorite song or some other inappropriate material before your message. Indeed, some candidates never get to interview just because the potential employer is sufficiently turned off by the message to hang up and call the next candidate. Make sure your message is clear and concise.

It's good to give potential employers options for reaching you. E-mail will be the preference for some people, so make sure you provide a current e-mail address. Some telephone answering services now allow people to leave messages even when you're online. You may want to invest the few extra dollars a month for this service to ensure that you don't miss important messages.

Pagers and cell phones have become more affordable and they are great options for instant communication with potential employers. A word of caution here: Make sure you turn them off when you are interviewing to avoid embarrassing moments. One station personnel director tells of an interviewee who interrupted an interview by answering her cell phone. Needless to say, she didn't get the job. ★ ★ ★ ★

■ **At the Station**   Arrive at your interview a few minutes before the designated time. The interview starts as soon as you enter the station. Other employees may be busy, but they notice newcomers. Act as if you know what you're doing and don't do anything that indicates nervousness or lack of professionalism. The walls and cubicles have eyes and ears.

Once you arrive in the waiting area, assume that you could go in for the interview at any time. Be friendly with the reception person or whoever greets you because he or she might relay information about you to your interviewer. Use whatever waiting time you have to review potential questions and try to relax. Once the interview begins, always do the following:

- *Greet the interviewer with direct eye contact and a firm handshake.* This will be the first impression he or she has of you. A decision about whether you are a serious candidate will probably be made in less than a minute.

- *Continue to make direct eye contact with your interviewer.* Don't look down at the floor or let your eyes wander as you think about answers.

- *Pay attention to your nonverbal communication.* Just as you do when performing in front of the camera, sit straight in the chair without looking stiff. Tilt your head forward a bit to indicate interest in your interviewer. Don't clasp your hands in front of you on your lap: feel free to gesture as you would in normal conversation. Smile and try to maintain positive facial expressiveness. Remember that your feet are the most honest part of your body and can give away nervousness. Give the impression that you are enjoying the interview.

- *Avoid one-word answers.* On the other hand, be brief and to the point. Remember that many of those interviewing you are used to dealing with soundbites; they want complete yet concise responses. Highlight two or three key points when you respond to keep you on track. There's nothing wrong with pausing for a few seconds to organize your thoughts before you respond. This also helps you be thorough and concise.

- ***Be prepared to audition.*** If the potential employer is serious about hiring you, he or she may want to take you into the studio for a cold reading of a difficult script or news copy. Practice your cold reading in advance with difficult-to-read material. If asked to audition, you should see this as a positive opportunity to showcase your talent.

- ***End on a positive note.*** The conclusion of the interview is as important as the beginning. End it with a firm handshake and smile. Just as the interview begins as you enter the station, it ends when you are outside and in your car. Station personnel may still be watching you after the interview. Also, if you get the job, some of these people will be your coworkers.

Above all, view your interviewer as an advocate and not an adversary. In most cases the station needed someone yesterday to fill the position. The interviewer wants to find the right person for the position as soon as possible. Make the person's job easier by giving him or her every chance to hire you. Feel good about yourself because you got an interview; many others applied for the job without making it to this stage.

Send a thank you note or letter after the interview because interviewers are taking time from other responsibilities to talk to you. A note or letter shows your gratitude for their time, while sending a message that you follow up and are attentive to details.

Job Fairs

Industry insiders believe that competition for performers' jobs is still intense; however, a recent development in television hiring has been the rise of **job fairs** in many major markets. Like those in other professions, these fairs feature representatives from a number of television and radio stations in a hotel or convention center. Information concerning internships as well as jobs is available at job fairs. Television stations have tables or booths where you can meet and network with station personnel. This is an excellent opportunity for you to find out the latest industry information as well as internship and job opportunities.

When you go to a job fair, treat it as you would an interview; dress professionally and have a printed resume. It's also a good idea to have some business cards with your name, address, and contact numbers to distribute to interested individuals. Some stations at job fairs will look at your resume tape and give you constructive feedback. Take notes while people critique your tape regarding its strengths and areas for improvement.

Local organizations such as Bay Area Star provide networking opportunities at job fairs.

Media job fairs are often advertised on radio stations and in newspapers. Local broadcasting websites will also give you information about these fairs. Even if you don't get a job or internship at a job fair, you may discover valuable information that will help in your job search.

Market Size

You may intern at a large-market station but in all likelihood your first job will be in a small market. You may find this outcome discouraging after working hard during your academic career and job search. If you have experienced the excitement of a large-market station, a small-market job may seem like several steps back. Also, the prospect of making a low salary when you have college loans, moving expenses, and other financial obligations may not seem very inviting; however, working at a small-market station can be one of the best experiences you'll ever have.

Small-market stations are wonderful training grounds because you get to do a little of everything. In many cases, what you do in front of the camera is only part of your responsibilities. You'll also shoot and edit videotape, because smaller markets are often free of union restrictions that prohibit you from using equipment. And you'll get training from station personnel at these stations, whereas major-market stations expect you to know everything.

Even recent college graduates can get anchor positions and other high-visibility performance opportunities in smaller markets. In some cases you may anchor, do general assignment reporting, and cover weather all in the same day.

Another advantage of small-market stations is that fewer people will see your mistakes. On the other hand, there will be opportunities to feature your talents in a variety of situations, which you can use to update your resume tape. Anchoring, general assignment reporting, reading public service announcements, and hosting interview programs may be included on your resume tape.

There are some major advantages to living in smaller cities, such as lower cost of living, greater ease of getting to know people, and a less frantic lifestyle. Moving to a smaller city can be an adjustment if you are used to big-city life, though, so target the areas where you'd like to live. Look at the surrounding area to see if there are recreational opportunities and points of interest. Remember, small doesn't necessarily mean boring.

Small-market television also doesn't mean that you will starve. Although it is generally true that stations in smaller markets pay lower salaries, there may be intense competition for talent at these stations. Don Fitzpatrick and Associates claim that market size doesn't always play a role in salaries.

Another item to consider with small-market stations is contracts. If station executives like you, they will try to keep you. Most smaller stations try to sign people to two-year contracts. Industry insiders advise trying to sign a one-year contract with what is called a "top 40 out" meaning that if you get an offer from a station in one of the top forty markets you can take that job. Contracts are legally binding, so you face the possibility of being sued if you don't have an "out" in your contract. Don't risk legal problems by not planning in advance for the possibility of other job offers.

Many people find that they are happy working in small and medium-sized markets because they offer a comfortable lifestyle and a good environment for family life. It is not unusual to find television performers who spend years in these markets with no intention of moving. Other people want to move "up market" as quickly as possible and won't be happy until they land jobs in New York or Los Angeles. Evaluate what is best for you and your career goals, and remember that you may change your mind along the way. Don't be driven by other people's advice if you are happy working at a station in a particular market. Only you can determine what feels right.

Unions

If you move on to a major market station, you'll probably join a union. Most performers at major market stations are members of the American Federation of Television and Radio Artists (**AFTRA**). AFTRA represents those who perform live or are recorded on tape for radio and television. You need no previous experience to be an AFTRA member.

Film performers are members of the Screen Actors Guild (**SAG**). These may be freelance performers appearing in film commercials and other productions. Membership is restricted to those who have appeared in a film production. Trying to become a SAG member thus raises an old dilemma: "You can't get in without experience, but how do you get experience?" You can circumvent this problem by joining AFTRA, which then makes you eligible to be a SAG member. In either case, be prepared to budget part of your paycheck for union dues.

Agents

If you move up to a major market, you may want to hire an **agent.** Most performers in major markets are represented by an agent who negotiates salary, benefits, and other contract items with station management (although some performers negotiate contracts without an agent). In most cases, you won't need an agent when you're starting your career.

Agents can help you with some finer negotiating points and contract legalese. Another advantage is that they can be the go-between from you to station management. Agents charge a percentage of your salary for their services. A reputable agent can be a good investment in your future. Get advice from your colleagues and those you trust in the industry for the names of credible agents.

Ratings

A harsh reality of the television business is ratings. Ratings can determine who stays at a television station and who will be unemployed. The A. C. Nielsen company gathers information on how many people are watching a station at a given time.

A **rating** is the percentage of all possible viewers in an area (televisions turned on and off) who may be watching you. An 8 rating means that 8 percent of all homes with television are watching a program. A *share* is the percentage of people with their televisions turned on who are watching you. If you have a 12 share, this means that 12 percent of people watching television are watching you.

The ratings game is the way the television industry does business, because the higher a program's ratings, the more that station or network can charge for commercial time. You may be an outstanding performer, but if you show's ratings are low you may be out of a job. Most performers are philosophical about this, assuming that if they do their best work, the ratings will take care of themselves; this is probably the best attitude for any video performer.

Consultants

Once you've landed a job you may come in contact with **consultants.** These are people hired by the station to give advice about news and program content as well as stylistic elements like graphics, set design, and other production values. Consultants also give station executives advice about performers' delivery styles, clothing, hair, and so on. If you notice that your favorite anchor, reporter, or other performer has suddenly changed his or her hairstyle or fashion choices, it may be due to a consultant's advice.

Consulting firms provide valuable information to station executives regarding news and other programs; however, there are some consultants who give little more than basic cosmetic advice. Most of the performers interviewed for this book had little good to say about consultants.

The fact is, however, that consultants are here to stay and performers have to coexist with them. If you work with a consultant, listen to what he or she has to say and assimilate the information together with advice you receive from others. Try to evaluate all advice in an objective way; then make decisions that work for your style.

Evaluation and Growth

No matter how much you know, you never know enough. Good performers see self-evaluation as a dynamic process; they are constantly looking at their tapes for areas that still need work. They also develop new skills and knowledge and change with the times.

The last 20 years have seen reliance on computers for everything from research to graphics. Some older performers who did not develop good computer skills were left behind in favor of younger, computer-literate colleagues. New technologies will continue to emerge in the future, so performers need to develop a working knowledge of them. But whatever technology develops, it is still people who are developing and communicating content. Technology is simply a tool to enable people to communicate information in a clearer and more stimulating way. It is up to performers to take advantage of innovations in the years to come. Nothing can replace well-read individuals who know what they are talking about and can communicate information with clarity.

Rewind and Fade to Black

In many ways the conclusion of this entire book is really a beginning. You are in the early stages of the exciting process of becoming a video performer or trying to improve your skills in using video in the corporate world. Maybe you have wanted to perform in front of the camera for years or just discovered your interest in performance. In either case, you're on the way to one of the most exciting careers anyone can have. Many video performers say they can't imagine doing anything else. This book has attempted to give you some of the information necessary to become a video performer; you will learn many more lessons in the "real world" of television.

There are obvious financial rewards as you become more experienced, but the true reward for many is sharing information with thousands of people. Consider this: a local public affairs program with a 1 rating in a major market may have 40,000 viewers—enough to fill a baseball stadium. You could spend your entire life trying to communicate a message to as many people individually.

There are hurdles along the way and intense competition for jobs; but there is still room for those who work hard, are reliable, and have talent. More stations, networks, and cable services exist than ever before, and they all need talented people.

Establish goals and pursue your career as a performer. As the great jazz musician Duke Ellington once said, "A goal is a dream that has an ending." True!

Exercises

1. Prepare a scannable resume and get feedback on it from an instructor, career placement center, or colleague.

2. Visit the websites of three television stations. What did you learn about the station, its personnel, and its programs? How could you use this information in a job interview?

3. Prepare a resume tape as soon as you have enough material to do so. What could you include on a resume tape at this point in your experience?

4. Visit a broadcasting job fair if there is one in your area. Make sure you follow the advice given in this chapter concerning professional appearance and preparation when you go.

5. Select three small markets you would consider working in for your first job. Find out all you can about these areas and decide whether you would be comfortable working in these locations.

INTERVIEW

Joyce M. Tudryn

President of the International Television and Radio Society Foundation

The International Radio and Television Society (IRTS) Foundation is a membership organization that stages educational events about electronic media. Based in New York City, IRTS offers educational luncheons, seminars, workshops, and other services. One of the organization's foremost activities is a summer internship program in which college students have an opportunity to work at media corporations throughout New York City. In this interview, IRTS President Joyce M. Tudryn talks about the IRTS Summer Fellowship Program, other IRTS services, and general tips for those looking for their first jobs.

Question: What are some of the internships available through IRTS?

Joyce Tudryn: For over 30 years, the IRTS has sponsored the Summer Fellowship Program. It is a national competition that attracts over 600 applicants from around the country. We typically choose 35 top juniors, seniors, and graduate students to participate in the program. These students receive an all-expenses-paid trip to New York. We cover travel, housing, and pay them a stipend.

Each student is assigned an internship that parallels his or her career goals. The eight-week work experience is preceded by a one-week orientation to the business to make sure students are familiar with the industry as a whole before they go off on their internships. During that time, they might shadow account executives on their calls to advertising agencies, hear CEOs explain their corporate business strategy, interview network journalists about the changing face of broadcast news, meet the creative team behind a great production, or see how an Internet company partners with traditional media. Throughout the course of the summer, we continue to plan seminars for them, net-

working opportunities, and even social activities, which might include baseball games, television show tapings, and theater tickets contributed by our friends in the business.

While the fellows get a lot out of the professional contacts they make in the industry, there is something to be said about getting all these young superachievers together. Strong bonds are formed, and fellows look out for one another as they advance in their careers.

Q: It sounds as if you adapt the internship to the student's interest; for example, if a student was interested in television sports, you would try to get him or her an internship in that area.

JT: That's right, but I would advise students looking for an IRTS fellowship or any internship to decide whether they want to reinforce or redefine their career goals. If you wish to reinforce your goals, you look for an experience that complements what you have already done. For example, if you have had some news experience at the local level, perhaps you should sample news at the network level when you come to New York. On the other hand, a student already well rounded in one aspect of our business may be smart to do something that is 180 degrees different to make themselves more marketable in a tough economic climate. In this case, the student with a lot of production experience might want a sales or marketing internship to better understand how that side of the business drives revenue and attracts viewers to help ensure the success of the program. I've seen many students change their goals after gaining exposure to a different arena and/or gain a competitive edge by having a more comprehensive understanding of our business as a whole. This type of exploration is more difficult to do once you are looking for a job and experience becomes a prerequisite, but while you are a student, you can get through many doors to sample different areas of our business via an internship.

Q: What is the process you go through to help a student decide if he or she should reinforce or redefine?

JT: The application tells us a lot about the student and his or her experience in general. Our years of experience in running this program help us recognize what we feel would be a perfect placement for a student. We then make that recommendation to the student and let him or her know why we feel a particular placement is in his or her best interest. It's not a forced situation, but those who trust our instincts are generally satisfied.

Q: What things do you look for when selecting students for your program?

JT: They are certainly not clones of one another. Each student is a little bit different in what he or she brings to the program. In general, you're looking for someone who has a strong overall background. The person has probably done quite well academically and he or she has had some previous internships, demonstrating some level of work experience. These students

tend to be leaders. It is not unusual for them to have worked as manager at their college radio or television stations, or have been officers in student organizations.

One thing that sets our students apart is an overall knowledge of the industry. The application we send out has some very simple questions to answer. In fact, the first application doesn't take long to complete, but it is very revealing. You can easily access a copy on our website at *www.irts.org*, from September to November. We have to have a way to sort through hundreds of applications to pick the semifinalists who will be subjected to a more intense second round. The second application is so time-consuming for the readers that we purposely make it easier the first time around. For example, one of the questions we ask is, "If you could ask any industry figure a question, whom would you ask and what would the question be?" Many students might choose Bryant Gumbel or Lesley Stahl and proceed to spell their names wrong. Instant elimination! Then those who spell the names right might ask a question that took very little time to think up. Also, are you more impressed to hear a student ask Oprah a career-related question, or ask FCC Chairman Michael Powell a regulatory question. This reveals a deeper understanding of the business.

It is so important to pay attention to details such as spelling, grammar, correct titles, etc. Many times I ask students to tell me something to bolster my confidence in their attention to detail and accuracy. The answer is often, "Well, I always use spellcheck." Spellcheck is not going to help you spell Bryant Gumbel or let you know that the research you did on the Internet is old news based on what appeared in today's paper. It's disheartening to us when applications that show great potential are eliminated because of lack of accuracy.

Q: It sounds like the screening you're doing is the same thing that would happen in the industry. Someone's resume or entire package could be thrown out due to lack of attention to detail.

JT: That is so true. Sometimes students fail to realize why it is so important. For example, say you are typing a name on-screen with the character generator and it is put on air during a newscast. If that name is wrong, the repercussions could be as serious as subjecting your station to a lawsuit. That's why these things are so important.

Q: Have IRTS fellows gone on to positions at stations in New York or to the network level?

JT: Yes. We have quite a number of success stories. A few that come to mind are ESPN anchor Suzy Kolber, NBC Vice President of Alternative Programs Curt Sharp, and WB Director of Programming/East Coast Ed Johnson. Of course, fellows can be found across the country, ranging from KARE anchor Rick Kupchella in Minneapolis to Melissa Jordan Grey in Redmond, Washington, who formed a company that was purchased by Microsoft.

Ann Lagorie is one of my favorite stories. Ann was someone who was determined to be on air without having to leave New York to go to a smaller market. She was a pro at networking and got Madison Square Garden Network to pick up her show *Interview with Ann Lagorie* by not only producing the show, but also by delivering the advertisers willing to support it. See what I mean about how that knowledge of several disciplines in our business can work to your advantage? Today, Ann can be found on the Sports Channel and Fox Regional Networks, the Golf Channel, and WFAN Radio. Ann even published a book, *Passion for Golf,* which was inspired by fascinating interviews she would have with celebrities ranging from Arnold

Palmer to Kevin Costner while she played the course with them. Now that's what I call using your skills to your best advantage.

Q: On the other side, do you ever get people who go through your internship program thinking that television is something they want to do and they find out it's not for them?

JT: Those situations are rare, but they do happen. We think of that as a very positive thing. It's great to be able to discover that at this juncture of your career before you make a deep commitment. I'll take your question one step further. It may be that someone thinks he or she wants to work at the network level, but after experiencing network decides to move up through the ranks and stay in a large market without crossing over to network. Think about how wonderful it is to come to a market like New York as an intern and learn early on what you do or do not want to do in this business. Sometimes it's depressing for an intern to come to this realization early in an internship, and it takes some time before he or she can understand that this is a positive discovery.

Q: Are there other positives to internships?

JT: Internships are important for a couple of reasons: Getting that experience in advance will help you get a competitive edge when you are looking for a job, but it's also true that the best way to get a job is to network. The company where you intern may not be able to hire you, but these people get calls all the time from other folks in the business looking for referrals. Job openings have a tendency to come up very suddenly, and it is a real chore to have to look for a new person to fill a position. Your first instinct as an employer is to call your friends in the business and ask them if they know a good candidate looking for a job. You know that you can trust your friends for an honest referral, and it makes a difference when a colleague talks about someone they met in person as opposed to someone who is represented by a piece of paper. Resumes don't tell half the story.

I strongly suggest that students conduct informational interviews. Even though IRTS interns have access to major industry professionals during the summer, we still ask them to conduct informational interviews on their own.

When you call a potential employer, it is easy for them to say that there aren't any openings at the time and turn down your request to be interviewed for future consideration. However, it would be difficult [to turn down] someone who asked the following: "Thank you for taking my call today. As I complete my last semester in college, I am in the process of trying to learn as much as I can about the business to help me bring my career goals into focus. You are someone who has achieved the type of success I would like to have some day, and I am hoping you might grant me 20 minutes to meet with you for some career advice. I have a number of questions I would love to be able to ask someone like you at this point in my life."

When you get your foot in the door for an informational interview, there's less pressure than when you are at an interview for a job, although you do need to do your research and come prepared with good questions. These experiences will make you much more knowledgeable when you are in the hot seat for a real job. And it's surprising how many people will remember you when you are looking for a job or will be willing to refer you to a friend.

Q: Depending on what job advice you read, some people say that informational interviews have fallen out of favor because people just don't have the time to deal with people who are in the job market.

JT: Time isn't what it used to be and people are busy. You have to be more persistent than in the past. If you can't find your way into a company, then you should attend industry events sponsored by organizations like IRTS. In that situation you'll meet people who aren't held hostage at their desks, and it may be easier to connect. As for persistence at a company, you should be sure to acknowledge that you realize the executive is extremely busy. If he or she . . . cannot spare 20 minutes, volunteer to bring a coffee and a bagel, as even busy executives deserve a coffee break. You can say, "Please let me bring you a snack."

If he or she is adamant about not having the time, don't let that connection with the company end. Ask if there is another person you can be referred to within the company. Even an assistant is worth seeing, as those are the folks who may well be on their way to a promotion, which sometimes creates a job opening. By talking to younger people in the company, you can find out where the openings are most likely to be.

Q: There's probably a little more empathy with younger people in a company because they have just been through the job search process.

JT: Exactly. We urge our summer fellows to begin the informational interview process by contacting former fellows who have walked in their footsteps. It's best to start off with people you feel comfortable contacting because you share something in common. Perhaps the contact is an alum from your school or previously worked at the station where you are now interning. Once you start interviewing, you discover it is really not that difficult to get in touch with people. We are always astounded by the level of executive our fellows are meeting near the end of the year.

Q: What other services does IRTS offer?

JT: Our membership is based here in New York. I would urge those who see themselves eventually headed to "the Big Apple" to join IRTS. We have a reduced membership fee and a fee for those under 30 years of age. We offer free monthly Q and A seminars where you can keep your finger on the pulse of our business by questioning key executives in a panel format. Of course, the reception before the panel provides a fabulous opportunity for networking.

Q: It sounds as if you are using the same skills as when you were trying to get your first job.

JT: Yes, and it never ends. Once you're employed, networking benefits your company, as you might be looking for clients, vendors, or even other prospective employees. Networking skills are important throughout your career, whether you are using them to climb up the ladder or look out for the best interest of the company for which you work.

IRTS also sponsors an annual Minority Career Workshop. This two-day workshop begins with an orientation to the business featuring seminars and speakers and a networking reception. The following day, students have an opportunity to interview for jobs or internships with more than 25 major communication companies. These companies then interview the students for internships and jobs.

It's difficult to track the success of the workshop, but we know that at least 20 percent of the students get hired or get an internship as a direct result of the workshop and others may. Just the other night I met a man who attended the workshop 16 years ago and is enjoying a great career at NBC because of it. That's an example of the success stories that are out there that we don't know about, because students tend to be so transient during the first few years of their careers.

IRTS is proud to have made a difference in the lives of so many students and professionals, and we wish those who are reading this book great success in their future endeavors.

IRTS programs allow students to meet television performers such as Charles Osgood of CBS Television and Radio.

Nielsen Media Research Local Universe Estimates

Rank	Designated Market Area
1	New York, NY
2	Los Angeles, CA
3	Chicago, IL
4	Philadelphia, PA
5	San Francisco-Oakland-San Jose, CA
6	Boston, MA (Manchester, NH)
7	Dallas-Ft. Worth, TX
8	Washington, D.C. (Hagerstown, MD)
9	Detroit, MI
10	Atlanta, GA
11	Houston, TX
12	Seattle-Tacoma, WA
13	Minneapolis-St. Paul, MN
14	Tampa-St. Petersburg (Sarasota), FL
15	Cleveland, OH
16	Miami-Ft. Lauderdale, FL
17	Phoenix, AZ
18	Denver, CO
19	Sacramento-Stockton-Modesto, CA
20	Pittsburgh, PA
21	Orlando-Daytona Beach-Melbourne, FL
22	St. Louis, MO
23	Portland, OR
24	Baltimore, MD
25	San Diego, CA
26	Indianapolis, IN
27	Hartford-New Haven, CT

Rank	Designated Market Area
28	Charlotte, NC
29	Raleigh-Durham (Fayetteville), NC
30	Kansas City, MO
31	Nashville, TN
32	Cincinnati, OH
33	Milwaukee, WI
34	Columbus, OH
35	Greenville-Spartanburg, SC-Ashville, NC-Anderson, SC
36	Salt Lake City, UT
37	San Antonio, TX
38	Grand Rapids-Kalamazoo-Battle Creek, MI
39	Birmingham (Anniston, Tuscaloosa), AL
40	Memphis, TN
41	Norfolk-Portsmouth-Newport News, VA
42	New Orleans, LA
43	West Palm Beach-Ft. Pierce, FL
44	Buffalo, NY
45	Oklahoma City, OK
46	Harrisburg-Lancaster-Lebanon-York, PA
47	Greensboro–High Point–Winston-Salem, NC
48	Louisville, KY
49	Providence, RI-New Bedford, MA
50	Albuquerque-Santa Fe, NM
51	Las Vegas, NV

Rank	Designated Market Area	Rank	Designated Market Area
52	Wilkes Barre-Scranton, PA	88	Jackson, MS
53	Jacksonville, FL	89	Cedar Rapids-Waterloo-Iowa City-Dubuque, IA
54	Fresno-Visalia, CA		
55	Dayton, OH	90	Davenport, IA-Rock Island-Moline, IL
56	Albany-Schenectady-Troy, NY	91	Burlington, VT-Plattsburgh, NY
57	Little Rock-Pine Bluff, AR	92	Colorado Springs-Pueblo, CO
58	Austin, TX	93	Tri-Cities, TN-VA
59	Tulsa, OK	94	Waco-Temple-Bryan, TX
60	Richmond-Petersburg, VA	95	Johnstown-Altoona, PA
61	Charleston-Huntington, WV	96	Baton Rouge, LA
62	Mobile, AL-Pensacola (Ft. Walton Beach), FL	97	Evansville, IN
		98	El Paso, TX
63	Knoxville, TN	99	Youngstown, OH
64	Flint-Saginaw-Bay City, MI	100	Savannah, GA
65	Wichita-Hutchinson, KS	101	Lincoln-Hastings-Kearney, NE
66	Lexington, KY	102	Harlingen-Weslaco-Brownsville-McAllen, TX
67	Toledo, OH		
68	Roanoke-Lynchburg, VA	103	Charleston, SC
69	Green Bay-Appleton, WI	104	Ft. Wayne, IN
70	Des Moines-Ames, IA	105	Springfield-Holyoke, MA
71	Tucson (Sierra Vista), AZ	106	Greenville-New Bern-Washington, NC
72	Honolulu, HI	107	Lansing, MI
73	Paducah, KY-Cape Girardeau, MO-Harrisburg-Mt. Vernon, IL	108	Tyler-Longview-Lufkin-Nacogdoches, TX
74	Rochester, NY	109	Reno, NV
75	Omaha, NE	110	Tallahassee, FL-Thomasville, GA
76	Shreveport, LA	111	Sioux Falls-Mitchell, SD
77	Spokane, WA	112	Peoria-Bloomington, IL
78	Springfield, MO	113	Augusta, GA
79	Portland-Auburn, ME	114	Florence-Myrtle Beach, SC
80	Syracuse, NY	115	Ft. Smith-Fayetteville-Springdale-Rogers, AR
81	Ft. Myers-Naples, FL		
82	Huntsville-Decatur (Florence), AL	116	Montgomery-Selma, AL
83	Champaign-Springfield-Decatur, IL	117	Santa Barbara-Santa Maria-San Luis Obispo, CA
84	Madison, WI		
85	Columbia, SC	118	Monterey-Salinas, CA
86	Chattanooga, TN	119	Traverse City-Cadillac, MI
87	South Bend-Elkhart, IN	120	Fargo-Valley City, ND
		121	Macon, GA

Rank	Designated Market Area
122	Eugene, OR
123	Boise, ID
124	Lafayette, LA
125	Yakima-Pasco-Richland-Kennewick, WA
126	La Crosse-Eau Claire, WI
127	Amarillo, TX
128	Columbus, GA
129	Corpus Christi, TX
130	Bakersfield, CA
131	Columbus-Tupelo-West Point, MS
132	Duluth, MN-Superior, WI
133	Chico-Redding, CA
134	Monroe, LA-El Dorado, AR
135	Rockford, IL
136	Wausau-Rhinelander, WI
137	Beaumont-Port Arthur, TX
138	Topeka, KS
139	Terre Haute, IN
140	Wheeling, WV-Steubenville, OH
141	Medford-Klamath Falls, OR
142	Erie, PA
143	Columbia-Jefferson City, MO
144	Sioux City, IA
145	Joplin, MO-Pittsburgh, KS
146	Wichita Falls, TX-Lawton, OK
147	Lubbock, TX
148	Wilmington, NC
149	Bluefield-Beckley-Oak Hill, WV
150	Albany, NY
151	Odessa-Midland, TX
152	Minot-Bismarck-Dickinson-Williston, ND
153	Rochester, MN-Mason City, IA-Austin, MN
154	Anchorage, AK
155	Bangor, ME
156	Binghamton, NY

Rank	Designated Market Area
157	Biloxi-Gulfport, MS
158	Panama City, FL
159	Palm Springs, CA
160	Abilene-Sweetwater, TX
161	Sherman, TX-Ada, OK
162	Salisbury, MD
163	Quincy, IL-Hannibal, MO-Keokuk, IA
164	Idaho Falls-Pocatello, ID
165	Clarksburg-Weston, WV
166	Gainesville, FL
167	Hattiesburg-Laurel, MS
168	Utica, NY
169	Billings, MT
170	Missoula, MT
171	Elmira, NY
172	Dothan, AL
173	Lake Charles, LA
174	Yuma, AZ-El Centro, CA
175	Rapid City, SD
176	Watertown, NY
177	Marquette, MI
178	Alexandria, LA
179	Harrisonburg, VA
180	Jonesboro, AR
181	Bowling Green, KY
182	Greenwood-Greenville, MS
183	Meridian, MS
184	Jackson, TN
185	Parkersburg, WV
186	Grand Junction-Montrose, CO
187	Great Falls, MT
188	Twin Falls, ID
189	Laredo, TX
190	Butte-Bozeman, MT
191	Eureka, CA
192	St. Joseph, MO
193	Charlottesville, VA

Rank	Designated Market Area	Rank	Designated Market Area
194	Lafayette, IN	203	Fairbanks, AK
195	Mankato, MN	204	Victoria, TX
196	San Angelo, TX	205	Presque Isle, ME
197	Casper-Riverton, WY	206	Juneau, AK
198	Cheyenne, WY-Scottsbluff, NE	207	Helena, MT
199	Ottumwa, IA-Kirksville, MO	208	Alpena, MI
200	Bend, OR	209	North Platte, NE
201	Lima, OH	210	Glendive, MT
202	Zanesville, OH		

GLOSSARY

AFTRA The union American Federation of Television and Radio Artists, whose members perform live and taped radio and television work.

actual malice Information communicated with the knowledge that it was false or with reckless disregard as to whether it was false or not.

ad-lib Spontaneously deliver information without a script.

agent Person who represents a performer in contract negotiations.

anchor Main newscaster on a television news program.

animatic Video storyboard of a commercial. Still images from the storyboard are edited to a soundtrack.

articulation Physical formation of spoken words by means of tongue, teeth, and lips working together with the soft palate and gums.

assimilative nasality Vocal quality in which *a*'s sound too pinched or tight.

assignment editor Main person in charge of the newsroom's assignment desk.

assistant director Person who helps director with timing and other program details.

aspect ratio Proportional dimensions of the television screen.

associate producer Person who assists producer with various tasks.

attribution Reference within a story to the source of that information or story.

audio console Electronic device used by the audio engineer to mix, route, and amplify sounds.

audio engineer Person who operates the audio console and is responsible for sound elements during a production.

audio track Area on a videotape used to record audio information.

b-roll Background video, usually rolled into a production while performers are talking in a studio or on remote.

boom Device that holds a microphone so that it is not seen on the screen. Booms are usually on dollies, allowing for directional control of the mic.

boom microphone Mic attached to the end of a pipe or adjustable extension pole.

boom operator Person who maneuvers boom microphone in studio,

booth announcer Person who reads live station identifications and promotional announcements.

bumpers Lead-ins to commercials.

buses Rows of buttons on a video switcher for cameras and other video inputs.

cardioid Heart-shaped microphone pickup pattern.

character generator Device that creates electronic graphics and titles for the television screen.

chroma-key Electronic system that allows information on the screen to be replaced by other sources. (In most cases a chroma-key background is blue or green and another image appears over the color. One of the most common uses for chroma-key is weather maps and other graphics during a weathercast.)

chronological resume   Resume presenting work experience organized in order of time.

cliche   Type of character, usually used in reference to commercials.

close-up (CU)   Subject or object framed tightly. In extreme close-ups only the facial features of a person are seen.

chief engineer   Person in charge of the technical aspects of a video production.

competency-based resume   Resume that shows various skill areas, useful for people with little or no work history.

controller   Device that allows one to choose edit points in video editing.

consultants   People hired by a television station to give advice concerning news content and stylistic elements such as performer's dress, graphics, set design, etc.

control room   Area where the director and other technical personnel conduct the business of getting a program on air or on tape.

control track   Area of the videotape used for synchronizing information.

copy   Material written to be read for a taped or on-air performance.

cover letter   Letter that accompanies a printed resume and resume tape.

cover shot   Medium to large television shot showing a news or interview set; also a shot showing an interviewer and guest.

cover video   Images providing an orientation for viewers as to where a story is shot.

cross shooting   When cameras shoot subjects or objects crossing each other.

CU   Abbreviation for "close-up." You will often see this marking on scripts.

cue cards   Cards used to convey information to on-camera performers. Can be entire scripts or bulleted items.

cut   Instantaneous change from one image to another; also a director's command to stop the production.

cutaways   In most cases reaction shots of a reporter or interviewer, used in editing to cover jump edits while an interviewee is speaking.

demographic analysis   Characteristics of the audience such as age, gender, racial-ethnic background, income, and others that can be used in audience analysis.

depth of field   Area in front of the camera that appears in focus.

diaphragmatic breathing   Use of the diaphragm (the muscles between the chest and abdomen) for inhaling and exhaling; the type of breathing used in speaking and singing.

dissolve   Gradual transition from one image to another, with the images overlapping for a brief period of time.

director   Person who calls the shots and gives commands for audio and video during a production.

dub   Copy a videotape or audiotape.

EFP   Electronic field production.

ENG   Electronic news gathering.

emphasis   Highlighting or prioritizing words that are read.

equalization   Ability to enhance audio quality via the audio console.

executive producer   Person who has financial responsibility for a production.

extreme close-up (ECU)   Camera shot that shows only facial features.

eye-to-lens contact   Making direct eye contact with the camera lens.

ESPN Entertainment and Sports Programming Network.

Federal Communications Commission (FCC) The governmental agency that oversees radio, television, and other electronic communication industries in the United States.

fade Go from or to black.

field interview Interview done on location.

field production Any production that happens outside the studio.

flag Device placed on a handheld microphone that identifies a station or network.

floor manager Person who relays director's cues to talent in the studio. May also be involved with studio preparation.

functional resume See *competency-based resume.*

funnel Interview organizational scheme beginning with general questions and proceeding to more specific questions.

generation Number of dubs away from the original tape.

gray scale How colors are translated to various shades of gray, ranging from white to black and shades in between.

green room Area where guests wait before going into the studio for an interview.

hand signals Signals used to communicate information to performers without speaking. In most cases these are used by the floor manager to communicate with performers.

hard news Breaking news or news happening at that point in time.

headset microphone Microphone built into a headset, allowing a performer to keep his or her hands free.

head shot Close-up that focuses on the head of the performer.

High Definition Television (HDTV) A video system that produces high-quality video images.

hitting the marks Moving to exact predetermined areas during a performance. In a studio, marks are often designated by tape.

hypernasality High, pinched, tight vocal quality.

hyponasality Vocal quality that makes a person sound congested or as if he or she has a stopped-up nose.

IRTS International Radio and Television Society.

informational interview Informal discussion in which a person gathers information about a company.

infomercial Extended commercial or sales pitch with product demonstrations and, in some cases, audience participation.

internalization Process by which the performer attempts to give an accurate and believable performance of a script.

interruptible foldback (IFB) Small earphone used by news anchors and reporters through which instructions are comminucated by producers and directors.

inverted funnel Interview organizational scheme starting with specific questions and proceeding to more general questions.

job fair Open convention at which numerous station representatives provide information concerning jobs and internships.

jump cut Image appearing to move or jump due to improper editing out of the sequence.

keys In most cases, printed information that appears on a screen from a character generator, such as a person's name or title.

lavaliere microphone   Small microphone that can be clipped onto the performer's clothing.

libel   Untrue statement that causes hardship to a person's reputation.

linear editing system   System that uses videotape as the editing medium and does not allow for random access of shots.

live shot   Image of a news story from the scene.

long shot   Subject or object seen from far away or framed very loosely.

major market   Metropolitan area with a potential viewing audience of one million or more.

makeup   Cosmetics used to improve the performer's appearance during a video production. Makeup is often needed due to lighting and other conditions of the video environment.

market   Area of reception for a radio or television station: major, secondary, or small.

mediated interview   Interview in which the host talks with multiple guests in multiple locations.

medium shot   Objects or subjects seen from a medium distance; in the case of a performer, usually from the waist up.

microphone   Electronic device that changes sound waves to electronic energy.

moire effect   Radiating or vibrating pattern that appears on the screen due to checks, stripes, or small patterns on the performer's clothes.

monitor   High-quality video receiver used in television control rooms and studios. The monitor allows control room and studio personnel to see what each camera is shooting and what is being recorded or put on air. Can also be a speaker that carries program sound.

mood   Emotional state communicated by the performer.

multidirectional microphone   Microphone that has an adjustable pickup pattern.

nasality   Vocal quality that sounds as if it is coming through the nose instead of the mouth.

natural sound   Ambient audio of people and things recorded on the scene.

news director   Executive in charge of the news division.

news planner   Person who selects news events to be covered from various press releases, letters, e-mails, etc.

news writers   People who write news copy based on wire service reports and network stories, as well as leads and transitional material.

nonlinear editing system   System in which video and audio are stored on computer disks allowing for random access of shots.

nonverbal communication   Communication involving facial expressions, gestures, and movement.

omnidirectional pickup pattern   Microphone pattern in which sound is picked up well in all directions.

on mic   Performers are on mic when they are speaking inside the ideal area of microphone coverage.

over-the-shoulder shot   Image obtained by shooting over one person's shoulder (back of the head is in view) toward another subject.

package   In news, a complete story prepared by a reporter that needs only a lead-in by the anchor.

peripheral vision   Ability to use the corners of one's eyes to see signals and commands given by studio personnel.

phrasing   Group of words expressing a thought, image, or movement.

pickup pattern Area around the microphone where sound is heard.

pitch Tone of voice determined by the frequency of vibration of sound waves.

plosives *p, b, d, g, k,* and *t* sounds.

popping Sound caused by speaking too close to the microphone (often saying *p* sounds).

presence Degree to which it sounds as if a person is speaking into the microphone.

press kit Package of information prepared by an organization to give to the press.

primary movement Movement in front of the camera.

producer Person who creates and organizes a video production.

production assistant Person who takes care of various odd jobs before, during, and after the production.

pronunciation Way of speaking words; also an accent or dialect.

prop (property) Objects other than sets or costumes used in a television production.

public service announcement (PSA) Announcement that promotes a charity or other nonprofit organization.

psychographic analysis Method of determining people's attitudes toward certain issues.

qualitative significance Significance based on the first or best of something.

quantitative significance Significance based on specific numbers or statistics.

rating Measurement showing how many people are watching a particular station or network.

reaction shot Cutaway shot that shows one person reacting to another.

reporter Person who reports news stories away from the station.

resonance Intensification of vocal tones due to vibrations in the nose and cheekbones.

resume Document presenting a person's work experience, qualifications, and educational background.

resume tape Videotape with examples of a person's performance work.

retracted voice Sounds that remain in the back of the throat and are swallowed.

rising inflection Rising of pitch, usually at the end of a sentence.

robotic cameras Television cameras that function without human camera operators.

SAG Screen Actors Guild, a union for film actors.

scannable resume Resume that can be scanned by a computer for key words and terms.

screen space Positioning of people and objects for proper spacing for the television screen.

script Printed document that contains what the audience will see and hear.

secondary market Area with 200,000 to one million potential viewers.

segment producer Person in charge of a specific portion of a program.

sibilance Hissing sound produced when pronouncing *s* and *sh.*

slate Visual identification of a program, established at the beginning of a tape, containing information such as program title, date of recording, air date, and the number of the take.

slice-of-life commercial Type of commercial in which a performer is often faced with a problem.

small market Area with fewer than 200,000 potential viewers.

soft news   Events such as meetings, press conferences, parades, etc.

soundbite   Brief statement made during a news story by someone other than the reporter; a video quotation.

sound check   Testing in which the performer speaks into a microphone prior to the production so that the audio engineer can set proper sound levels.

stand-up   Appearance by a television reporter on camera with a statement, often used to wrap up a news story.

still storage   Electronic device that stores a variety of images to be used during a production.

streaming video   Video delivered via the Internet.

super or **superimposition**   Simultaneous overlay of two images on the same screen.

sweeps   Ratings periods (February, May, August, and November) used to determine the advertising rates for a television station or network.

switcher   Video console that allows an operator to cut and dissolve between cameras as well as performing other effects and functions; the title of the person operating this piece of equipment.

tally light   Red light on top of the camera that when lit indicates the shooting or "hot" camera.

tease   Brief promotional announcement for an upcoming segment or program.

technical director   Person who operates the video switcher, sometimes called a "switcher."

teleprompter   Device placed in front of the camera lens to display copy for performers.

tell stories   News stories in which the anchor appears on screen with no accompanying video and in many cases a corner graphic.

toss   Transitional statement made to hand off to another person or segment.

truck   Lateral camera movement by means of a mobile camera mount.

tunnel   Interview organizational scheme that combines a series of questions concerning the same topic.

unidirectional microphone   Microphone that picks up sound in one direction.

upcut   Error that occurs when performer starts speaking before the floor manager's cue, causing viewers to miss the first few words said by the performer.

video operator   Person in charge of overall video quality.

videotape recorder   Recording device that stores picture and sound for later playback.

video track   Area on a videotape used to record video information.

vocal quality   Sound of a person's voice, including characteristics such as rasp, hoarseness, thinness, nasality, and huskiness.

voiceover   Narration in which the person is heard describing the story but is not seen.

word color   Technique of reading a word in such a way that the word sounds like the object.

wrap   Ending of a production.

RESOURCES

Books

Alburger, James R. *The Art of Voice Acting: The Craft and Business of Performing Voice-Over.* Woburn, MA: Focal Press, 1998.

Apple, Terri, and Owens, Gary. *Making Money in Voice-Overs: Winning Strategies to a Successful Career in TV, Commercials, Radio, and Animation.* Hollywood, CA: Lone Eagle Publishing Company, 1999.

Arva, Bob. *Thirty Seconds to Air., A Field Reporter's Guide to Live Television Reporting.* Ames, IA: Iowa State University Press, 1999.

Bender, Gary, and Johnson, Michael L. *Call of the Game: What Really Goes On in the Broadcast Booth.* Chicago: Bonus Books, 1994.

Berland Terry, and Ouellette, Deborah. *Breaking into Commercials: The Complete Guide to Marketing Yourself, Auditioning to Win, and Getting the Job.* New York: Plume Publishing, 1997.

Biagi, Shirley. *Interviews That Work.* Belmont, CA: Wadsworth Publishing, 1986.

Blu, Susan, and Mullin, Molly Ann. *Word of Mouth: A Guide to Commercial Voice-Over Excellence.* Rohnert Park, CA: Pomegranate Press, 1996.

Carroll, Victoria McCullogh. *Writing News for Television: Style and Format.* Ames, IA: Iowa State University Press, 1997.

Catsis, John R. *Sports Broadcasting.* Chicago: Nelson-Hall Publishers, 1998.

Coronauer, Adrian. *How to Read Copy: Professionals Guide to Delivering Voice- and Broadcast Commercials.* Chicago: Bonus Books, 1990.

Dougan, Pat. *Professional Acting in Television Commercials: Techniques, Exercises, Copy, and Storyboards.* Portsmouth, NH: Heinemann Publishers, 1995.

Elster, Charles Harrington. *The Big Book of Beastly Mispronunciations.* Boston: Houghton Mifflin Company, 1999.

Farris, Linda Guess, *Television Careers: A Guide to Breaking and Entering.* Fairfax, CA: Buy the Book Enterprises, 1995.

Foote, Joe S. (editor), Koppel, Ted, and Utley, Garrick. *Live from the Trenches: The Changing Role of the Television News Correspondent.* Carbondale, IL: Southern Illinois University Press, 1998.

Fridell, Squire. *Acting in Television Commercials for Fun and Profit.* Victoria, BC: Crown Publishing, 1995.

Hausman, Carl, O'Donnell, Lewis B., and Benoit, Phillip. *Announcing: Broadcast Communicating Today.* Belmont, CA: Wadsworth Publishing, 1999.

Hedrick, Tom, McKenzie, Mike, and Castiglione, Joe. *The Art of Sportscasting: How to Build a Successful Career.* South Bend, IN: Diamond Communications, 2000.

Hyde, Stewart. *Television and Radio Announcing,* 9th ed. Boston: Houghton Miffin Company, 2001.

Kerchner, Kathy. *Soundbites: A Business Guide to Working with the Media.* Superior, WI: Savage Press, 1997.

Matelski, Marilyn J. *TV News Ethics (Electronic Media Guides).* Woburn, MA: Focal Press, 1990.

McCoy, Michelle, Hopkins, Page, Utterback, Ann S. (contributor). *Sound and Look Professional on Television and the Internet. How to Improve Your On-Camera Presence.* Chicago: Bonus Books, 2000.

Reese, David E., Beadle, Mary E., and Stephenson, Alan. *Broadcast Announcing Worktext, Performing for Radio, Television, and Cable.* Woburn, MA: Butterworth-Heinemann, 2000.

Rhodes, John, and Caldwell, Brad. *Videoconferencing for the Real World.* Woburn, MA: Butterworth-Heinemann, 2001.

See, Joan. *Acting in Commercials: A Guide to Auditioning and Performing on Camera.* New York: Watson-Guptill Publishing, 1998.

Shaw, Bernard Graham. *Voice-Overs: A Practical Guide with CD.* New York: Routledge Press, 2000.

Shook, Fredrick. *Television Field Production and Reporting.* Boston: AddisonWesley Publishing Company, 2000.

Smith, Ronald, A. *Play-By-Play: Radio, Television, and Big-Time College Sports.* Baltimore: Johns Hopkins Press, 2001.

Utterback, Ann S., and Freedman, Michael. *Broadcast Voice Handbook.* Chicago: Bonus Books, 2000.

Weaver, Dan, and Siegel, Jason. *Breaking into Television: Proven Advice from Veterans and Interns.* Lawrenceville, NJ: Peterson's Guides, 1998.

Wolfe, John Leslie, and Mc Donough, Brenda. *You Can Work On-Camera: Acting in Commercials and Corporate Films.* Portsmouth, NH: Heinemann, 1999.

Yorke, Ivor. *Basic TV Reporting.* Woburn, MA: Focal Press, 1997.

Zettl, Herbert. *Video Basics 3.* Belmont, CA: Wadsworth Publishing, 2001.

■ Organizations

The following organizations offer internships, newsletters, networking opportunities, and other possibilities. In many cases they have local chapters that you can join. Here is a representative sample of organizations serving television professionals:

The Association for Women in Communication
780 Ritchie Highway Suite 28-S
Severna Park, MD 21146
www.womcom.org
410-544-7442

AWC has numerous local chapters and job lines, and offers excellent networking opportunities.

American Women in Radio and Television
1595 Spring Hill Road, Suite 330
Vienna, VA, 22183
703-506-3290
www.awrt.org

AWRT features a career line for members and special membership rates for students and has chapters in 40 cities around the country. Membership is open to both men and women.

Asian American Journalists Association
1182 Market Street Suite 320
San Francisco, CA 94102
415-346-2051
www.aaja.org

AAJA maintains a job bank with postings from around the country.

Bay Area Star
855 Battery Street
San Francisco, CA 94111
www.bayareastar.org
415-765-8702

While Bay Area Star serves industry professionals in northern California, there are a number of similar local organizations for networking around the country.

International Radio and Television Society Foundation
420 Lexington Avenue, Suite 1714
New York, New York 10170
212-867-6650
www.irts.org

The services offered by IRTS are covered in detail in the interview with Joyce Tudryn in Chapter 12.

National Academy of Television Arts and Sciences
111 W. 57th St., Suite 1020
New York, New York 10019
212-586-8424
www.emmyonline.org

The people who bring you the Emmy Awards have 17 regional chapters and internship programs for students who want to learn more about the industry.

National Association of Black Journalists
8701A Adelphi Road
Adelphi, MID 20783-1716
301-648-1270
www.nabj.org

The NABJ has internships, scholarships, and a job line. The organization also features an outstanding website with information about minorities in the industry and links to other websites.

National Association of Hispanic Journalists
1193 National Press Building
Washington, D.C. 20045
202-662-7145
www.nahj.org

National Cable Television Association
1724 Massachusetts Avenue, NW
Washington, D.C. 20036
202-775-3550
www.ncta.org

NCTA offers a publication called *Careers in Cable.*

Radio-Television News Directors Association
1000 Connecticut Ave., Suite 615
Washington, D.C. 20036
202-659-6510
www.rtnda.org

Numerous regional chapters of the RTNDA conduct workshops for students.

TVSPY.Com
www.tvspy.com

This website includes Don Fitzpatrick's advice on resumes and resume tapes plus other valuable job hunting information.

INDEX